HOME IS WHERE THE RV IS

GERRI ALMAND

BROWN POSEY PRESS

an imprint of Sunbury Press, Inc.
Mechanicsburg, PA USA

an imprint of Sunbury Press, Inc.
Mechanicsburg, PA USA

Copyright © 2020 by Gerri Almand.
Cover Copyright © 2020 by Sunbury Press, Inc.

Sunbury Press supports copyright. Copyright fuels creativity, encourages diverse voices, promotes free speech, and creates a vibrant culture. Thank you for buying an authorized edition of this book and for complying with copyright laws. Except for the quotation of short passages for the purpose of criticism and review, no part of this publication may be reproduced, scanned, or distributed in any form without permission. You are supporting writers and allowing Sunbury Press to continue to publish books for every reader. For information contact Sunbury Press, Inc., Subsidiary Rights Dept., PO Box 548, Boiling Springs, PA 17007 USA or legal@sunburypress.com.

For information about special discounts for bulk purchases, please contact Sunbury Press Orders Dept. at (855) 338-8359 or orders@sunburypress.com.

To request one of our authors for speaking engagements or book signings, please contact Sunbury Press Publicity Dept. at publicity@sunburypress.com.

FIRST BROWN POSEY PRESS EDITION: September 2020

Set in Adobe Garamond | Interior design by Crystal Devine | Cover design by Lawrence Knorr | Edited by Lawrence Knorr.

Publisher's Cataloging-in-Publication Data
Names: Almand, Gerri, author.
Title: Home is where the rv is / Gerri Almand.
Description: First trade paperback edition. | Mechanicsburg, PA : Brown Posey Press, 2020.
Summary: A formerly reluctant rv wife is now settling into the nomadic routine with her recently retired husband but the laughs continue.
Identifiers: ISBN : 1-978-620064-27-6 (softcover).
Subjects: TRAVEL / Special Interest / Family | TRAVEL / Special Interest / Senior | TRAVEL / Essays & Travelogues | HUMOR / Topic / Travel | TRAVEL / United States / General.

Product of the United States of America
0 1 1 2 3 5 8 13 21 34 55

Continue the Enlightenment!

23	Smoke Gets in your Eyes	144
24	Sweet Places to Live	152
25	The Meaning of RVing	158
26	Marital Trials and Tribulations	165
27	Holidays on the Road	170
28	Woodstock, At Last	182
29	A Porta-Potty of our Own	186
30	Why Janis Sang the Blues	193
31	How Many Can Fit?	198
32	A Very Sweet Spot	201
33	Sitting on the Dock of the Bay	209
34	Taking Stock	213
35	The Long-Suffering Caregiver	216
36	My Friends Got Here as Fast as They Could	221
37	A Juke Joint is Calling Me Tonight	225
38	Not everything in Texas is Big	231
39	My Worthless Bottle Tree	238
40	Well, Duh!	244
41	Reluctant No More	249

About the Author   254

CONTENTS

CHAPTERS

1	The Damaged Duo	1
2	On the Road Again	5
3	Finding RV Parks	10
4	Black Tank Initiation	16
5	A Rogue Wave	20
6	Where is Home?	24
7	Finding My Tribe	29
8	Cobbled RV Abodes	33
9	Pesky Intruders	37
10	Scary Encounters	42
11	Tourist Busts	49
12	Serendipities	55
13	It's Not Always Pretty	65
14	Dueling GPSs	75
15	Deliberate Living	82
16	The Philadelphia Folk Festival	87
17	*Easy Rider*, Old Coot Style	96
18	It's Too Hot!	103
19	Nest Building	109
20	If Only It Could Last	114
21	Simple Pleasures	120
22	Better to Say No	138

CHAPTER 1

The Damaged Duo

"I went to the woods because I wished to live deliberately, to front only the essential facts of life, and see if I could not learn what it had to teach, and not, when I came to die, discover that I had not lived. . . . I wanted to live deep and suck out all the marrow of life, . . ."

—Henry David Thoreau, Excerpt from *Walden*; or *Life in the Woods* [Boston: Ticknor and Fields, 1854]

My rallying cry for life, and RVing, came from my Transcendental hero, Henry David Thoreau. Pardon me, Henry, but I would like to paraphrase your opening and say, "I went off in my RV because I wished to live deliberately, . . ."

I first read Thoreau in my late teens. That image of "sucking marrow out of life" lodged in my brain and stayed there. Decades later, I thought Thoreau might have chosen an RV over a cabin had he lived in the twenty-first century.

Some might think it was a stretch to compare traveling around the country in an RV to Thoreau's retreat to a tiny cabin in the woods. After all, the RV came with a microwave oven, heating and air-conditioning, and dozens of electronic devices, whereas Thoreau's retreat left him in a barren cabin in the middle of a forest next to a pond. I believed the comparison was legitimate. Thoreau did exactly what I had always wanted to do with my life: reduce it to the essentials and eke out meaning from what remained.

When I looked back, I was chagrinned at how distracted I had become by the many superfluous accouterments of the modern world. I had lost my way. But now, through the freedom I learned as an RVer, I have returned to my mission to find meaning in everyday life.

I could never have predicted RV travel would have triggered all these changes.

"Oh, my God!" I had tried to roll out of bed but froze in surprise and agony.

It was the morning after my accident, the one in which I had tripped over a garden hose and smashed my lower back against a raised brick planter at the end of the swimming pool.

It was also a mere four days before my husband, Michael, and I planned to leave on another long road trip. Now into our third year of extended travel, we had RVing in our blood and the love of the open road in our souls.

"What?" Michael jerked awake when he heard my scream. "What's wrong?"

"I can't move. It hurts too much." I started systematically wiggling everything, beginning with the outer extremities of my fingers and toes and working my way in toward my torso. "Guess I can move after all," I finally admitted. I swiveled, eased to a sitting position on the edge of the bed, and stood up. "Actually, standing feels better than lying down."

I stretched and headed to the bathroom to look in the mirror. While I could not see my entire backside, I could see huge bruises. My heart pounded in sudden fear. "Michael, come look!"

"Swelling and discoloration usually mean a fracture," Michael said as he studied my bruises.

"This can't be happening," I whined. "We're supposed to leave in four days."

"It happened. You need to see a doctor."

"If I'd broken something, I don't think I'd be able to walk around like this." I strutted a little, trying to prove my point while stifling grimaces with every step. "I'm going to pretend it didn't happen. Once I'm up and about, I think the pain will go away, don't you?"

"I think you're a psycho. You need to see a doctor."

Two days later, I called my primary care physician. The pain was getting worse. I visualized shards of fractured coccyx floating around like seaweed in the ocean, gently wafting in the serum buildup in my lower back. I imagined my physician ordering X-rays and shortly afterward receiving an urgent call from the radiologist regarding my perilous medical situation. My doctor would order me to call an ambulance. EMTs would then rush me to the hospital for emergency surgery before a bone splinter punctured my kidney, gall bladder, or some other vital organ. *If only I can live until a surgeon performs the miracle that will keep me alive*, I thought.

I was both disappointed and relieved when the X-rays showed arthritis, not a fracture. I knew I had osteoarthritis everywhere, but it had not been bothering me too much lately. I had had knee replacements a couple of years earlier and had recently commented how nice it would be to take off in the RV without hurting anywhere. Since I had not broken any bones with my lanai fall, we had decided to take off as planned. My doctor predicted the pain would go away in three or four weeks.

I felt bad complaining about my bruised butt. My poor husband had had major surgery on his left shoulder six months earlier after tripping on a crack in the sidewalk. The hemiarthroplasty surgery had not been successful. He could now raise his left arm only as high as his ear. He still experienced pain, and the injury had affected his balance and gait. Given Michael's much more severe medical issues, I knew I needed to suck it up and stop whining.

Between the two of us, we presented one terribly pathetic pair—Michael with his poorly-healed broken shoulder and me with my bruised tailbone.

Pain notwithstanding, I would be the one loading up the RV for this upcoming trip. While my joints might hurt, they still functioned. I could bend, lift, and hustle up and down RV steps. I had done it with bone-on-bone arthritis in both knees, and I had done it many more times after the two replacement surgeries that had left me with titanium and polymer implants. Compared to all of that, what was a little bruising and fluid buildup around my tailbone?

While we were not taking off fulltime, we had resolved to spend six months on the road on this trip. To ensure we did not cave in early, we had bought tickets for four big events—three music festivals and the National Storytelling Festival. We had spaced the festivals about a month apart, thus making sure the earliest we could get back home without losing lots of money would be mid-October. Despite our damaged bodies, we planned to spend a long time in our small Class C motorhome.

There was something magical and liberating about the open road that pulled at us. The closer departure day came, the more excited we became. We shrugged off our aches and pains and refused to let our physical infirmities dampen our spirits. We were willing to wager we had many more years and thousands more miles on our personal odometers.

I hoped this time around, which would be our first trip up the Atlantic Seaboard, we would feel more like hippies living in a tent rather than what we really were—old-geezer RVers who lived in a motorhome. Regardless, there was marrow in life out there, and I planned to find it.

CHAPTER 2

On the Road Again

I threw too many clothes into my allotted four small bins in the RV, and I stashed even more clothes in the back of the car. It was hard to pack for a long trip, and I knew I would take things I would not wear and would want things I had not brought. We had many activities and climates on our agenda. How could I know what I would need for something like the Philadelphia Folk Festival? Or a first-time meeting with an online attorney writing buddy? Or even for the weather? We were leaving in early May and would not return until mid-October. We planned to go from Florida up the Atlantic coast to North Carolina, as far west as Minnesota, up into Canada, and then stay at least two nights in every state in New England. We planned to camp in the woods, in the mountains, on the beach, and on lakes and rivers. We anticipated rain, sun, wind, and temperatures ranging from the thirties to over one hundred degrees. How did folks plan for that kind of variety and keep their clothes to an appropriate RV amount? I did not know. It occurred to me that Thoreau would not have been impressed with my packing.

Several neighbors came out to the street to see us off. I wanted to believe I saw envy in their eyes, but probably not. They might have felt pity for us, or at least for me. They all knew that despite my excitement, I hated leaving my garden behind. But perhaps they silently cheered for

Michael and wondered why he put up with me. Still, I wondered if they sensed any sadness in my eyes as I surveyed my front yard a final time.

During those final minutes of preparation, I thought of my new favorite song, Alice Merton's "No Roots." I had declared it my theme song for the trip. During the past six months, I had thrown or given away about a thousand pounds of excess baggage from our house. I had also completely given away or sold the last of the 200 orchids I had loved and nurtured on our lanai. I had made these dents in ridding ourselves of 'stuff' despite Michael's injury and its disruptiveness to our lives. Granted, there was still much to do, but I had made progress in overcoming attachments to our possessions. I felt not a single stab of pain as I walked away from my house and its contents for this trip.

But Merton's song about not having roots did not ring true when it came to my plants. It felt ironic. I would miss the literal roots of the lush foliage and flowers in my yard and my potted plants. I wondered how I could be so much more attached to my plants than I was to the stuff inside my house, but this was not the time to think about my weirdness.

It was 11:00 a.m. by the time we pulled out of our subdivision.

"I'm exhausted already, and soaking wet," I said.

"It's eighty-seven degrees with eighty-seven percent humidity," Michael said.

By the time we hit I-275 fifteen minutes later, I had forgotten my little bout of plant-separation anxiety. Our adventure had begun.

"Tell me again why you wanted to come here," Michael said. It was the third day of our Low Country stay in St. Marys, Georgia.

"This is Pat Conroy country," I said. "It's unique to the South." We had both read a great deal of Conroy when we were younger, and I was currently plowing through *The Death of Santini: The Story of a Father and His Son*. We planned to move up the Georgia coast to Savannah and into Charleston, South Carolina. We had gone to the Okefenokee Swamp on Monday and Cumberland Island National Seashore on Tuesday. We had seen a fantastic array of wildlife in both places.

The main reason for coming to this area, I realized, had nothing to do with beautiful white beaches, crashing waves, and salty air. Nor with snake and alligator-infested swamps. For years I had heard about the wild horses on the beaches along the lower east coast, and those horses had drawn me here. The mountains out west seemed a more likely place for feral horses, not the ocean. A quick Internet search revealed that while there were more States on the west coast that had wild horses, the east coast had herds on the beaches in Georgia, Maryland, and Virginia.

Michael and I had taken the ferry ride to Cumberland Island National Seashore in Georgia the day before and had seen the horses there.

"Those malnourished horses are haunting me," I said to Michael.

"Yeah, but what's the answer? The National Park Service wants Cumberland Island to stay as it is. If they started bringing in food and supplies for those horses, it would upset the natural balance."

"But they don't even have clean water. They drink that brackish stuff. They're skinny and sick."

"It's nature. There's not enough food for them, and the saltwater damages their internal organs. But if the park service started feeding them and bringing in veterinarians, they'd start breeding like crazy. Then they'd overpopulate the island, eat all the foliage, and there wouldn't be enough food for the rabbits and the bobcats and all the other animals."

"What'd our guide say about the average life span of a horse? Wasn't it about thirty years? Those horses live only about twelve. Something's seriously wrong with this picture."

"An ethical dilemma, for sure. But how many parts of the country are still untouched by modern development? I'm with the National Park Service on this one. They need to leave Cumberland Island alone—let whatever happens there happen."

"I guess I agree," I said. "But still . . ."

Everywhere we went along the coast, tiny sand gnats, known as no-see-ums, found me and bit me.

"I'm going crazy," I said. "I itch all over."

By our fourth day in the Low Country, no-see-um welts dotted my arms, neck, and even my scalp. I had scratched so much I worried about infection. The pesky things defied window screens and had invaded the inside of our RV. DEET seemed to work, but I had neglected to dab it on my head until after they had already bitten me on the scalp. While mosquitos preferred dawn and dusk, or at least shady areas, these sand gnats seemed to be active twenty-four-seven in all kinds of light. When I realized the damned things were not biting Michael, I screamed at the injustice.

My hysteria mounted as my number of bites increased. Being hypersensitive to stinging and biting insects, I needed an antihistamine to calm the itching and my frantic scratching. Topical medications did not work on me.

"I'm going to become addicted to Benadryl if we don't get out of here soon," I said. I had had enough of this languid, listless South. Logging and fishing appeared to be the major industries in this southeastern corner of Georgia, and the poor appeared to outnumber the rich about a thousand to one.

"We're not leaving here until I get a Low Country Boil," Michael said. We had been reading about this local specialty and had already picked out a couple of possible restaurants in Charleston. The dish consisted of shrimp or crab legs, corn on the cob, potatoes, and lots of spices, all cooked together in a big pot. Michael could hardly wait. Not me. I did not eat shellfish. However, I loved fish and looked forward to dinner in a nice restaurant.

I had to admit the Southern charm was seductive. I sat at a picnic table in our RV park, watching Spanish moss waft in the breeze and listening to noisy, busy birds. The sound of our air conditioning hummed softly in the background. Occasionally, a vehicle sped down the main road a quarter mile away. Although almost ten o'clock in the morning, the campground felt abandoned. Where was everyone? Had the world ended, leaving only Michael and me? While almost every camping site had a rig of some sort, we appeared to be the only people around. A profound sense of loneliness washed over me. Yes, I had successfully de-cathected from all that stuff in Tampa, but this hot, humid, sand-gnat-infested coastal Low Country could never be my home.

I wanted to feel excited and energetic again. I had been free to wander, but where was the thrill now that I was doing it? If I was running away from the enslaving demands of my house and fast-paced life back in Tampa, this present moment should have felt liberating and euphoric. I had no demands, and time felt like it moved in slow-motion. Instead of feeling free and light, I felt hot, itchy, and sad. This was not the kind of deliberate living I had envisioned.

Did I need to return to some sort of spirituality? Maybe I should have joined the New Age woo-woo movement or found some pagans to hang out with? Would a Zen Buddhist infusion or some yoga meditation have set things right in my head? We were only four days into our road trip. Surely this was not yet another existential crisis popping up.

Or maybe it was. Someday, I vowed, I would stop my fretting and stewing and learn how to relax. Maybe then my husband would not think I was such a psycho.

CHAPTER 3

Finding RV Parks

Selecting an RV park to camp for a couple of nights was not rocket science, and it should not cause friction between a husband and a wife. Michael loved to plan and organize our trips. I had learned it was easier if I stayed out of the planning and let him proceed without my input. Where we stayed was not usually something I cared about. Plus, making reservations for campgrounds could be time-consuming, and there were other things I preferred doing, such as reading and writing. However, occasionally we landed in what looked like a dump. Then I complained that my smart and talented husband could have done a better job of picking out a place for us to spend the night.

When looking for campgrounds and other necessities on the road, Michael used an app on his iPad called AllStays Camp & RV. He clicked on the app, typed in the town we wanted to stay in, and options popped up—campgrounds, truck stops, grocery stores, and more. Once the selected town appeared on the iPad map, finger pinching either expanded or reduced the distance from the center of town. Click on a campground icon and links appeared, including the park website and a link to Google Maps for directions and anticipated travel time from one's current location. The technology behind this information boggled my mind.

Finding RV Parks

Michael swore by his AllStays Camp & RV app and used it with almost worshipful adoration. I found the app impossible. On my iPad, I somehow managed to destroy my selected options for notifications on every attempt. Plus, the required finger pinching to expand and contract the parameters of the search flummoxed me. But the most important reason I disliked the app was that it offered a limited number of options. I could find more campgrounds on my iPad by merely googling "RV campgrounds near me." With my Google search, I generally found twice as many options as Michael found with AllStays. My stubborn husband refused to admit this truth.

We had stayed in hundreds of parks and campgrounds during our years of RVing. I knew we had not seen everything, but we had seen a sampling of everything from top-of-the-line luxury resorts to bottom-of-the-barrel cesspools. We told ourselves it was all good, that we were flexible, adaptable, and resilient people at our cores.

However, occasionally one of those sight-unseen selections from AllStays did not look like a place where I wanted to stay. I did not always handle it well when that happened.

"This isn't it, is it?" I asked.

Michael had slowed the rig and turned the blinker on. We were waiting for a traffic break to turn left into a seedy-looking trailer park on Highway 301 in Wilson, North Carolina.

"Believe it is," Michael cheerfully said. "I'm ready to settle in for the night. This was not an easy travel day."

"Michael, look at this place. I don't think we ought to stay here."

"Why not? They've mowed the grass. I don't see garbage piled up anywhere. What's the problem?"

"Their sign is falling down. The office looks like a dump, and there are huge potholes in the road. I think we could find a nicer place." I could have added that the parking slips were mud and grass instead of concrete and that there were not any trees to provide shade from the searing sun and the ninety-plus degree temperatures. I did not add that God only knew how far we were from the closest grocery store.

"I've already told you. This was the only place I could find between here and Kitty Hawk, North Carolina. There are no RV campgrounds in this part of the state."

We had been driving for six hours. The humid ninety-four-degree temperature outside did not improve my disposition. We were both weary and overdue for our five o'clock cocktails.

"It'll be fine," my husband said. He pulled to a stop in front of the campground office.

I grabbed Michael's arm as he turned off the ignition. "You've already put down a deposit, right? Why don't we stay tonight and find another place for tomorrow night?" We had four nights to hang out before our reservation began at Kitty Hawk. In keeping with our plan to do more living and less driving, we had deliberately scheduled a few breaks from places we considered tourist destinations. We wanted to hang out in unknown locations and try to get a feel for what folks were thinking, what life might be like living there. It would be our own twenty-first-century John Steinbeck *Travels with Charley* sort of journey. Per my initial impression, Wilson, North Carolina, certainly seemed to fit the definition of off-the-beaten-path, though not necessarily in a charming and delightful way.

"Would you please stop worrying. And whining," Michael said. He jerked his arm out of my grasp and stepped down from the truck. I quietly followed him into the office, still hoping I could intervene.

The two large, cigarette-smoking, snaggle-toothed North Carolina women behind the counter acted as if we were crazy to want to reduce the number of nights in our four-day reservation.

"I mean, we can reduce it to one night, but you'll be sorry," the one with the red hair said. "This is summer, after all, and places fill up. If you don't go ahead and pay now, I can't promise there'll even be a place for you by tomorrow night. We get busy."

"Oh, okay," Michael said. "We'll leave the reservation at four nights." He pulled out his Visa card and passed it over the cluttered counter to the redhead.

I was not happy but bit my tongue. We did not speak as we left the office. As soon as we unhooked the car from the RV and connected to the utilities at our campsite, I booted up my laptop and googled *RV parks near me*. At least we had Internet and cell phone service in this campground, an amenity I never took for granted in rural areas.

"You and your damn AllStays app," I said. I could not stop myself from pointing out to my husband that I found seven other RV parks in Wilson, North Carolina. "That app doesn't list everything. When I google campgrounds on my laptop, I get twice as many listings as your app shows. When are you going to accept that your beloved AllStays is not the best way to find a campground?"

"My app works fine," Michael said. I could tell he felt miffed, but I did not know whether it was because he knew he had been wrong about park availability or whether he was disgusted with my obnoxious behavior of pointing it out to him.

"Wait until you see the bathhouse." I had checked it out while Michael hooked up the cable so he could watch the ABC Evening News. "You're crazy if you think I'll take a shower in that dark, dirty dungeon." Michael later agreed that management could have put a few more light fixtures in the bathrooms. Lighting in the men's room would prove so inadequate that Michael had trouble shaving. While I relented and used the ladies' room for my shampoo showers, I used our tiny RV shower on non-shampoo nights.

The next morning, I bucked up and reconciled myself to a four-day interlude in what I considered our marginal RV campground. We pulled out our iPads and started looking for exciting things to do for the next three days.

We discovered Vollis Simpson's Whirligig Park and Museum in downtown Wilson. Simpson (1919-2013) had been a local farmer/house-mover/machine shop operator who salvaged scrap metal and created large, kinetic structures with moveable parts activated by the wind. He called his fanciful, colorful pieces whirligigs. Some were as simple as cowboys and bicycles, while others were as elaborate as airplanes and windmills. The town relocated Simpson's structures from his farm to a downtown park in 2004 and started holding an annual whirligig festival the first week of every November. Proclaimed a brilliant intersection of art and science, North Carolina declared whirligigs the official folk art for the state in 2013. My head still spins with memories of all those spinning whirligig parts.

We stumbled upon a newly opened microbrewery (217 Brew Works) and spent a couple of hours drinking beer and listening to a great three-piece jazz ensemble. I was surprised to find something so hip in this small town. We took a mile-long, self-guided tour of Historic Wilson and saw Civil War era houses. Some were decaying while other structures had been restored to their original states. During a day trip to Raleigh, we hiked three miles along the Neuse River, explored the City Market area, and moseyed through four huge buildings of produce and other products at the State Farmers Market. Rain drenched us during an unpredicted thunderstorm during a hike in the Flower Blossom Nature Preserve, and we laughed with the delight of being comfortably cool for the first time in weeks. Finally, we took a docent-led tour of a Country Doctor Museum under the guardianship of East Carolina University. The museum even had a garden and grew the medicinal herbs used by doctors in the past. The excitement our millennial docent conveyed when talking about eighteenth and nineteenth-century pharmaceutical, surgical, and home-remedy medical interventions impressed and amazed me. Months later, I still thought about that young man and wondered if he was making progress towards his dream of becoming a doctor.

In retrospect, Wilson, North Carolina, was not the armpit I had originally dubbed it to be. Nor did the Wilson RV Park prove to be the run-down, degenerate-filled campground I had feared. The only legitimate thing I could, and did, blame the RV park for was the dark bathhouse. They could have found higher watt lightbulbs or maybe added a couple more fixtures. By the light of day and with the exterior doors propped open, the bathrooms did not even appear dirty.

One unanticipated and welcomed surprise of Wilson, North Carolina, was the absence of insects. We had arrived in Wilson after spending two weeks in the Low Country. Welts from both sand gnat and mosquito bites covered me from head to toe, and I had scratched myself raw in places. Topical creams had been useless, and Benadryl had limited effectiveness. It took some time to realize that in terms of biting, stinging insects, Wilson had been insect-free. The almost-infected welts I had arrived with finally had a chance to heal.

It took a few months for me to sort out all these experiences and admit that Wilson, North Carolina, had not been bad at all. Michael had made a good choice for a pit-stop between tourist attractions, after all. Sometimes it took some distance to reach a reasonable perspective, and sometimes the distance made me realize how judgmental and obnoxious I could sometimes be. Chalk one up for RV travel helping to make one a nicer, kinder person.

CHAPTER 4

Black Tank Initiation

"What?" Michael's voice reflected his shock.

"We don't have a bathhouse here," the manager of the Kitty Hawk RV Park said. "I thought you understood that when you made your reservations."

Michael's mouth hung open.

"You have a bathroom in that thing," the manager continued, gesturing toward our Four Winds. "What's the problem?"

"We've never stayed in a park that didn't have bath facilities," Michael said, his voice now under control.

"This is the beach. You have any idea how many homeless folks hang out around here? How nasty a bathhouse would get in a place like this?" The manager became animated, started gesturing with his arms and pacing. "There'd be folks sleeping on the floor, hypodermic needles all over the place, puke in the sinks." The manager stared at Michael like he thought he was crazy. "The owner of this park lives in that big house right over there. He doesn't want riffraff even tempted."

"Guess I can see that," Michael said, "and you're right. We've got full facilities, so we'll be okay. It's a bit of a surprise."

I could see the despair in my husband's eyes.

Black Tank Initiation

The RV park manager had no way of knowing that after almost three years of RVing, we had never graced our sacred black tank with anything other than liquids. The black tank caught the waste from the toilet and the bathroom sink, while water from the shower and the kitchen sink went into a grey tank. Somehow, when we bought our motorhome, Michael heard or overheard stories about RV owners who maintained pristine black tanks to avoid problems down the road. After much persuasive talking, Michael convinced me that we would be triggering untold grief and complications if we ever deviated from a liquids-only policy for our black tank.

Despite my determination to not let my husband make this RV thing any more difficult than it already was, I had agreed to his black-tank vision. Nevertheless, I often pointed out to him all the other RVers who did not appear to follow these precautions.

"It's not fair," I would say in exasperation, my voice rising. "These RVs are made for our use and convenience."

"I'm telling you," Michael said, "in time, our toilet will get clogged up."

"Then we'll get it unclogged. There must be services that clean out these things if they clog up that easily. Michael, you're being impossible."

We had had this conversation or some variation thereof too many times to count. I enjoyed getting overly dramatic and seeing my husband's reactions. Maybe I triggered those conversations for my amusement. I suspected my husband enjoyed our little repartee as well, but I could have been wrong. I had not decided whether or not I would ever tell him that I secretly believed what he said about problems down the road with the black tank.

Sometimes foul odors arose from the toilet, even though there was nothing but urine in the tank. "What the hell, Michael? Why does it stink?"

Michael would shrug. "Must be the enzymes I've been using. I'll try another brand next time."

To help prevent odors and clogs, our Lazy Days saleswoman at the outset had sold us an expensive gallon jug of a probiotic enzyme to break down odor-producing bacteria. Measuring and adding the enzyme proved cumbersome, so we switched to dissolvable pods that we dropped in the toilet. On the rare occasions when we talked about tank management with other campers, they assured us odor problems were common. But while RVers did not tend to talk about black tank waste and its management, our non-RVing friends expressed great curiosity. I chuckled to think that black tanks were like a verboten topic in the RVing world.

Getting back to our current situation, I grinned at my husband while laughing to myself. Yes! Finally, we would cross the barrier. I hoped Michael would be the first to use our motorhome throne.

The next morning on what would be our first full day in Kitty Hawk—it happened. My disappointment was that I had crossed the line first. I cursed my early morning call of nature.

Thirty minutes later, Michael buckled his sandals and said, "I'm going to take a ride." He stood up and reached for the car keys hanging over the door. "I'm going to that Dunkin' Donuts down the street."

"Why? We've got coffee here, and I know you don't want doughnuts."

"They've got nice, clean restrooms," Michael said. He grinned at me as he sauntered out the door and to the car.

It cannot last, I thought. He will break down. Or maybe he will experience an emergency and have no choice but to use the toilet in the rig. Maybe I should hide the car keys one night. Then he would have no choice but to join the Black Tank Club. I would not dare do that, though. I was sure he would succumb before we left this place.

But it did not happen. Michael continued to make trips to Dunkin' Donuts, the 7-Eleven, and even to Home Depot for the remainder of our five-day stay in Kitty Hawk. He grinned at me with every trip.

That RV park in Kitty Hawk remained the only place we have ever stayed that did not have showers and toilets. We both continued to find the absence of a bathhouse in that RV park surprising.

I figured with our black tank situation, once we had crossed the line, there would be no going back. It was sort of like losing one's virginity.

Black Tank Initiation

Either you had done it, or you had not. Unless we had parked right next to a bathhouse and the weather was good, I continued using the RV toilet for its intended purposes. But Michael maintained his abstinence of black tank desecration, and an end was not in sight. I was impressed but also embarrassed. I wished my husband would do what God and the RV manufacturers intended RVers to do in their motorhome bathrooms.

CHAPTER 5

A Rogue Wave

"But people love the beach," I had argued to Michael when we had planned our trip. "There's got to be something we're not understanding." We sat in our RV in Kitty Hawk, North Carolina, eating breakfast. Michael had made a bologna sandwich for himself, and I had instant oatmeal with walnuts and cinnamon. We could almost hear the waves from the Atlantic Ocean, which was less than a block away.

"I can't imagine why we chose to come here," Michael said. "I hate everything about the beach. The sand hurts my feet, the sun stings my eyes, and the wind burns my skin. Tell me again why we're going up the coast."

"So you could put stickers on your stupid sticker map. We needed a South Carolina sticker, which is how we ended up in Charleston, although we didn't go to the beach there. To answer your question, Charleston leads right into Kitty Hawk. I've heard about the Outer Banks all my life, and I want to see the wild horses there."

I realized too late that I had not needed to see more wild horses since we had already seen the sick, starving ones on Cumberland Island in Georgia. When we planned the trip, we had not realized we would be duplicating wild-horse sightings. But our logic, or the lack thereof, was typical for us. We would pick a place we had never been and plan the stops along the way to get there.

Michael and I had been through this before. "Maybe this time will be different, and we'll like all that salty air and sunshine," I said to him.

"Do we have to put on bathing suits and get in the water?"

"Nope. I didn't even bring my bathing suit."

"Thank God," Michael said.

We forced ourselves to walk along the beach in Kitty Hawk. It felt compulsory, since our RV park was across Ocean Boulevard, with only dunes separating the road from the Atlantic Ocean. So, I could say I had done it, I removed my shoes and stepped into the water. "Yikes! What do you think the water temperature is—fifty degrees?"

"Don't be ridiculous," Michael said. "According to the news, it's fifty-four. I can't believe how you exaggerate everything."

"Hahaha. At least I know why no one's swimming." Not only had the water felt freezing, but the surf also looked strong and scary.

A few days later, we learned how strong and scary those waves were. It began when Michael and I walked over to the dunes at dusk one evening before turning in for the night. We wanted a final look at the ocean, a sight that never failed to generate awe. We were surprised to see something new at our crossover spot—someone had nailed a red mailbox to a post. That was when we began to piece together the story from old newspapers, the Internet, and conversations with locals.

The incident had happened on April 25, 2018, about a month before we arrived in Kitty Hawk. We both freaked out when we realized we had probably walked along the exact spot where the horrific incident had happened. It may have even been where I ventured barefoot into the water's edge.

A New Hampshire mother and her four-year-old son, Wesley Belisle, had been walking ankle-deep along the water's edge when a powerful, four to six-foot rogue wave knocked them down. A second wave followed and separated the mother and child. Forever. A riptide had caught Wesley and ultimately deposited him thirty miles to the north at Carova Beach five days later.

The community of Kitty Hawk mobilized with an outpouring of support and sadness. Private citizens combed the coastline long after the Coast Guard called off the official search. Residents created a huge heart out of seashells on the beach, filling the inside with balloons, teddy bears, flowers, and all sorts of gifts. Someone created a time capsule, filled it with collected notes, and threw it into the water.

"Wow," I had said. "These stories are bringing tears to my eyes."

"The story received national coverage. Whoever heard of such a freakish accident? It makes shark attacks and alligator bites seem like every-day occurrences," Michael said.

Now, exactly one month later, an anonymous member of the community had nailed a red mailbox to a platform on the beach and had left notepaper and magic markers inside the box for visitors to write messages to Wesley and his parents. Orange had been Wesley's favorite color, and the mailbox donor had painted seashells orange and arranged them at the mailbox's base, creating a second option for folks wanting to leave messages. Already, with the mailbox there for less than a day, folks had written dozens of messages in the notebooks. Michael left a note from us, expressing condolences.

"Wow," I said a couple of days later. "That could've happened to me."

"What are you talking about?"

"A rogue wave. A riptide. I had my feet ankle-deep in that water. A wave could have swept me away like it did Wesley. You could have lost me forever, right here in Kitty Hawk."

"You're being absurd," Michael said.

"Oh, yeah? Probably if Wesley's mother had heard a story like that, she'd have thought it ridiculous, too. But look what happened. Why'd they ever call it a *rogue wave* anyway? That doesn't seem to fit."

Later, I sat down with a thesaurus and, for the life of me, I could not find a word that described that unexpected, ferocious, deadly wave any better than the word *rogue*.

A Rogue Wave

A few days later, as we drove out of Kitty Hawk, I made a mental inventory of all the things we had experienced thus far on the east-coast leg of our RV trip. We had been on the road a little over three weeks, and we had encountered ungodly temperatures that soared to the upper nineties during the day and dropped only to the mid-to-upper-seventies at night. Even with sunglasses, my eyes burned from the sun's penetrating glare. Sand had gotten into my clothes, shoes, eyes, and hair. The wind never seemed to stop along the coast, and my hair tangled every time I stepped outside. Sand gnats and mosquitoes had attacked me for three weeks, leaving my arms, legs, and scalp covered with itchy welts and a few red, inflamed areas where I had gouged off skin with my frantic scratching. Now I could add a killer wave and undertow to the list of things I did not like about the beach. Our seashore camping jaunt had not changed Michael's aversion for the beach, either.

But in looking at our sticker map plastered to the RV freezer door, I knew we would be looking at the Atlantic Ocean a few more times before we filled in every state with a sticker. Where else would one go in Delaware or New Jersey or Rhode Island if not to the beach? We had to go to these States, or our map would have gaps.

Michael was having the time of his life, despite his dislike of beaches. He was thrilled to see the open road out his front windshield and feel the tires rolling beneath him. His ear-to-ear grin had become semi-permanent on his face. I needed to readjust my attitude if I wanted to be a good traveling companion on this long RV trip.

I needed something bizarre, not a *rogue wave* necessarily, but something unexpected or serendipitous to awaken a sense of awe in me. The road ahead held the potential for incredible adventures that would change my life. I hoped I would recognize those significant events when they occurred. When I thought about what a serendipity it had been that we even heard the story about Wesley Belisle and the rogue wave, I worried I would miss important stories unfolding around us. I was not sure how to make every moment count, but that was what I wanted to do. To do less would have been cheating myself.

CHAPTER 6

Where is Home?

Despite growing up on a farm in a flat agricultural area, I thought of myself as a mountain person. I loved forests with trees so thick they limited visibility. I loved trickling, ice-cold streams that dotted mountainsides, at times producing sparkling whitewater rapids as they rushed over rocks and glinted in the sun. I loved the occasional sound of leaves rustling as an unseen animal scampered out of sight. I loved the smell of all that vegetation in various states of growth and decay. The regeneration, death, regeneration, death cycle. Ad infinitum, with no help from us humans.

I had a lightness in my heart and joy in my soul as we left Kitty Hawk, North Carolina, and headed towards the Blue Ridge Mountains in Virginia. I remembered the first time I went camping—in late May 1972. My husband (the first one, not Michael) and I went with another couple in their tiny Airstream to the Shenandoah National Park in the Appalachian Mountains. We had lived in Maryland at the time, and spring had arrived. Every shrub and tree had sprouted new growth, and many plants had burst into bloom. As the four of us drove into Virginia and began our ascent up the mountain ridge, I noticed that the vegetation become more barren and less green the higher we climbed. By the time we got to the park, I marveled that spring had not yet arrived at this higher elevation. The first night we were there, it snowed! Now it was

Where is Home?

May 2018. Would I see snow again during this camping trip, forty-six years later?

🚐

"Hey, slow down." I jerked to attention. Michael had been looking out the window rather than ahead and had not appeared to notice the sudden slow-down in traffic. We had crested a hill and looked down at flashing lights. Michael hit the brakes.

"Looks like they're diverting traffic. What the hell?" There were maybe three vehicles in front of us, with a highway patrolman talking through rolled-down windows to each driver in turn. Every stopped vehicle made a U-turn across the median and headed back in the direction from which we had all come.

We had been following U.S. 33 heading west toward Elkton, Virginia, toward the campground where we had reservations. The location sounded perfect for hiking along the Appalachian Trail and for seeing the famous Luray Caverns. We were hoping for cooler temperatures. Finally, we reached the head of the line of stopped vehicles.

"This road is closed," the Virginia State Trooper said. "There've been three mudslides—the road is impassable. Turn around here and head back towards Ruckersville. You'll be able to pick up U.S. 29 and get to the park from there." We made a U-turn as instructed by the trooper.

"Mudslides?" I asked, the question rhetorical. I was incredulous. "I know it's been raining every day, but that blows me away."

"Sounds like they happened within the past few minutes. Be glad we didn't get trapped between them. I have no idea how long it'd take to clear a mudslide off a road, but I wouldn't want to have to sit and watch them do it."

I pulled out my trusted *Rand McNally Road Atlas*. "Why don't we head north? Maybe try to find a place in the Front Royal area? That'd put us at the north end of the Shenandoahs, closer to Harper's Ferry."

"Fine with me."

While mudslides made our entry into the mountains feel unusually auspicious, this was the kind of event that perked me right up. It was bizarre, which was precisely the kind of experience I had been wanting. Mudslides fell into the category of adventure, and these three mudslides affected us personally, despite us not having seen them.

We found spring in full force in the Shenandoahs when we arrived. Was it because of global warming, or had that May snowstorm forty-six years earlier been a fluke? We found a campground in Front Royal. We also found temperatures in the low nineties, at least until it started raining. And rain it did, for what felt like forty days and forty nights. As we drove along the scenic Blue Ridge Parkway, we found our views obstructed by rain, fog, and mists. While the rain dropped temperatures to a more tolerable level, at times, it still felt like we were in a sauna. I often thought of that May 1972 snowstorm during my first camping trip. It left me with stronger and more exciting memories than this heat and rain ever would.

We checked out a couple of entry points to the Appalachian Trail from the Parkway and hiked short distances during rain breaks. The trail sometimes required climbing over boulders, balancing on tree logs, and tiptoeing across rocks in small streams. All these maneuvers challenged my orthopedically asymmetrical husband. We would return to the car from these jaunts with mud on our jeans and shoes. We managed to log several miles each day, but our performances were laughable even to us.

However, we were proud to have taken the heat and rain in stride. It would have been easy to shrug, sit in the air-conditioned motorhome, and read books or play Rummikub. We felt hardy and proud, strong and rugged. Nothing would stop us from our outdoor camping adventure.

Our resolve did not last. After three nights, the ongoing deluges in the Front Royal area of the park drove us out. We headed north to Harper's Ferry, West Virginia, hoping to get away from the low-pressure weather system stalled over our heads.

I remembered Harper's Ferry and the confluence of the Shenandoah and Potomac Rivers from a previous camping trip in a pop-up camper. It had been in a previous life with my first husband and a couple of young children, circa 1982 or 1983. I remembered the quaint historic town and the convergence of the rivers as one of the most beautiful places on

Where is Home?

the planet. I had been euphorically happy and peaceful at that spot. I wondered if the area would be as I remembered it and if those feelings would return.

The rains continued with enough breaks for us to visit the town and see the rivers. I had not remembered the footbridge over the Shenandoah River, where one could walk across to Maryland. We did not take a walk, being too hot and tired from our drive from Front Royal and setting up in a new campground. We checked out the John Brown Museum, browsed some shops and restored buildings, and ate lunch in a charming little café.

It was fortuitous that we visited Harper's Ferry that first afternoon. It rained throughout the night and flooded the riverbanks. Officials blocked entry into the town the following day for five or six hours until the water receded. We headed to higher ground, hiking in the woods, and seeing battlefields that were too high to flood.

My ho-hum reactions to the Shenandoah Mountains and the village of Harper's Ferry surprised and dismayed me. My memories of earlier visits were strong, so why did I not feel excited or joyful at what should have been homecomings?

I could only conclude that maybe I had become jaded. Maybe I had traveled too much and seen too many things. In the past couple of years, we had seen both the Colorado and the Canadian Rockies. Both of those ranges dwarfed and rendered pathetic these old Appalachian Mountains in the east. But still, mountains are mountains. The beaches along the east coast—St. Marys, Savannah, Charleston, and Kitty Hawk—had not been places I felt at home or found meaning. Now the mountains disappointed me as well.

Would I ever find a home-away-from-home in this damned RV while traveling across the United States? I realized I had been searching and waiting for a place that resonated as a spot where I belonged. I had always felt awe that Georgia O'Keefe reported finding her spiritual home the minute she set foot on Ghost Ranch in Abiquiu, New Mexico. I longed to feel a connection like that to a place on the planet. I wanted to find my true spiritual home. Maybe it would never happen. Maybe, given my pain from osteoarthritis, it was time for me to go back home to Tampa, back to my real home and a life I understood. But I knew Michael would never agree.

Could I muster the courage to go home without him? I knew I was wading into dark and dangerous waters with thoughts like these, waters that could potentially contain rogue waves and fatal riptides. The combined stresses of the still-itching sand gnat bites, the strong nonstop winds and brutal sun of the beaches, and now the constant rain that pummeled us daily in the mountains had taken their toll. I felt sorry for myself and hated the feeling. It was not what I had wanted or planned.

But maybe life did not require that one find a special place where the stars converged in perfect alignment and the elements resounded in harmonic synchronicity. Perhaps I was asking too much from my universe. Did others feel settled and contented in their homes? Was there something abnormal about me that led to this constant searching and questioning? Perhaps a more relevant question for our current RV trip might be what the hell kept me from accepting and enjoying whatever I saw in the moment? My real home, the one where I had planted deep roots, both literally and figuratively, was back in Tampa. What was my need to find meaning and connection everywhere I went? I needed to rearrange my thinking, and I needed to do it soon.

CHAPTER 7

Finding My Tribe

It took almost a month, but I finally stopped mourning my life back in Tampa and started relaxing into the trip. I even admitted to having fun. After our first couple of years and several long road trips, I wrapped my arms around the notion of RVing and fell into the rhythm of the road. I welcomed the unhurried pace. I loved moseying from one place to the next, the spontaneity of changing plans when something new popped up that interested us. Most of all, I appreciated the simplicity of the lifestyle—no schedules, no appointments, no telemarketers. We pretty much ate when we felt hungry, slept when we felt tired, and followed our whims with books and movies. My writing was even going well.

Michael's mission to put a sticker on every possible state on our sticker map took us to areas we might not have previously chosen. We wanted to go to the Rock & Roll Hall of Fame in Cleveland, Ohio, and we scoured the Internet trying to find things of interest to do between Harper's Ferry and Cleveland. We did not find much. The shortest possible driving route was 341 miles, more miles than we wanted to do in one day. RV travel was harder and slower than automobile travel. Plus, we were old and retired and had no reason to push forward like a bat out of hell. We liked easing slowly into each day and gliding into an even slower finish by mid-afternoon. But right now, we needed to find a place to stop for the night.

"This is certainly not an RV-friendly state," Michael said.

"What do you mean?"

"There are no RV parks. Nothing for miles and miles."

"Can't be. You're on RV AllStays, right? Let me look on the Internet," I said.

My usually productive Google search for campgrounds proved as barren as Michael's RV AllStays. We did, however, find an almost infinite number of mobile home parks. I had known as a social worker in Florida that Ohio transplants landing in the Sunshine State usually headed for the trailer parks, sometimes after transporting the entire family of six and all their belongings in a beat-up station wagon with peeling wood panels on the sides, mattresses strapped to the roof, and the kids buried among the pots, pans, and pillows in the back of the car.

"What are we going to do?" I asked. "I don't want to sign a three-month lease to stay overnight somewhere."

"I'll find something." We sat in the rig in a service station parking lot where we had stopped for gas and coffee. Michael had been on the phone for almost an hour already, calling various mobile home parks to ask if they had any spots for overnighters. It felt like dialing for dollars. Most of the parks had a few sites set aside for travelers like us. The problem, we learned, was that Ohio was building an oil pipeline through its center and seasonal construction workers employed by the pipeline company had booked all the short-term spots.

We were well into our third year of RV travel, and this was the first time we had had trouble finding a place to stay other than during holidays. We had always been able to find something, even if it was a few miles out of town. But this time, we were having trouble finding anything at all.

"Why don't you try government parks?" I asked. "It doesn't look like there are any private RV parks anywhere in this damned state."

"Why don't we ignore Ohio and head straight to Michigan? We could do another four hours of driving."

"And miss the Rock & Roll Hall of Fame? No way." I could not believe my husband had suggested such a thing. "Plus, you know as well as I that you're not going to leave a hole in that sticker map." I laughed. "You're too obsessed about it."

It took another hour of telephoning, but eventually, Michael found us a spot for the night in Cadiz, Ohio, about midway between Harper's Ferry and Cleveland. The small county park, called The Sally Buffalo Campground, sat on top of a rolling hill and looked down on a couple of small lakes. From our campsite vantage point, we could see camper sites around the lakes and inlets below. The farther down the hill we looked, the more established and permanent the campsites seemed. Many of the campsites had private docks, elaborate decks, and outside storage sheds. A significant number of the rigs looked as if no one had moved them in decades. Our top-of-the-hill location looked pretty settled, too, and I suspected we might have been the only one-nighters there. We saw storage sheds, large BBQ pits, and decks impossible to take apart for relocation.

By dusk, the park had come alive with country music. Men stood around drinking beer and talking smack, while smoke sifted from their BBQ grills and smokers. Women went in and out of the rigs, some setting up picnic tables for supper, others chasing down children. Party time! However, by nine o'clock, every trailer was dark, and the park had become eerily quiet. Construction worker hours, for sure.

The next morning it looked as if two-thirds of the residents left the park between seven and seven-thirty in the morning. We guessed they might have been temporary oil pipeline workers there for a season with their families. Or maybe they had long-term leases on their sites and stayed year-round, even during the winter with freezing temperatures and snow. As we walked through the park later that morning, I realized I found those campsites and how people lived in them more interesting than anything I had seen so far on this trip.

The realization that people interested me more than plants or animals should not have been a 'well, duh!' moment. I had been a social worker for forty years, after all.

These campers appeared to have created a sense of community on this mountaintop of travel trailers and the occasional motorhome. They seemed to share a lifestyle, and they did not appear to be trying to impose their values on anyone.

That I should feel a twinge of jealousy on that hilltop surprised me. Would I have been able to fit into a community like this one? I sensed that they had found something I had been searching for and that had eluded me my entire life. I wanted and needed community, and this one felt stronger than the one I had back in Tampa.

The culture I glimpsed in the working-class community of the Sally Buffalo Campground reminded me of that feeling of community I had had as a child in my small hometown. Those hard-working, hard-partying Sally Buffalo folks were like the folks I grew up with. They were my tribe of origin, except the accent was not quite as Southern as mine had been. I felt a restlessness coming on, not quite as happy and contented as I had been before. We had pulled up roots to take a road trip. Now I suddenly ached for roots, and I knew that buying an orchid for the RV was not going to satisfy my longing.

CHAPTER 8
Cobbled RV Abodes

Sometimes the creativity people showed in arranging and adapting their homes to suit their needs stunned me. Before I retired from social work, I had made home visits for almost the entire forty years of my career. I thought I had seen about everything—from sprawling mansions to two-room hovels, from places with minimal furnishings to houses with goat paths winding through ceiling-high piles of stuff. I had seen floors so clean I would eat breakfast off them to ones littered with two-week-old dog poop. I had a colleague who once made a home visit and found a cow standing in the family's kitchen. One time I sat on an over-sized sofa with stuffing oozing out of a torn cushion and struggled to maintain a poker-face when mice scurried out of the cushion and dashed across the floor to a hole in the baseboard.

The Sally Buffalo Campground in Cadiz, Ohio, interested me much as those long-ago social work home visits had done. At Sally Buffalo, I witnessed a hilltop community of RVers who seemed united in values and lifestyle. The uniqueness of the rural Ohio setting interested me. I never learned where those people went when they left the campground at 7:00 every morning. It was not important, anyway.

HOME IS WHERE THE RV IS

I was not ready for our next Ohio campground. While the Sally Buffalo perked my interest, the Willow Lake Campground in Medina, Ohio, boggled my mind. Located an hour south of Cleveland, this campground was the closest we could find for our trip into the city to visit the Rock & Roll Hall of Fame. While the park maintained a seasonal schedule, open from April through October, most of the rigs stayed on the property year-round. We were not surprised to learn this since few of the trailers or RVs looked roadworthy anyway. Most looked as if they would fall apart if anyone tried to move them two inches. I started to get a sense that full-timers inhabited RV parks in Ohio more than seasonal residents, and that fulltime and seasonal residents greatly outnumbered traveling guests. It felt like an epiphany when I realized many people possibly lived fulltime in RVs because they could not afford to live in houses or apartments. Sometimes I wondered why I was so slow to figure these things out.

Many of these cobbled-together homes in the Willow Lake Campground looked like structures erected in a Third World Country, sometimes with only the shell of the former recreational vehicle still recognizable. Many had no wheels and sat on cinderblocks, while others had flat tires. People had tossed tarpaulins across the roofs of a few of the RVs, and several inches of leaves lay decomposing on the tarps. Green roofs now grew naturally where seeds had settled and germinated in the rich organic compost. Some of the homes had broken windows, with the openings boarded up with plywood or covered with plastic. One bivouac did not even have a door—it had only a blanket hanging across the front entrance. Did the owners booby-trap the entrance to scare off trespassers? Or maybe they did not bother because they had nothing of value for anyone to steal.

Residents in some of these structures had expanded living areas with add-ons to their original shells. Some had enclosed front decks, creating screened rooms almost the size of the house. Others had added a room or two at the front, the end, or the back of the rig. Almost every site had a freestanding shed or lean-to. These supplemental structures stored a wide variety of items, anything from bicycles to chain saws to refrigerators.

Cobbled RV Abodes

We saw occasional pens of animals, usually chickens or rabbits. I understood the poultry—someone might have wanted organic eggs from free-range chickens, and they could have butchered pullets and eaten them. But the rabbits? Surely, they were not growing them for food. But maybe they were. I had grown up in a rural area, and my family had eaten rabbit when I was a child, but my dad and brother had hunted those rabbits. We had not raised them as pets. However, I had grown up with folks who raised and bred rabbits for food, just as they would raise chickens to butcher and put on the table. It was more than fifty years ago. Did people still live like that? What did they do with these animals in the winter when temperatures dropped below zero, and four feet of snow covered the ground?

My social work colleagues and I used to share stories about the broken appliances and disabled cars that littered the front yards of places we went to. The Willow Lake Campground brought back all kinds of home-visit memories, except now I had no reason to go up to any of these front doors and knock. The mere act of stealing glances as we walked along the campground roads made me uncomfortable. I imagined folks inside, peeking out at us through small slats in the blinds or from tiny slits in the curtains, watching us scope out the fronts of their places.

Could these people in the Willow Lake Campground look at me and know I was a social worker? My profession triggered fear in some groups when the parents had something to hide. In other households, parents embraced social workers as a resource for services and goods, making us feel loved and appreciated.

The people in Willow Lake probably looked at us and wondered what we said to each other. My hunch was they had felt suspicious. I imagined what some of those folks might have thought about middle-class RVers like us, obviously traveling rather than sedentary, and probably the owners of well-maintained houses with everything in good working order back home.

If I compared the two parks, the Sally Buffalo Park in Cadiz looked like something in a developing country, and the Willow Lake in Medina looked Third World. If a community had existed on that hilltop in Cadiz, it probably gelled like airplane glue in Medina, though we did not stay long enough to find out. The staff at Willow Lake had assigned us to the transient part of the campground that sat apart from the permanent-resident section. We never got to see what went on at the end of the day when people returned home. During our mid-day walks, the campground felt deserted and abandoned, with no one out despite beautiful weather.

Our transient section of the campground sported motorhomes, fifth wheels, and travel trailers, all operational and roadworthy. We were at Willow Lake for two nights, and ordinarily, in that amount of time, we would say hello to at least a couple of our neighbors. Here we never did, and we never saw any of our neighbors speak to each other either.

The atmosphere in the park held a nervous edge, creating a tense, agitated rather than relaxed atmosphere. Although it was not "the South," this place felt like backwoods, much like the rural area where I had grown up. Although I knew this place was not home, I nevertheless felt like I knew these people.

To find a place to call home had become my unspoken mission. I looked around everywhere we stopped and wondered: *Could I be happy living here? Could this be my home? Are these my people?*

I had an awakening in the Willow Lake Campground in Medina, Ohio. While I might have thought it was as cool as homemade wine to ride around the country in our little peanut-sized motorhome and celebrate our freedom, not everyone would view us as the unfettered and untethered harmless old coots we viewed ourselves as being. The fact that we did not belong in Willow Lake had jolted me when I saw its truth. I felt embarrassed to have indulged my obnoxious, middle-class voyeurism with our walks through that campground. Those folks did not need to have their privacy invaded and evaluated, certainly not by the likes of someone like me.

CHAPTER 9

Pesky Intruders

Many uninvited guests have invaded our RV. Flies were the most common and getting rid of them could be challenging.

Our first fly invasion occurred in a campground in St. Charles, Missouri. The ordeal began when Michael spotted a housefly, and then three more appeared. We were not sure how they had gotten inside.

"Not a problem," I said. "We'll pick up a fly swatter when we go to the grocery store."

In the store, I spent more time thinking about flies than food. I could not find a swatter anywhere. "What? You don't have fly swatters?" Michael said to the cashier at checkout. She directed us to a small hardware store down the street.

The hardware store had sold out of fly swatters, and the clerk had no idea where to send us to look. We returned home without an efficient weapon for getting rid of the pesky things, whose population had now risen to about eight or ten. We tackled those intruders with paperback books, folded newspapers, and whatever else we could grab. Our efforts proved only mildly successful.

That night, flies found me in the dark as I tried to sleep. They paraded across my forehead and arms and made me almost crazy. By the third or fourth time I woke up with that creepy, tickly feeling of little fly legs on my skin, I felt like screaming. I finally buried my head under the covers, hoping I would not suffocate. If the damned things bothered my charmed husband, he never gave any indication.

At least one week and twenty-seven stores later, we finally found a fly swatter at a truck stop in Arkansas. I still did not understand why such a simple, low-tech, inexpensive, frequently used item had been so elusive.

Our scariest flies were the huge black biting ones in the Upper Peninsula of Michigan. We had pulled off a deserted road in front of a small store. Michael got out, leaving the window open on the driver's side of the truck.

When I went into the RV, I screamed. "Michael, close the window! Flies are coming in." It looked like at least a dozen, zipping Kamikaze-style inside the house.

I grabbed our swatter to begin the slaughter. Except it did not happen quite like that.

"They're not landing," I said. "Oh, my God. It's like something from a horror movie." I could not hit them, despite frantic swats. They were too fast.

"Stay calm," Michael said. "You're probably scaring them with your hysterical jumping around."

"Then why don't you come in here and kill them?" I noted that while Michael had closed his driver's window and walked back around to the house, he had not opened the door and climbed in. He stood outside and calmly watched me through the window as I tried to deal with this terrifying invasion.

The black flies in the Upper Peninsula were not ordinary. They were huge—about an inch long—and had reputations for painful bites. One had bitten Michael, and he verified that it hurt. I had not gotten a bite and did not want one, thus explaining my frenetic jumping and jerking with the fly swatter while these flies zipped around almost too fast for the human eye to track. One rarely landed, and if it did, it did not stay still long enough for me to aim and fire.

Pesky Intruders

It took almost fifteen minutes of supreme swatting before I pronounced the house free of the invaders, and it took at least thirty minutes for my pulse to return to normal. It had felt like a war zone, and I feared a post-traumatic stress disorder from the horrific battle.

It did not seem to matter where we were or what the weather was like, flies found us. We never figured out how we could lose a fly swatter in such tight quarters, but we had. At some point, our dependable orange swatter with its sturdy wire handle disappeared. I insisted that we find a replacement at once. We had no trouble this time—the first Home Depot we walked into had them. We bought two just in case. I had come to understand a fly swatter was as vital to me as my toothbrush, and I never wanted to be without one again. My mental health depended on it.

Several small critters other than flies have invaded our home and disrupted our serenity. We have seen occasional spiders, and they scared me. I had gotten spider bites at home while working in my garden, and my physiological reactions were systemic. While I had never seen a spider web inside the RV house, spider webs often popped up on the outside of the rig. One would think that in a campground, spiders could find trees or bushes and not have to build their homes on the rearview mirrors of our truck or the ladder on the back. I struggled to figure this one out.

One time we had an ant invasion while parked under a fruit-laden pear tree in Georgia. We determined they had entered through small cracks underneath the rig. We saturated the floor and walls with Raid Ant Killer, probably damaging our lungs and activating dormant cancer cells. At least it took care of our ant invasion.

In terms of things that bit, my worst experience had come with the no-see-ums along the Georgia and South Carolina coasts. Those invisible sand gnats bit me everywhere, including on my scalp underneath my hair. They never bit Michael. Although I tried to stay slathered with insect repellant, I would sometimes forget or wait too long between applications and get more bites. The damned things were so tiny they could squeeze through screens, and it felt like I got almost as many bites while inside as I did outside. Logic said that could not be true. Once we had driven out of the Low Country, it took a full week and massive doses of Benadryl and topical anti-itch creams before the welts disappeared.

I thought our sand gnat biting days were over as we moved inland. They were . . . until we reached the top of Whiteface Mountain near Lake Placid in the Adirondack Mountains in upstate New York. It was mid-September with unseasonably warm temperatures in the low eighties. At our campground ten miles away and six thousand feet lower in elevation, we had had not a whisper of any kind of insect.

"Oh, my God!" I had just walked into a swarm of tiny black insects, a ball of clustered, frenzied activity. "Michael, these bugs are biting me." I frantically began rubbing, swatting, brushing—trying to get the damned things off. We had been climbing the steps to the Summit of Whiteface, a vertical distance of about one-fifth of a mile.

"I'm not going up." I turned and started boogie-shoeing back down those steps as fast as I could. Other tourists moved to the side, giving me a wide berth.

"They're really bad today," a man said to me. "We were warned at the bottom that they'd be out."

"What the hell are they?" I asked. "They're tiny, but the bites really hurt."

"Yeah, I don't know what they are, but the bites feel almost like bee stings," the man said.

Down below, another guy said, "Come stand in the shade. They won't bother you if you stay out of the sun."

He was right. The shade provided protection.

In the gift shop, I asked the clerk what kind of bugs they were. She shrugged. "We call them no-see-ums," she said.

"But you can see them," I said. "They're black, not invisible at all. The no-see-ums down in South Carolina really were invisible. I don't get it."

The clerk shrugged again. "It's unusual to have them out this late in the season. I'm allergic to them. My arms stay covered with welts." She held out her arms to show me.

"Our chemistries must be similar," I said. "I have bad reactions to them, too."

I again spent a week slathering myself with topical anti-itch creams and popping Benadryl every few hours. In time, all the welts shriveled up and stopped driving me crazy. It occurred to me that I would give up RVing without a backward glance if no-see-ums were everywhere. I could not live with such insane itching and scratching.

CHAPTER 10

Scary Encounters

Of all the bugs that bit and stung, Michael won the prize for our scariest insect assault so far. On a hot summer's day in late June, we had gone hiking in a state park in Chippewa Falls, Wisconsin. The trail was wide, shaded, and followed the shoreline of a lake. We both wore shorts, and neither of us remembered brushing against bushes or foliage.

Later that day, I noticed a streak of dried blood under Michael's armpit. I had been sitting on the sofa, and he had been at the other end of the RV.

"What's that under your arm?"

Michael walked over to the pantry mirror and turned to see the spot where I had pointed. "Must have scratched myself." He shrugged and pulled on his t-shirt.

The image nagged. The next morning, I said, "Let me look at that place on your side again. Something's bothering me about it."

Michael pulled up his t-shirt.

"Oh, my God. It's a huge tick." The thing freaked me out. It was fat and swollen, engorged on my husband's blood. Disgusting. But I knew I needed to stay calm. "Let me find the tweezers. I think I can yank it out, but I want to check online to make sure." I grabbed my iPad and made a quick Google search for proper tick removal.

"Jeez," I said, tugging with the tweezers. "This thing's really attached." Pulling it off was more like a tug of war than a simple jerk. "Look at this." I held the tick up for Michael to see. "He's got a big chunk of your skin in his mouth. Look at him wiggle—he's still alive." I would have thought all my squeezing and tugging would have killed him, but it had not.

"Get a baggie," I said. "We need to take him to the doctor with us." Not knowing how doctors diagnosed Lyme Disease, I did not want to destroy evidence.

Meanwhile, blood still oozed down Michael's side. With the tick secured in a plastic bag, I pulled out the first aid kit, cleaned the area with hydrogen peroxide, and applied a Band-Aid.

An hour later, we walked into an emergency clinic. Michael's tick was still very much alive and hyperactive inside the baggie. The physician pronounced him "very engorged" and told us the disturbing findings from a recent study of ticks in the Chippewa Falls area—90 percent of them were carriers of Lyme Disease. Michael left the clinic with a ten-day prescription for the recommended antibiotic, doxycycline, and with instructions to follow-up with a blood test six weeks later. I assumed the doctor put the tick in her garbage—we did not bring him back home.

We scoured the Internet when we got home from the clinic to learn more about Lyme Disease. The next morning, I screamed when I saw the tell-tale bull's eye mark around the site of the bite. Thank goodness we had gone to the doctor.

It took over three weeks for the bite mark under Michael's arm to heal. He did not talk about it, but I was sure he worried about the damage that tick bite might be doing to his health. He faithfully took his antibiotics, not pleased that he was supposed to take it easy with the beer until he finished the medication.

Seven weeks and hundreds of miles later, Michael went to an emergency walk-in clinic in Hatfield, Pennsylvania, for blood work. The doctor called the next day and gave him a clean bill of health. We had not realized until after the phone call how anxious we had both been for the past couple of months.

I still became hysterical over bug bites. I complained, and scratched, and talked ad nauseam about my discomforts. After Michael's tick bite, I felt guilty when I considered my dramatic over-reactivity. But maybe I should not have. He never itched or felt a single bit of physical distress from his tick bite. Maybe next time, I should hope for a tick rather than all the mosquitoes, black flies, and sand gnats that seemed always to find me.

We have read of other varmints, like rats and mice, that made nests and raised families inside RVs. The rumor was that rodents were adept at chewing through RV building materials and squeezing their way inside. When I first read about these rodent invaders, I vowed to do a daily exterior inspection of our rig to look for signs of entry. I quickly forgot, however.

We have camped in areas with warnings posted not to leave any trace of food outside at night because of raccoons and bears. For tent campers, that meant packing up all food and securing it inside an automobile or, if remote backpack camping, suspending it from trees. Raccoons were especially adept at opening coolers and plastic containers to get their grubby little paws on food stored inside. Although we had heard many stories about them, we had yet to see a raccoon at a campground.

The bear warnings scared the bejesus out of me. I looked at tent campers in awe in the Northwoods areas where campgrounds posted those warnings. I worried that a hungry bear would smash our RV windows and come inside our house—metal, aluminum, and other building materials notwithstanding. If I had been camping in a tent, I doubt I would have slept five minutes in total.

One night in a remote campground in the Catskills, I thought a bear had visited us during the night. We had a Weber Q-1000 grill, a small but heavy cast-iron gas cooker. We had set it up at the end of our picnic table and grilled steaks the night before. After it cooled, I put the plastic cover on to protect it from rain and dew. The next morning, I received a surprise when I peeked out the window.

"Michael, look outside. I think we've had a bear at our campsite." The Weber grill lay on its side on the ground.

When we inspected the grill, we saw that the aluminum drip pan from underneath was on the ground and had been either wiped or licked clean.

"Raccoons," Michael said. "A bear wouldn't have had the dexterity to take the drip pan out like this."

"But raccoons would not have had the strength to push the grill off the table," I argued. "They're not big enough."

"I've seen some pretty big raccoons, like forty or fifty pounds."

"Maybe a couple of them worked together," I said with a shrug. "I certainly wouldn't want to meet up with a raccoon big enough to push this heavy thing off a table. Glad I didn't see it happen. I'd have had nightmares for a week."

But even monster raccoons could not have produced the kinds of nightmares triggered by our next invasion, which felt like yet another terrifying horror movie. It began in Jonesborough, Tennessee, where we camped at a lovely little mom 'n pop RV park beside the Nolichucky River. Our site was idyllic with its unobstructed view of rushing white water against rocks, where one could almost hop, skip, and jump from one to the next to get to the other side. Temperatures were ideal, and we had slept for four nights with the air-conditioning off and the windows open, listening to the crash of water against rock. We had landed there for our final scheduled event—The National Storytelling Festival—of our long, five-and-a-half-month road trip. From Jonesborough, we would drag ourselves back home to Tampa.

We packed up and moved on with reluctance, dreading the long, hard drive back home with nothing exciting on the agenda. That first day, we drove over 300 miles and almost seven hours before stopping overnight in a KOA Campground in Cartersville, Georgia. That was when we got the first inkling that we had a problem.

"Hey, what are these things?" I pulled back the curtain, separating our bedroom area from the rest of the RV. "Come, look at this." We had pulled into our site twenty minutes earlier and connected the electricity, water, and sewer. My husband was programming the cable for the TV, eager to catch the *ABC Evening News*.

"Hold on; I'm in the middle of something."

"You're not going to believe this. Where's the fly swatter?" I practically screamed. "Michael, we've got a problem." I found the swatter buried behind raingear in the front closet and jerked it out. I returned to the curtain and started swinging.

"There are dozens of them," I yelled. My husband sat nonchalantly programming his TV. In addition to freaking out at what I saw on our curtains, my anger flared at my husband. His beloved television and national news dominated his entire friggin' life. "Would you please come over here and look? We've got stinkbugs."

"Huh?" Michael finally got up and walked over to look. "Wow," was all he could manage to say.

There were maybe a dozen stinkbugs attached to the inside of the curtain, and they all hung there without moving. Every time I swatted, they flew to another spot. Despite my frenetic aiming and swinging, I could not seem to hit and kill one. I seemed to simply rearrange them. It became reminiscent of the black flies in the Upper Peninsula, except these stupid stinkbugs were much slower. Thank goodness they appeared to have no evil intentions towards me. And unlike the stinkbugs I had encountered in my garden back in Tampa, these stinkbugs did not even stink.

After fifteen or twenty minutes of futile swatting and swinging with the fly swatter, I switched to paper towels for a capture-and-squish final solution. I hated being such a cold-blooded killer, but I hated having stinkbugs in the RV even more. I was not certain, but my total executions by bedtime were around thirty-seven.

I drifted off to sleep that night exhausted but confident I had taken care of the invasion.

I patted myself on the back too soon. The next morning, we awoke to find dozens more stinkbugs and dozens after that. I characterized our three-day trip from North Georgia to Tampa as war—my heroic but ultimately unsuccessful battle to rid our home of the external invasion. Every time we stopped, we found more stinkbugs crawling in from our slide and resting on the curtain. I lost count, but by the time we hit our driveway, I figured I had squished several hundred.

We unloaded the RV fully aware that we could potentially be bringing the damnable insects into our house. We kept our fingers crossed and hoped for the best. We unpacked, hightailed it to our U-Haul Storage site, parked the RV, and released a fogger-bomb twice the size recommended for our square footage. When we returned two days later, dozens of stink bugs lay dead on the floor, the bed, the stove, the furniture, all over the damned house.

I am not sure I will ever pull the RV curtain separating the bedroom from the rest of the house again without thinking about stinkbugs. In the overall scheme of things, those stinkbugs were probably the most benign of all the insects and critters we had encountered. They did not bite, they did not vector diseases, they did not leave droppings, and they did not even stink. The enduring horror was how they kept coming, and coming, and coming. Every time I thought I had killed them all, I would find more.

There were lots of other possible camping intruders that could invade our little RV—snakes, scorpions, tarantulas, grizzlies, and God-only-knows-what else. I understood and accepted that those risks came with the territory. When we took off in the RV for the unknown, we hoped to be open to whatever came our way. We did not want to equivocate or cower. We wanted to stand tall and brave and say, "Bring it on. We can deal with anything!"

However, in the still of the night when only the crickets and owls and the occasional thrashing of some unknown animal in the bushes interrupted the silence, I snuggled deep under the covers, a pillow over my face, and realized I did not want it all. I did not want insects biting and stinging me or walking across my flesh as I tried to sleep. I did not like wildlife rummaging around my campsite at night and licking the fat out of the drip pan in our BBQ grill. I did not want ticks sucking my blood and vectoring Lyme Disease into my already old and compromised body.

 I admitted to myself, when alone with my thoughts in the night that I would be unable to cope with much more than what I was already dealing with. RVing filled me fuller than I ever wanted to be filled without all these campground intruders added to the mix.

CHAPTER 11

Tourist Busts

If one is touring in an RV, then tourist destinations would seem to be where one should go. But if one is living in an RV, then it seemed to me one should go, or not go, wherever one wanted. For me, I could easily spend endless days reading, writing, doing some yoga stretches, and walking a few miles along wooded trails. In the evenings, I would enjoy either a TV series episode, such as *House of Cards* or *Breaking Bad* or maybe a movie, before reading myself to sleep. I would enhance all these evening activities with a couple of glasses of my favorite nectar from the goddess—cabernet sauvignon.

In contrast, my husband wanted to see and do and go and experience things first-hand, not vicariously through reading or from watching something on YouTube or TV. His RV traveling goal was to do at least two cool things a day. Lucky for me, a nice hike qualified as a cool thing in his mind, as would a game of miniature golf or a stroll down a street in a quaint little tourist town, like the Village of Lake Placid in New York.

Sometimes, the absurdity of what we chose to do left me stunned. Frequently, I did not even see it coming.

For example, our Tahquamenon River Trolley and Boat trip to the Tahquamenon Falls in Newberry, Michigan, in the Upper Peninsula (the U.P.) came to mind. To give a context, we found the Upper Peninsula rather short on things to do, and the few things that existed were many miles apart. But then, the U.P. was nothing but remote and desolate, and that was the way those hardy, rugged, outdoorsy folks up there wanted it to stay.

The Tahquamenon Falls was located on the Tahquamenon River in the northwestern part of the U.P. near Lake Superior. One side of the Falls was visible from the Tahquamenon State Park and was easily accessible by car. Because this waterfall was one of the largest ones east of the Mississippi and located in such a remote place, we chose to take a longer trip to the falls. The alternative route took us along miles and miles of the Tahquamenon River and deposited us across the river from the state park. We excitedly signed up by phone, paying ninety-five dollars per person, for the seven-hour train/trolley/boat excursion to the waterfall. We believed we would see incredible scenery and wildlife that most folks visiting the Upper Peninsula would miss.

Except it was not cool at all.

It took seventy-five minutes each way from our campground in Sault Ste. Marie, Michigan, to the excursion office in Newberry, Michigan—a total of one hour and thirty minutes. The train ride from the office to the boat dock took thirty-five minutes each way—a total of one hour and ten minutes. The boat ride to the falls was two tedious hours—a total of four hours. The actual time at the Tahquamenon Waterfall, which included the time it took to get on and off the boat and to hike the three-tenths-mile-long rocky uphill trail to get to the viewing area was a mere one hour and fifteen minutes. Several of our fellow passengers found they were physically unable to make the trek, so they ended up having paid the exorbitant fee of ninety-five dollars each and never getting to see the famous Tahquamenon Falls.

But the final indignity for the folks like us who made that grueling hike was that we could only see the back and smaller side of the Falls. We looked with envy and chagrin at the folks on the other side of the river in the Tahquamenon State Park as they walked along a wooden suspension bridge spanning two-thirds the width of the falls, with almost the entire waterfall in full view.

Tourist Busts

By the end of the day, I calculated a total of seven hours and fifty-five minutes for our excursion. Now throw in another thirty or forty minutes for the time waiting around in the morning upon our arrival and the boarding and exiting of both the train and the boat, and we figured we wasted almost nine hours of an otherwise perfectly beautiful day in that Northwoods paradise.

We laughed at ourselves on our drive back to the campground. Three months later, the only animal I could remember seeing on the boat ride was an American Bald Eagle, which was a pretty cool thing to see but not the first time we had seen one in the wild. While that thick bug and varmint infested swamp on either side of the river during our four-hour boat ride was indeed primeval and refreshing, after about ten minutes, we realized it was unchanging and remained so for the entire trip.

While not as expensive as the Tahquamenon Falls trip, I remembered an especially frustrating couple of hours in downtown Tulsa, Oklahoma, searching for an elusive Center of the Universe. Described as a mysterious acoustic phenomenon, there was a small circle where one could stand and talk. The noise echoed back to one's ears at a much louder volume than spoken. Anyone standing outside the small circle heard nothing at all. The spot was an actual sound chamber without walls. On our drive through Tulsa, Michael and I agreed it would be interesting to visit this spot.

Except we never found it. Unfortunately, the circle was downtown, and it was not easy to maneuver our Four Winds with the C-Max in tow. After going in circles on busy, narrow streets and making many righthand turns for what felt like forever, we found a parking lot that offered both space and accessibility for our oversized rig. We knew that getting into places was sometimes easier than getting out of them with this RV. We parked with trepidation and paid triple since our rig took up more than two parking spots. We took off on foot and spent another hour trying to find that damned Center of the Universe.

Perhaps the acoustical phenomenon existed, but you could not prove it by us. When I later read about it online, I was sorry we did not persevere a little longer and try a little harder. Perhaps if we ever go to or through Tulsa again, we will take a second stab at seeing this curiosity.

At least we were able to extricate ourselves and our equipment from the small, crowded parking lot without scraping another vehicle or having to unhitch the toad.

When we had first started RVing, we were avid bicyclists who rode fifteen or twenty miles a day, four or five times a week. Or at least we tried. We had a bicycle rack on the C-Max and routinely brought our Treks with us, despite the hassle of trying to keep them covered from rain and road grime, locked up when not in use, and cleaned and oiled from the abuse of travel. We knew of the growing movement to create greenways in urban areas for pedestrian and bicycle traffic, and we assumed these newly created trails, often along rivers, would be a fantastic way to experience new places while getting fresh air, sunshine, and exercise.

Our first attempt to find one of these newly created bicycle gems was along the Cumberland River in Nashville, Tennessee. On our trip to Nashville in July, both the temperature and the humidity soared into the nineties. Michael could not believe I wanted to find a section of Nashville's miles and miles of advertised greenway in such brutal weather, but I did.

Finally, we found the downtown route. We also found lots of traffic, construction, detours, steep inclines, and finally, a section of a bike path along the Cumberland River. Unfortunately, it appeared that druggies and the homeless had also found this cleared path, which consisted of a byway running directly under overpasses and bridges, great shelters from the sun and rain for people who might need them. I did not feel safe riding my bicycle in this part of town.

Memphis, Tennessee, was equally disappointing with its greenways for walking and bicycling. I searched on the Internet, and then we scouted in the car. Eventually, we found Tom Lee Park right on the Mississippi

River, and it looked promising. When we got out of the car and went to the trailhead to study the route, we realized the path was a mere one mile long, not even worth the time and effort to take the bikes off the rack.

We hoped the size and placement of the greenway in St. Louis, Missouri, would be more to our liking. Like the greenway in Memphis, this one also ran along a river, the Mighty Mississippi. While we persevered and rode about fourteen miles on the trail, we were not impressed. The trail passed factories that belched pollution into the air, landfills and garbage dumps, gang-graffitied walls and tunnels, and congregations of homeless people.

While I applauded the efforts of these urban areas for providing paths for recreation, I could only sigh with the outcomes. Perhaps down the road, gentrification and revitalization would come to those riverfront paths. It was easy to imagine parks, bars and restaurants, and trendy shops along the riverbanks.

Who could have visited St. Louis, Missouri, and not have gone to the famous Gateway Arch? Not us. However, we experienced an unfortunate confluence of unforgettable and unpleasant events when we went.

The arch was a signature landmark that opened in 1965 to commemorate the country's westward expansion. It remained the largest arch in the world. We had made our way to St. Louis's famous shrine on a day of ungodly high temperatures and humidity. Unfortunately, both the air-conditioning and one of the two lifts taking people up and down the arch had stopped working on the day of our visit. We ended up trapped at the top of the arch, with visitors packed together like Dasani water bottles in a case. Our bodies pressed and sweated against the bodies of strangers for more than an hour. We cheered when we finally boarded the one functioning people-conveyor that took us to fresh air and freedom at the bottom.

I have read that St. Louis renovated the Arch not long ago, after our visit. The renovation included replacing the glass windows that had barely offered visibility when we had been there. Maybe the next time we went through St. Louis, we would try again, and I would have a more favorable report.

Still, I considered us blessed that our major disappointments in tourist attractions have been few, especially considering the numerous places we have been.

CHAPTER 12

Serendipities

How delightful to stumble upon places that pleased rather than disappointed, experiences that stood strong in one's memory long after they should have, by all rights, faded into a file folder of 'not that important.' Why did some stories and images linger? I believed, based on things I had learned from public speaking, storytelling, and writing, it was ultimately about emotional connections. The way the new experience touched feelings, fitted into one's history bank and settled in among all those other memories determined whether it resonated in the soul.

Michael and I have knocked around the country in our RV for a few years, looking for places and events off the main roads. I resisted many of the tourist attractions. I liked to think of myself as a lowly disciple of Robert Pirsig or William Least Heat-Moon, someone searching for the meaning of life and my purpose in it. Our road trip was simply the surface story of the journey.

Not everything that happened on the road was amazing and memorable. Much of what we saw and did was mundane, unimportant, and quickly forgotten. But a few places and encounters stayed with me. I thought of them as serendipities of which the universe had graciously gifted me.

HOME IS WHERE THE RV IS

"Hey, I think I've found something that might be interesting," I said, interrupting my husband's road trance.

We were traveling backroads through God-forsaken Oklahoma. Our impossible-to-follow Route 66 guidebook lay open across my lap. It was a chilly, windy day in November 2016, and we were on our first big RV trip across the country, trying to follow the Mother Road from Chicago, Illinois, to its end at the Santa Monica Pier in California. Due to deterioration, destruction, and relocation of the original Route 66 highway, we were having many navigational difficulties.

"Anything's got to be better than this. I'm not even sure where we are. What'd you find?"

"It's called the Hogue House. Listen to this." I read from our guidebook. "Back in the early 1900s, Sears Roebuck & Company sold precut houses, and this is one of them."

"Sears sold houses? You're kidding, right?"

"Nope," I said. "Let's find it." It took a few minutes and several wrong turns before we finally found the house, which now sat a mile north of the original Route 66 Highway. The physical address was 1001 South Olive Street, Chelsea, Oklahoma. The population of Chelsea, per the 2010 Census, was 1,964 people.

We stopped in front of the house, hopped out, and began taking cell phone photos. The house looked a couple of stories tall with a dormer at the top. A front porch wrapped around to one side. It looked in good repair, and I saw a couple of automobiles out back.

I froze when the front door flew open, and a petite, silver-haired woman rushed down the front steps, a long-haired Dachshund in her arms. "Welcome to my home," she called out, striding down the driveway towards us. I felt embarrassed, like she had caught us doing something that was not right. Maybe she had not liked us taking pictures of her house. It suddenly felt wrong.

"We didn't mean to intrude," I said, afraid she felt threatened or invaded despite the big smile on her face. After all, we were strangers standing on her property.

"Nonsense," the woman said. "I'm Polly, and I bet you'd love to see the inside of this old house."

We chatted a couple more minutes in the driveway. We learned that Polly and her three-generation family had recently moved into the house, which they had rented from descendants of the original Hogue family that had built the house.

"I'm a nurse, and we're new to the area. My husband owns a pool company and is opening a branch in Tulsa, fifty miles from here." Polly caught her breath. "Come on in. We're still unpacking. We've only been here a couple of weeks." She led us up the front steps and inside.

The first thing Polly pointed out was the framed certificate from the Oklahoma Historical Society certifying that the Hogue House was on The National Register of Historic Places. The history Polly related and my Internet research findings told the same story. Sears Roebuck and Company sold precut houses from 1907 to about 1940. The company shipped the houses by rail from lumberyards. The houses arrived in staggered installments, beginning with framing materials and progressing through plaster, plumbing and wiring materials, and finally, glass and shingles. Assembly was a do-it-yourself undertaking in which buyers followed written instructions printed in a leather-bound manual shipped with the first delivery. The wooden building materials were solid oak and came precut, notched, and numbered. With the final shipment, owners received an engraved plaque with their names inscribed in gold. Polly pointed out the Hogue family's plaque, which hung along a stairwell leading to the second floor.

We heard stories about both Polly and the house as we climbed up and down narrow, twisting staircases and stepped over and around unpacked boxes and children's toys.

"Long way from your husband's work, isn't it?" I asked.

Polly laughed. "It's rural here. He can get to Tulsa in thirty-five or forty minutes." As we toured, Polly interrupted her personal story to tell us about the house. "It's undergone multiple upgrades and remodels through the years to comply with changing code requirements."

I later learned that The Hogue House was Oklahoma's lone survivor of those Sears Roebuck prefab houses. Joe Hogue, a Chelsea cattleman, had seen a model home in Chicago in 1911 and ordered one for $1,600. At the time, Sears offered a variety of architectural styles, ranging from a little over $500 up to about $5,000. It also sold a complementary outhouse for an additional thirty bucks. I do not know whether Mr. Hogue took advantage of the outhouse deal or not. Hogue and his six brothers completed the construction of the house in 1913. Although folks may have pooh-poohed the houses back in the early 1900s as look-alike cracker-boxes, today people consider them chic. Our hostess Polly certainly did. We did, too.

"I couldn't resist the history of this place when I learned it might be available," Polly said. "The Hogues started a tradition back in the twenties and called this place the Café of Life. They'd cook huge meals and serve them outside on the porch every Thursday evening to anyone who wanted to come to eat. They requested a donation, but only if someone had the money. It was during the Depression, and many families were going hungry." She paused, caught her breath, and continued. "I want to start that tradition up again. It sounds so wonderful!"

After we got back home from our three-month RV trip, I searched on the Internet to verify Polly's story of the charitable community dinners every Thursday night. I found only a Facebook report of the City of Chelsea shutting down "a charitable practice at the house due to zoning violations."

I now felt confused about Polly's story. Zoning violations? What were they for—too many cars parked in the driveway? Operating a business without a license? Health and safety violations from the Department of Agriculture? I did not believe those Thursday night dinner guests would have disturbed the peace by getting noisy and rowdy. That did not fit at all.

Polly's story had touched my heart, though. I wanted to follow her progress on the Internet. I rechecked the Hogue House Facebook page about a year later. With this Facebook search, I sent a request for updated information via Messenger. No one answered.

Serendipities

I returned to my Internet searches several months later. This time I found a few new historical items about the house, but the Facebook page, previously posted by the Hogue family, had disappeared. The clip about zoning violations had also disappeared, leaving not even a hint of big Thursday night dinners on the front porch during the Depression.

I wondered about Polly and her family. Were they still in the house? If so, were they still renting the house? Maybe they had been able to buy it. Or maybe Polly's family moved out, and members of the Hogue family or some other family moved in. Polly had told us hers was the only non-Hogue family to ever live in the house. It was hard to imagine a family letting such a beautiful historical home slip out of its possession.

But it was more than the physical house that haunted my memories.

In my mind, the Café of Life story captured a community's caring and generous attitude. It reminded me of bygone days—times when life moved slower, when the world felt less complicated, and when individual action could make a difference for an entire community. A time before rules and regulations governed even our most basic of charitable offerings—that of offering food to a hungry person.

I hoped Polly made her dream happen. Something told me though, if it was not at the Hogue House, she would leave her generous mark somewhere else. Polly made me feel like a slacker not to have made more contributions of my own toward making the world a better place.

The next time Michael and I took off across middle America in search of adventure, I wanted to stop again in Chelsea, Oklahoma. Next time, I would head straight up the steps and knock on the Hogue House front door. I would not hesitate or apologize. I needed the next installment in this century-long saga. It might feel like returning home.

We landed in Las Cruces, New Mexico, almost by default. We abandoned our Route 66 route in Santa Fe, New Mexico, when the temperature dropped to seventeen degrees one late November night. We headed due south, as far as we could go without crossing the border to Mexico. Welcome to Las Cruces, a border town that had never been on my radar screen. Weary from our frantic race across the country trying to follow a famous national road that now lay in ruins in many places, we decided to spend a couple of days catching our breaths. The temperatures here were a bit more tolerable, dropping only into the low forties at night. We learned these temps were Las Cruces' definition of a brutal cold snap. Like the weather in Florida. Our kind of weather.

As we checked into the RV park, Michael asked the manager about things to do in the area. She recommended the White Sands National Monument in the Chihuahuan Desert, twenty miles north of Las Cruces. Trip Advisor had given it great reviews.

When Michael mentioned the place, my response had been lukewarm at best. "Are you sure you want to go there? Isn't that where the military tested all those nuclear missiles?"

"This monument is way out in the desert, something other than the military base. It's the largest gypsum sand-dune concentration in the entire world. We need to check it out." Michael was the Internet researcher in our family.

I had fallen in love with the deserts of the southwest. Even though the wind howled and penetrated my warmest layers of clothes, I agreed to the road trip. I often brought my iPad and did my own research on our way to and from places, but there was no Internet service out in the desert. I had to wait until later to read up on this amazing place that sat in the middle of nowhere.

The White Sands National Monument consisted of rare white gypsum. The elevation was over 4,200 feet, despite being in the middle of a desert, and the area covered about 275 square miles. The gypsum rested in huge dunes that resembled sand dunes along beaches. The dunes were as high as three or four-story buildings and looked like hills with flat tops.

A winding, twisting, climbing road permitted visitors to drive a big loop of maybe ten or twelve miles through the dunes. Pullouts were situated every few miles. Developers of the national park designed boardwalk connectors between some of the dunes and placed interpretive exhibits focusing on animal, plant, and geological features. I had no trouble understanding the inclusion of geological blurbs at the interpretive stops. It was an astounding thing to see. But animal and plant life? The area looked so barren and stark I could not imagine it supporting any kind of life, but obviously, it did. The interpretive exhibits reported that microscopic plants and animals lived in the dunes. We saw an occasional bird and deduced there must have also been insects of a size large enough to attract a bird's attention. Maybe even small reptile or mammal prey. Otherwise, why would birds be in the area?

Our visit to those gypsum dunes had felt like something out of a science fiction movie set in an alternative universe. 'Moonscape' was a lame way to describe the area. But what boggled my mind the most were the hiking trails that began and ended at the pullouts, with places for hikers to register if they planned to be out overnight or longer. Overnight? The trails were barely visible to my eyes three feet from where I stood. How could a hiker possibly follow an almost invisible trail out into such desolation to stay for a night or more? Where were the landmarks to prevent hikers from getting lost? There were certainly not any trees with painted tin markers hammered into the trunks with arrows pointing the way. I later realized hikers probably used GPS coordinates, compasses, or the movement of the sun to navigate their way and avoid going in circles.

We saw hikers in the distance, way up on far-away dunes, weighted down by heavy backpacks. Occasionally, we saw a lone hiker. Talk about a setting that forced one's thoughts inward. If the desolation itself did not prove a stark-enough experience, I thought about how low the temperatures must drop at night. It was the desert in late November, and temperatures farther south at sea level had already chilled my Florida bones.

On the other hand, what a glorious sky those overnight hikers must have seen. They possibly bore witness to a million stars, meteor showers, comets, the moon, and every constellation ever recorded, and there were no city lights, tall buildings, or other manmade intrusions to obstruct their views. What an opportunity it would be for one of those peak experiences of a lifetime, one that changed you so profoundly there would be no way of ever returning to who and what you had been before. Hiking through those limited, self-contained gypsum dunes would be like pushing the envelope in ways a little stroll along the approximately 2181-mile-long Appalachian Trail could not begin to touch.

I felt a sadness for all the things in life I had missed and would never have the chance to do. In my younger days, I had always thought I lived on the edge. There was nothing like a good immersion into another world to bring home how limited and sheltered my life had been. The White Sands National Monument was one of those serendipitous stops, both in what we saw as well as in what I learned.

Our list of pleasant surprises on the road was much longer than our list of disappointments. Take the discovery of the Whirligig Park in Wilson, North Carolina, with kinetic wind sculptures made from pieces of old farm machinery by Vollis Hollis, a retired machine-repairman-turned-artist. Or the renowned Cadillac Ranch outside Amarillo, Texas. Or the local gems we discovered in Rapid City, South Dakota, while waiting nine days for a manufacturer to deliver a new awning for the RV. Or the Saguaro National Park in Tucson, Arizona, where I fell in love with the cacti. (But not with all the rattlesnakes that made the Saguaro Desert their home.)

Not all our discoveries were tangible or of things we could record in photographs, however. One example was my discovery in the small town of Endicott, New York, when we visited with our Alaska Caravan friends, Ray and Kathy, a year after the trip ended. These folks were not RVers. Instead, they had felt both excited and trapped as co-travelers in a motorhome with Kathy's sister and brother-in-law. Ray and I initially connected over our shared reluctances to go on this Alaskan trip. Before long, Ray and Michael got to know each other and became friends.

Ray and Kathy were the opposites of the vagabonds Michael and I were turning out to be. They had both grown up in the area where they now lived. Their families lived a couple of streets apart. They had dated in high school. The relationship ended when Ray entered the military. They each went on to pursue other lives, eventually both divorcing their long-term spouses when they re-discovered each other decades later.

Serendipities

They returned to their family-of-origin neighborhood and reconnected with old childhood friends who had either never left or who had now returned in their retirements.

We hung out with Ray and Kathy a couple of nights. We heard their stories. They took us to dinner in a local restaurant where they knew the owner and the employees. They took us to a biker bar, where we met a couple of their friends whom they had known for decades.

I experienced a profound sense of loss as I sat in the bar that night. A local band played in the background, and patrons of questionable singing talent picked up the microphone for karaoke every few songs. I listened to Kathy and her friend talk about their adult children, grandchildren, bridal showers, and weddings for daughters of other women they knew, teachers in their grandchildren's classrooms at school, and what had happened to the local bakery on Preston Street that suddenly closed. I felt a hole, a sense of emptiness. They had something I did not and had not even realized I wanted. They had a community.

During my childhood and until I left home at age eighteen for college, I had had a community. After leaving my hometown, I never looked back. I never wanted to. My childhood memories of that small, rural town were not good ones. I cringed at the thought of going back, of having those memories jiggled in my mind. I did not want to revisit things I had spent years and traveled miles trying to forget.

I now lived in a large metropolitan area where I knew a handful of my neighbors. I had friends who do not know any of their neighbors, so I felt pretty good about knowing a few of mine. In fairness, though, I had other friends who knew all their neighbors, so I felt in the middle of the spectrum. But in Endicott, New York, for the first time, I saw small-town living from a different angle. At this age and point in my life, that glimpse of a small-town community presented a charming and nurturing invitation.

I wondered if five months on the road, with no roots and no grounding other than my husband and our little tin-can house, might have led me to exaggerate how attractive a small town might be. While traveling, everything around me changed, sometimes by the hour. Loneliness, lack of significant personal connections, a sense of isolation—all these things could attack and occasionally bite. Did Endicott, New York, look so enviable and appealing as a way of life, or was it circumstantial and because we had been on the road for four months already?

Eventually, I reached an understanding of what an alternative RV lifestyle meant for me. Or at least my thinking solidified for the time being, and it felt good. With a sense of surprise, I understood I was exactly where I needed to be, doing exactly what I needed to be doing at this point in my life. I could not live Ray and Kathy's lives, nor could they live mine. Nor would I ever be able to find what they apparently had, nor would it fit on me the way it seemed to wrap so perfectly around them.

I stopped yearning for home. I stopped counting the days until we got back to Tampa, where I could resume what I fondly referred to as my 'real life.' I started living in the present, feeling appreciative of all that I had and loved.

I had to laugh with the additional insight that this was only the thirty-third time I had reached this very same bottom-line, deep-in-the-gut, ultimate truth of who and what I was, on this trip alone.

CHAPTER 13

It's Not Always Pretty

Campgrounds ranked among the most peaceful, happy, and safe places we had ever been. Sometimes, I secretly thought of every park as a Lake Wobegon facsimile, like Garrison Keillor's fictitious but perfect hometown 'where the men are all strong, the women are all good-looking, and all the children are above average.' RV parks felt that way.

Our impressions came from over three years of spying on our neighbors in RV parks. We rarely heard anything other than happy and friendly words, except for the occasional crying baby or young child. Somehow even the behavior of children in campgrounds seemed better than average. Those kids rarely talked back or misbehaved. We overheard conversations everywhere—in campground offices, at the swimming pools, in laundry rooms, on benches outside the recreation hall in the sunshine. All that eavesdropping had strengthened our beliefs that maybe we had found Nirvana. RV parks began to feel like an instant community, and we came to believe that almost any randomly selected RV park could be a prototype of the last small town in America.

Those overheard campground conversations stayed away from religion and politics. Instead, people talked about places they had been and places they wanted to go, weather and traffic, and occasionally life back home.

Michael and I realized early on that RV couples seemed to get along well. Our observation strengthened as we continued to observe folks interacting, facing challenges, and getting on with the business of day-to-day living. We also learned from our first-hand experiences.

"What do you think would happen if I reacted to every stupid thing you did that irritated me?" Michael asked.

"Stupid things that I do? Do you have any idea how many times a day I wonder if I'm going to need stitches in my tongue?" I could not help but raise my voice.

As we talked about our relationship, we had come to understand that RVing had changed us. It had made us aware of the critical, unkind words we sometimes spoke to each other. We both wanted to keep things on an even keel. It was imperative when living in such small quarters. An even more astounding epiphany was that if one ignored one's spouse's irritating mannerisms long enough, after a while, they no longer irked. In fact, one stopped noticing.

I had never heard a raised voice or a cross word in a campground for almost three years. Until one day I did.

"You son of a bitch, worthless piece of crap!" I heard angry shouting from the other side of the park. "You were supposed to be watching your son!"

I had been chatting with a retired Texas minister in a travel trailer next to our Four Winds. Our conversation stopped, and we both turned to look in the direction of the voice. Across the lawn on the next street over, a distraught-looking, obese woman of about thirty screamed into the face of a bearded man of comparable age and size. The man stood with his head down, silent. A stocky boy, maybe eight or nine, stood watching and listening.

"You asshole. You fucking dickhead." With those words, the woman stepped forward and pushed the man. She shoved him so hard he stumbled backward.

Oh, my God. Please do not let him hit her back. I caught my breath. I slowly exhaled when the man's arms remained at his side, and I felt certain he would not retaliate.

The woman's venomous verbal assault continued for another minute or so, with language I felt sure made the minister's ears burn in disgust. The woman physically pushed the man several more times before her rage seemed to dissolve. She turned and stomped back down the road toward a destination I could not see. The man followed, his posture stooped, his head bowed, an outward appearance of remorse. The child followed the man, shuffling his feet and kicking rocks on the graveled road.

"That's the first argument I've ever heard in an RV park." I finally found my voice. "More than an argument. That was domestic violence, and right in front of the child," I said to my retired Texas minister neighbor. I wondered if, as a social worker, I should have intervened. Obviously, I had not, and now the scene had ended.

The minister stared off into the distance, maybe at the parents and child, maybe at nothing. "It certainly didn't seem to help anything, did it now?" The minister asked, his Texas twang exaggerated. We both knew his question was rhetorical.

Silence mushroomed between us. What was there to say after witnessing such an uncomfortably private and painful domestic scene?

After a few moments, I mumbled, "Nice meeting you," and made a retreat toward my quarters. The unexpected, angry incident had upset me. I needed to go home and process it. Michael had unknowingly sat through the disturbing interactions. With the air conditioning running and the windows closed, he had not heard a thing.

When I shared my observations with Michael, he said, "Office staff have told us before. Not all the people who come to RV parks, even nice ones like this KOA (Kampgrounds of America, a large national chain of RV parks), are happy, successful, and financially secure folks. We have no idea who any of these people are or what their circumstances might be."

The transient and homeless families I had seen through the years as a social worker flashed through my mind. Anything was possible. Maybe that little family left the park to return to a pup tent outside the park property line. Maybe they slept in campgrounds once a week for showers, the rest of the time in their car or wherever they could find shelter.

I knew Michael was right. It would be wrong to assume that people vagabonding across the country in an RV represented a cross-section view of the camping population. I had been away from social work for a long time. After the anger I had witnessed, I vowed to set aside a few minutes of each day to mourn the human condition and to thank the universe for my blessings. It seemed the least I could do.

RV travel did not always land one in exciting, glamorous spots. Some places, regardless of what they looked like, left a bad taste in the mouth. Yuma, Arizona, was such a place.

Yuma, known as the Salad Bowl Capital of the United States, grew tons of winter vegetables, especially lettuce. Although it sat in the middle of a desert, engineers found a solution for Yuma's lack of water—they dammed the Colorado River and diverted water across thousands of acres via a system of ditches and levees. With irrigation, farmers now mass-produced vegetables and shipped them to all four corners of the country. For the reason of damming the Colorado River alone, I did not like Yuma, even before we got there. Its economy sounded motivated by human greed and a squandering of natural resources.

We arrived in the area late one cold November day and found an RV resort nestled in an ocean of lettuce, with only an occasional settlement of a few houses and stores. We could see the Colorado River in the distance across a lettuce field to the east and Mexico a quarter of a mile to the south. Resort staff told us border-patrol agents cruised the area at night, searching the banks of the river for illegal immigrants.

"You might hear a gunshot," the RV resort employee said. "But don't worry. Coyotes and wolves also prowl around here. If you hear a shot, agents are probably shooting at an animal, not a Mexican." The employee laughed.

When we left the office, I threw what my husband called one of my hissy fits. "I'm not staying here. I want you to go back in there and demand a refund. I'm not staying in a place where locals laugh about shooting Mexicans as they cross the border."

"I don't like it either," Michael said. "But it's too late to try to find another place. Let's stay tonight and get the hell out early in the morning."

Reason told me my husband was right. We had driven over three hundred miles that day, and temperatures were dropping like a stone. Neither of us felt like moving.

We watched the Yuma news that evening and learned that local farm labor consisted of Mexicans working below minimum wage. While hundreds of commercial transport trucks came and went every day, an almost equal number of old school busses transported thousands of Mexican workers to and from their little villages south of the border.

"I am disgusted. That is so wrong on so many levels. I bet they're paying those Mexicans diddly-squat, probably five dollars an hour or something equally insulting. Bet there's no health care, no paid sick leave or vacation time." My voice grew louder, my outrage escalating. "The truck drivers belong to unions, probably make fifty bucks an hour with excellent benefits, including retirement pensions. You don't find all of that sickening?"

"That's corporate America for you." My husband shrugged. "What can you do?"

I felt relieved the next morning to realize gunshots had not awakened us during the night. My distress about Yuma, however, was not over yet. My disgust turned to outrage when the morning news reported a story about a charitable event designed to show appreciation for the Mexican workers. The charity sponsored a big, all-you-can-eat sausage and pancake breakfast. But because they did not want the growers to lose valuable work time, organizers started the event at 4:00 a.m. so the Mexicans could be on-the-job, as usual, by 6:00 a.m.

The situation worsened, in my mind, when the reporter went on to say that each worker had received a gift—a pair of socks.

"A pair of socks? Can you believe that crap?" I exploded in indignation. "How much more offensive and insulting can this get? They want to do something nice for them, and then they make them get up two hours earlier than normal and deprive them of precious sleep." My pulse quickened. "And the socks? One pair of measly socks that cost a dollar? It's outrageous because it's so small. If they wanted to give a gift, how about a fifty-dollar gift card to Walmart or somewhere? At least make the gift large enough not to insult the receiver."

The reporter explained the reasoning, though. Fieldwork was a wet, messy business, and shoes and socks were sopping by the end of the day. "Now," the reporter had said, with a big smile on his face, "workers will have a clean, dry pair of socks to put on their feet each morning."

"Honey," I said to my husband a few days later, "I'm not sure I ever want to eat another salad. I almost wish I didn't know how those Yuma vegetables are grown."

"Not sure you could get around it. It's how food is grown in this country."

I knew my husband was right, but I could not sort it out morally in my head. I understood there were no jobs in Mexico for those workers brought across the border every day to work on the produce farms. If corporate America did not employ them at substandard wages, the men would probably not have jobs at all. Did that make it okay? Was it right that American businesses profited while taking advantage of those Mexican workers' unfortunate circumstance of being born two miles south of the border rather than two miles north of it? I figured my best strategy would be to check labels and not buy anything grown in Yuma, Arizona. It would not solve the dilemma, but at least I would not feel I participated in it. I did not want a bad taste left in my mouth, especially not from a salad.

🚐

While most of the folks in RV parks appeared to be in good health, we had come to understand that things were not always as they appeared. One of our favorite guys from our Alaska Caravan trip in 2017, in his early seventies and as spry as an elf, dropped dead from a heart attack seven weeks after the Caravan ended. He was in an RV resort somewhere in

Arizona when he passed away. We saw it on Facebook and were shocked, as were our other fellow RV travelers.

We learned firsthand that death indeed happened in these idyllic RV resorts, despite outward appearances that everything was perfect. It happened in our Saugerties/Woodstock KOA Campground in New York. We had come to visit Woodstock for an immersion into the Sixties Hippiedom we had missed in 1969.

I had noticed a couple angled across the road from us our first day for several reasons. The first, and most obvious, was the huge, fully dressed, sparkling clean Harley-Davidson parked at the end of their small travel trailer. The four-passenger, huge pickup truck that pulled the trailer sat at the opposite end of the RV. I assumed they hauled the motorcycle in the truck-bed.

The second thing that made the couple memorable was the Florida license plates on the truck, the trailer, and the bike. I remembered thinking that if it worked out, I would ask where they were from. They might have been neighbors from two miles away in Tampa. Stranger things had happened.

My first glimpse of the occupants of that campsite came early the next morning. A white-haired, pony-tailed man squatted beside the bike, a polishing cloth in his hand, making the chrome on his Harley sparkle in the early morning sun. Two little blonde-headed girls sat on the bike, chatting and laughing while grandpa worked.

In the early afternoon, we saw the family again at a Shop Rite grocery store in Saugerties. One of the little girls sat in the buggy's child-seat while the other one rode on the front, grandpa pushing while grandma selected the grocery items. She, too, appeared in her early sixties with long, straight salt-and-peppered hair pulled into a ponytail. Both husband and wife wore t-shirts and jeans, and she wore a denim work-shirt as a jacket. Later in the afternoon, I saw the grandma walking with the little girls back to the trailer from the campground's heated swimming pool. The little girls wore bathing suits and swim rings. Grandma was still in her jeans and t-shirt. Maybe grandpa had stayed home to take a nap? Both the bike and truck were in the campground, so he had to be somewhere close by.

Labor Day eve arrived, and we excitedly started our bonfire late in the afternoon. Michael's sister Anne had joined us for the holiday weekend, and the campground had filled. We had had a great day shopping in the village of Woodstock. I now wore my new, consignment-shop Vintage bell-bottoms, and Anne sported a previously owned, batiked denim shirt. A few cocktails had smoothed any wrinkles off our faces and knocked any emotional loads off our shoulders. Life was good.

The wail of a siren interrupted our idyllic evening. "It's the fire station on the other side of the road doing a test," Michael had said.

"I'm not so sure," I said. "It's lasting a long time."

"It sounds like it's getting closer," Anne said.

Next thing we knew, an ambulance came into the KOA campground, a firetruck not far behind. After making an initial wrong turn down another campground road, the ambulance stopped right across from us at the Harley-Davidson campsite. The man had stood outside by the road, flagging the ambulance down. The two little girls stood beside him, clutching his skinny legs.

We tried not to look, out of respect, at the horror taking place in the campsite diagonally across from ours. Paramedics from the first bevy of emergency vehicles had brought the grandma outside under the awning and started administering CPR. The old-fashioned way, by hand. A second ambulance appeared, bringing more medical help. The CPR efforts continued. Another stretcher appeared, followed by two police cars. A black SUV appeared, and a younger woman jumped out and pulled the little girls into her arms. Everyone stood around gawking, as still as statues, silent, except for the two paramedics who continued their futile and ineffective efforts to bring life back into the inert body of the woman. Eventually, paramedics loaded the stretcher into an ambulance, and every vehicle slowly exited the campground. The young woman in the SUV left with the little girls. Grandpa hopped in his truck and left, less than a minute behind the ambulance that carried his wife.

"She's dead, you know," Michael said to Anne and me.

"Yeah, I know," Anne said. Michael's sister had three master's degrees in nursing, so she certainly would know.

"Why do you say that? What makes you so sure?" I asked. Michael had not spoken words I wanted to hear.

Neither Michael nor Anne answered. "Why do you think she's dead?" I would not let it go.

"It all took too long," Michael finally said. "Too long for the paramedics to get here, too many minutes working on her under the awning."

"No-one survives being without oxygen that long," Anne added. "She's gone."

When we woke up the next morning, the black pickup was at the end of the trailer. About 9 A.M., the man left the campground and was gone most of the day.

Our camper neighbor to our right told us later that the woman had died. "They reportedly worked on her all the way to the hospital, but she never came back."

The next morning when I got up about eight o'clock, I looked out to see grandpa sitting in a folding chair under the awning, leaning slightly forward, his face resting in his hands. He seemed to stare at nothing, mute and immobile. I could not imagine a more desolate and sadder image. The picture haunts me to this day.

Both the Buddhists and the Hindus had a concept of something they called 'a bad death.' It referred to a passing that came suddenly and without warning. One that gave no chance to get affairs in order, to tie up loose ends, to apologize for mistakes, or to tell anyone goodbye. Maybe those ancient religions came up with those bad-death concepts before modern medicine became adept at extending life far longer than we had any business living, oftentimes at a high price in terms of suffering and pain.

I did not see this woman's life as having had a bad ending, despite being unexpected and sudden. She died in the Catskill Mountains on a road trip, with two adorable little granddaughters and her husband at her side. I would have been satisfied with an ending like hers. She was alert and active, out in the world, and living a life many people would envy right up until the moment of her death.

Still, I found it jolting and unnerving to see someone die under an awning right across a dirt campground road from us. Was this the closest I had ever been to a person taking his final breath?

There were some things, although novel and potentially enlightening, one simply did not want to see or hear while RVing. Domestic violence, gunshots from the border patrol shooting coyotes or maybe even illegal immigrants, and sudden human death came to mind. I hoped my iteration of 'things not pretty' would remain short.

CHAPTER 14

Dueling GPSs

Call it neurotic, but I needed to know where I was and where I was going. I could not sit in our motorhome, even with a well-functioning GPS, without a *Rand McNally Road Atlas* sitting on my lap. I needed the big picture in addition to the zoomed-in, electronic visual of where to make the next turn. I wore out an atlas a year. I turned and dog-eared pages, I dropped and retrieved it from the floor, and I moved it in and out of an RV drawer crammed with manuals, insurance policies, and scotch.

When we bought our motorhome, our Lazy Days salesperson insisted we needed an expensive Rand McNally top-of-the-line GPS navigational system. She said it was the product truckers used and loved.

"We've got to have this GPS." My husband's eyes sparkled, and his volume rose. "Listen to all it can do. It'll route us around congested areas, tight corners, and low underpasses. It'll tell us the height restrictions of tunnels and alert us to accidents ahead. It does everything."

I rolled my eyes. "Look at the price, Michael. It's as ridiculous as its promises." I whispered to him, not wanting our saleswoman to know I did not believe every word she uttered. The sticker read $499.99.

"But it's marked down twenty-five percent."

I shrugged. Only the best for my husband, I had thought.

The GPS sat on the console for our first year of travel. Without warning, one day, Michael decided he wanted the GPS mounted on the front windshield. Our GPS battles began.

"I have to look down to see it. It's dangerous taking my eyes off the road."

"You don't have to see it. I do," I retorted. "I'm the navigator. I'll tell you where and when to turn."

"I need to be able to read the damned screen. For safety."

He moved the friggin' GPS. With it now mounted on the windshield and angled so the driver could see it, the passenger could not. Even if I leaned over as far as I could, the angle was such that I could not see the screen. The first time I tried to reprogram the GPS while the rig was moving, I could not reach it without unbuckling my seatbelt and standing up, an unsafe action to undertake with the truck barreling down the road at sixty-three miles per hour. Even if I stood up, removing the GPS from its mount proved difficult, and I found it impossible to return the thing to its bracket after reprogramming.

Not long after Michael repositioned his Rand McNally GPS out of my view, I remembered an old Garmin stashed in my C-Max. I had not used that antiquated GPS in years. I pulled it out, plugged it in, and voila! I was in business. I could track us on my GPS as well as on the road atlas. I no longer needed to see my husband's over-sized, over-rated, over-priced, and impossible-to-manage IntelliRoute Truck GPS.

The level of contention over routes skyrocketed. We now had two navigational systems, and they did not always agree. In fact, except out on open highways, they rarely agreed. I defended my little Garmin, arguing that the Rand McNally was overkill for our little 26-foot Class C motorhome. I maintained that our path should be the most direct one, the one that cars followed, not the truck route recommended for huge tractor-trailer rigs. Michael argued that his Rand McNally was up to date, pointing out that I had never once updated my Garmin in the ten

Dueling GPSs

years I had owned it. I stubbornly refused to concede he might have a valid point.

Our expensive, very smart Rand McNally GPS died unexpectedly during our second year of RV travel. Its demise stunned us both. First, the screen dimmed. Initially, the dimming was intermittent, but then it faded and turned black. Those changes happened over a ten or twelve-day period. We watched, not believing the damned thing would fizzle out. I sensed that Michael felt personally affronted by the failure of his GPS. He had defended the device intensely, and it had let him down. He wanted to throw it in the garbage.

"Hey," I said, "considering how much we paid for the thing, I think you should call Rand McNally. See if we can get a free replacement."

"Are you kidding? It's two years old."

"That's not that long, and Rand McNally is a huge company."

I stashed the GPS away, with Michael saying maybe he would make the call when we got home. I think we both knew it would not happen.

Neither of us could have predicted how much worse our navigational arguments would become. While I trusted my old, outdated Garmin, Michael did not. He bought a windshield mount for his cell phone and started using Google Maps for navigation. While I had had trouble reading the now-defunct Rand McNally seven-inch GPS screen from the passenger seat, reading Michael's tiny cell phone screen was impossible.

Our two systems disagreed—on routes, on distances, and on arrival times. It became a major source of dissension every travel day—big time. Before Michael pulled out his cell phone, I had thought my Garmin took us on far more direct routes than the truck GPS had done. Neither of us was ready for the direct-as-the-crow-flies route that Google Maps on the cell phone invariably selected.

As the main driver and the follower of Google Maps, Michael believed his system trumped mine. My observation was that Google often led us into troublesome spots, such as construction, heavy traffic, dead ends, and backroads. I confessed to absolute glee when Michael's beloved cell phone resulted in delays and wrong turns, and I refused to admit that my trusty old Garmin ever let us down. Not that we would ever know where my Garmin might have taken us, since nine times out of ten, Michael ignored my recommendations. I argued that my directions could not possibly have been any worse than some of the situations Google led us into.

In time, we agreed that the ongoing friction over routes needed to end. In the overall scheme of things, like many other things in my marriage, I did not care what route we took or how long it took to get there. I kept reminding myself it was about the journey, not the destination. The specific route did not matter.

I began to consciously practice sitting quietly in the passenger seat, eyeing my Garmin periodically while reading, working Sudoku, or looking at the scenery. I clamped my lips when Michael turned or did not turn at roads that differed from my GPS directions. While not able to claim 100 percent success at staying quiet, I got better.

But alas, non-participation in the navigation process was not what Michael wanted after all. With my new attitude and behavior, it took only a short period before my husband exploded.

"Goddamn it! I need some help here. I missed another turn."

I stared ahead, not answering.

"Gerri, would you please wake up? These highways are crazy, and these are the rudest drivers I've ever seen."

I looked at him and shrugged. "Thought you didn't want my input. My GPS would have had you turn three miles earlier." We were in the congested Northeast, somewhere between Washington, D.C., and Connecticut. While trying to skirt New York City and the heart of Philadelphia, we nevertheless had passed through Baltimore, Wilmington, Newark, and other hotbeds of insane urban congestion in our quest to put a sticker on every state in the country on our United States sticker map.

Dueling GPSs

"Shit! Did you see the way that truck almost clipped us? These drivers won't let me change lanes, and I can't tell which lane I need to be in." Michael's voice reflected a mixture of anger and frustration, both at the traffic situation as well as at me. "Stop being so smug and help me out, dammit. I'll follow your frigging Garmin. Just get us out of here."

"Aah, you need me, after all." It was a mean thing to say, especially under the circumstances, but I felt a sense of self-righteousness that my stubborn, intensely macho husband had finally admitted to an obvious truth: navigating one's way in a motorhome while towing a car through major metropolitan areas would go a bit easier with two heads rather than one.

It took a harrowing, death-defying trip through the Catskill Mountains for my husband and me to reach a point of GPS accord. Relying upon his trusted Google Maps, Michael drove us out of the Woodstock/Saugerties KOA Campground one sunny August morning and pointed us toward western New York.

"Aren't these roads getting more and more narrow?" I felt relieved we were not meeting head-on traffic, for Michael would have had to drive the rig onto the grass to let another vehicle through. "The houses are getting farther and farther apart. Where's the highway we're supposed to be on?"

"I'm sure it's ahead," Michael said.

"My GPS has been saying to turn left at every street we've passed for the last three miles. It doesn't like what you're doing."

"That old hunk-of-junk Garmin of yours doesn't know what it's talking about."

"Whatever." I sighed, biting my tongue not to start arguing about directions.

The ascent began, and Michael dropped the truck into a lower gear for climbing. "I think I saw a sign that this is Indian Head Mountain," he said.

I consulted my trusted road atlas and confirmed. "Yep, and it's three thousand, five hundred fifty-seven feet."

The road narrowed more, now barely wider than one lane.

"What the hell does 'limited use road' mean, Michael? Did you see that sign?"

"Guess maybe they close it down in the winter, or maybe it means big tractor-trailers can't go on it."

"We're more like a tractor-trailer than a car," I said. I felt panicky. "I think we should turn around. Like right now."

"Keep your eyes open for a spot."

The twisting, turning, switchback-filled one-lane road continued for eight miles and took us more than an hour to navigate. We never found a place to turn around. We never even found a spot to pull over to the side, if God forbid, we had met another vehicle coming from the other direction. What we found instead were hairpin turns on blind curves, drops of thousands of feet down mountainsides with no guardrails, and patches of road with no pavement and potholes the size of kitchen sinks.

Thankfully we seemed to be the only crazy fools on the little road that day.

By the time we reached a state road, Michael's knuckles were white, and his brow glistened with sweat. I had bitten two nails down to the quick, and it probably took thirty minutes for my pulse to return to normal. We pulled over at the first filling station we saw and sat in silence for a few minutes, thankful to still be alive. Google had once again taken us on the most direct route, but this time we agreed that Google Maps had put us at risk and that perhaps we should again consider a commercial GPS designed for tractor-trailers and RVs towing toads.

We traveled those days in an unsettled truce. I continued to ride with my Rand McNally Road Atlas in my lap and my antiquated Garmin on the console. Michael positioned his cellphone on the windshield, facing him, with Google directions programmed in. I monitored our route and took note of turns Michael made or did not make that disagreed with what my Garmin said. I inwardly gloated when we hit horrible roads, construction, congestion, or some other difficulty. I tried to stay quiet and calm. When Michael announced, "I need your help," I perked up, consulted my preferred GPS, and gave him directions based on my navigational system, not his.

I liked being a navigator. I could not believe my husband would discount the value of a second opinion when in unfamiliar territory driving a fifty-foot-long, six-ton rig through every conceivable traffic and road condition. The thought would hurt my feelings if I let it.

Living with almost constant togetherness in cramped quarters for months at a time could put a strain on even the best of marriages. We had both learned to choose our battles carefully and arguing over directions was something we stopped doing. I vowed not to say another word about Michael's cellphone and the absurd Google Maps directions it spit out. I did not want to drive. If I did, he would pull over and walk around to the passenger seat without another word.

I have come to understand that driving a rig in unfamiliar situations over time can be as stressful as facing yet another large and unfamiliar supermarket and not being able to find a damned box of Cheerios. No matter how much these new surroundings and challenges tickled the synapses in our brains and hopefully helped keep us young and mentally alert, they also took their toll in terms of stress.

Perhaps Michael and I needed to loosen up and laugh about our dueling GPSs. They both worked okay, and either one would ultimately get us where we needed to go. It did not matter which one we listened to. Both were competent and did their jobs without any hysterical emotionality. In fact, neither of them ever raised its voice, no matter how far off-kilter we may have gone. My husband and I could learn and grow from the self-control our navigational devices demonstrated.

I supposed our GPS truce could continue indefinitely, but at some point, one of us might get tired of the discrepancies and fork over several hundred dollars on a new, state-of-the-art Rand McNally GPS designed for trucks. We would eventually see, but I did not plan to pull out my Visa card anytime soon.

CHAPTER 15

Deliberate Living

I will read this book at least once a year for the rest of my life, I promised myself. I was nineteen and had finished reading Henry David Thoreau's *Walden*. My bones felt rattled, my core shaken. The book had changed my way of looking at the world. It was a profound 'once you've seen it, you can never go back' kind of awakening.

Despite great intentions and multiple attempts, I had managed to slog my way through the book again only once during the past five decades. I bought a new copy—crisp, white pages, and larger print—for our last RV trip. I picked it up a few times, but I failed to read a single chapter while we were on the road. Back home, I still had not opened it. How can this 1854 classic be so powerful and yet aversive at the same time?

Rambling along on a road trip through New England, I realized our route south would take us close to Concord, Massachusetts, the site of Walden Pond and Thoreau's original cabin. I perked up at once, energized by newly awakened memories and a sudden, overwhelming desire to go to Walden Pond. I needed to revisit this shrine. The desire felt as profound as hunger or sleep. We made it a plan.

Deliberate Living

We could not find a campground near Concord with openings. It was early August, peak tourist season. We finally found a place in Littleton, Massachusetts, about thirty miles away. We never dreamed those thirty miles would take ninety minutes to travel each way. Concord was a popular tourist destination, perhaps more for all the historical markers than for Thoreau's little cabin in the woods.

I had hoped visiting Walden Pond would reignite my passion for a deliberate life, one that valued ideas more than possessions. Thoreau had enamored me at nineteen with his ability to extract meaning out of simple daily activities. He had not needed an ever-changing horizon for stimulation. I wanted to reconnect with that younger part of myself and understand, at last, what I was doing riding around the country in a tiny, bouncy tin-can house. Rather than helping me find the ultimate meaning of life, I had sometimes suspected that RV travel was interfering with my search and possibly delaying my success at determining the purpose of my life.

Our challenge of getting to Walden Pond could be a metaphor for the difficulty of achieving the simple life Thoreau so valued. The difficulty went beyond the bumper-to-bumper traffic and construction delays between our campground and Concord. When we finally reached the turnoff for our destination, we found ourselves trapped in a long line of cars on the two-lane road in and out of the Walden Pond National Reservation. A uniformed employee greeted each car, spoke for a few seconds, and gestured toward a turn-around spot. When our turn came at the front of the line, we learned the parking lot was full. We could try again after two o'clock in the afternoon.

"How can they close a national landmark at eleven o'clock on a Tuesday morning?" Michael asked. I did not have an answer.

I had been to Walden Pond before when I was in my twenties. I remembered the replica of Thoreau's one-room cabin. His minimalism had made my heart flutter at that time, and I had stared at his house with awe and envy. My reaction this time was different.

"Oh, my God," I said to Michael with a laugh. We had walked up to the replica of Thoreau's cabin. "He could have been an RVer living in such a tiny bit of space." I peeked inside the cabin. "I don't see a rock on his desk. Remember that story of how he'd found the rock, thought it was pretty, and set in on his desk to look at each day? When he realized it was doing nothing but collecting dust, he tossed it out the window."

My husband, who thought Ralph Waldo Emerson (Thoreau's mentor) and Nathaniel Hawthorne were the Transcendental writing gods, did not respond. I found it unbelievable that my husband, whom I viewed as a smart, well-read man, had never read Thoreau. Despite having been a part of the civil rights, women's rights, and anti-war protests, Michael was unfamiliar with Thoreau's famous *Civil Disobedience* and the influence it had wielded during those turbulent sixties. He did not understand why I was so smitten with an old geezer who had lived alone in the woods back in the 1800s.

His loss, I had always thought.

The idea of reducing life to bare bones had always appealed to me. It was an aspect of RV living that suited me well. If I could get over the longing for the routine and the personal connections back home, I would have no problem with this RV thing.

While our RV, in some ways, reflected the pure essence of minimalism, our clutter of clothes, toiletries, and the tangle of electrical cords to charge all our electronic devices reminded me hourly of our twenty-first-century lives. Despite longing to the contrary, our current lives were anything but simple and minimal. I imagined Thoreau sitting quietly by the pond, which was so huge I would undoubtedly have called it a lake. I imagined his thoughts turning inward as he waited for a profound insight to pop into his mind, some profundity triggered by the stillness and beauty of the natural environment. In contrast, our already-overloaded minds suffered an ongoing bombardment of external stimulation every time we pushed an ON button connecting us to the Internet that made us one with the entire friggin' planet. The difficulty of replicating Thoreau's life in the twenty-first-century boggled my mind.

"Maybe it's the routine I miss when we're on the road," I said to Michael. "It's hard to settle into any kind of pattern when every day is different." It was an ordinary day—I had no idea where we were in our travels—but I had experienced a jab of homesickness.

"What are you talking about? You've got a routine. You get up every morning and write for several hours. Then we either get in the car and do whatever we're going to do that day, or we hook up the car and hit the road."

"It's not the same." I frowned. "Everything outside is constantly changing when we're on the road. I don't have a room of my own, a sanctuary that helps me generate ideas. I have that at home. I sit down in my office, and things happen. I can write. Here, sometimes it happens, and sometimes it doesn't."

Michael shrugged. "Sounds like a problem with your head, not your environment. You need to get over yourself." My husband was not one to mince words. "You can write in our RV, and you can write while we travel. You drafted an entire book last summer while we were on the road." He glared at me. "Stop whining. I'm not buying it."

"But it's not just the writing, Michael. It's the contact with people that I miss." I slapped my paperback on the table and stood up. I could not believe we were having this conversation again, the one that seemed to resurface every two or three weeks.

"There are people all over the place. Look out the window. Go talk to the people sitting over there if you're so starved for conversation with someone other than me." He pointed toward a couple, probably in their sixties or seventies, sitting at a nearby picnic table, drinking coffee and chatting. I heard a familiar irritation in my husband's voice. I was sure he viewed me as a broken record.

"Those people don't know me, and I don't know them. What would I say to them, other than asking where they're from, where they're going, and how long they planned to be on the road? I mean, really... who even cares about that crap?" I fought down anger that my husband refused to understand what I had said many times before. "I want conversations with people I have things in common with, and with people who know my history." How could my husband not miss our friends and family?

I walked outside, determined not to have yet another stalemated discussion with my husband.

Would achieving a Thoreau-like deliberateness be possible while living with another person? I began to imagine what life would be like if I lived alone, and what changes I might make to achieve a simpler lifestyle. The Thoreau mindfulness I admired went beyond merely reducing one's possessions. It was more than minimalism. It was a mindset, and I was having a tremendous amount of trouble achieving and maintaining it in an RV. But it was not as if I had found it back at home either.

Our visit to Walden, with all the memories it shook loose and the thoughts it generated, made me realize that Walden was a state of mind. Like everything else. I would have to continue searching. In the meantime, the least I could do was crack the spine on my still-virgin copy of *Walden*, the book that had changed my life when I was nineteen. Maybe it would change me again. I would make myself read a chapter or two. Tomorrow, yes?

CHAPTER 16

The Philadelphia Folk Festival

I had listened to Michael rave about the Philadelphia Folk Festival for over twenty-five years. Back in the sixties and seventies, he had lived in New England, a mecca for aspiring musicians. He had grown up an easy daytrip from Boston, Greenwich Village, Newport, and all the other metropolitan areas that had offered venues for unknown artists. Musicians like Bob Dylan, Richie Havens, Janis Joplin, and others had come to those places to perform and to make names for themselves.

When I thought of music festivals, Woodstock came to my mind. Not Michael. He would remember the Philadelphia Folk Festival, which opened in 1961 and was the oldest, largest, continuously running folk festival in the country. It took place on the Old Pool Farm in Schwenksville, Pennsylvania, a small village about thirty-five miles west of Philadelphia. The Philadelphia Folk Song Society produced the four-day festival the third weekend in August every year. Attendance was generally around 30,000. While most folks came with day passes, camping was also a popular means for total immersion into the festival scene.

The Old Pool Farm covered several hundred acres of rolling pastureland with permanent areas set aside for both RV and tent camping. After more than half a decade, The Folksong Society, made up of volunteers, knew how to get the job done. The volunteers loved folk music and were on a mission to keep the tradition alive. They did this by providing educational services year-round for children to ensure the festival's future into posterity.

We bought our RV in late 2015 and began taking long trips in 2016. We could not have considered attending a music festival back then—my arthritic knees were too debilitating. But by 2017, after two knee replacements, I was good to go. Michael made several attempts to get tickets for the Philly Folk Festival that year, but it was not to be. Somehow, tickets disappeared the minute they became available online.

As we began planning our 2018 RV adventure, we again considered the possibility of snagging tickets for the Philadelphia Folk Fest. We were looking at other music events and wanted to make music festivals the focus of our trip. This year Michael vowed to work smarter rather than harder to try to find tickets.

Michael learned that the secret to obtaining tickets for the 57th Philadelphia Folk Festival was to purchase an annual membership in the Philadelphia Folksong Society several weeks before tickets went on sale to the public. Our membership came with a guarantee of tickets for the entire event. However, being RVers, we wanted more than those day passes. We wanted a spot in the campground, where the after-hours action took place. We wanted to be insiders, a part of the scene. We did not want to fight traffic for miles every day and end up parking two miles away and walking to the grounds. We wanted to be on location, which only that sacred Folksong membership could ensure.

It came together at the last minute. Costly, but what the hell? We went for the gold with the full concert admission ticket, a site in the RV campground, reserved seating in chairs in front of the main stage, and special green wrist bands that allowed us to hop on golf-cart shuttles that ran back and forth between the campground and the mainstage area.

We had both missed Woodstock. For me, being in the rural South in the late sixties, I felt like I arrived late to the dance when I finally got out of North Florida, caught up with current social issues, and became politically involved. I lived a couple of miles outside Washington, D.C., during the turbulent anti-war, social justice movements of the early seventies. Lyndon B. Johnson was in office, and the Great Society promised to bring an end to all the country's social ills. We believed the Revolution was right around the corner. Finally, I had gotten on board.

Snagging those Philly Folk Fest tickets triggered all those old memories. For both of us, although Michael's memories differed from mine. We had not known each other back then. The festival became the primary focus for our 2018 trip, and we planned everything around this hallowed event.

As Festival time approached, the weather continued its ominous pattern. Global warming was turning both rainfall and high temperatures into daily records almost everywhere. Parts of Pennsylvania had been intermittently flooding for several weeks due to torrential rains the entire summer. As August 16, 2018, neared, relief did not appear on the horizon.

Knowing we would boondock for four days and that the festival would be exhausting, we arrived in the Philadelphia area several days early to rest up. We monitored the weather, dismayed to hear predictions of a record-breaking heatwave followed by severe thunderstorms during the festival weekend. Oh, well, we thought. It could be like Woodstock. Weather forecasts conjured those iconic photographs of hippies wallowing in the mud during a heavy rainstorm while Jimi Hendrix played a rain dance on the mainstage.

Except, of course, it would not be like that for us. We were sixty-eight and seventy years old and sleeping in a 26-foot Class C motorhome. Our experience would not be like the Woodstock footage showing miles of tents as far as the eye could see. Nevertheless, boondocking made us nervous. Our small RV had small tanks—for fresh water, grey water, and black water. Our four nights, from Thursday afternoon until Monday morning, would test the capacities of those tanks.

"I think we should try to get there around noon," Michael said. "There's a staging area a couple of miles from the campground for RVs. They let in a few campers at a time. Should be a smooth process."

We arrived at about 12:15 p.m. Volunteers waved us away, saying they were not letting in any more RVs right now. "Come back in an hour or so," they told us.

"What the hell?" I asked. "That staging area only had a dozen or so campers. Lots of room for others to pull in."

"Guess they know what they're doing," Michael said.

We ended up circling the surrounding farmland for a couple of hours, driving past the staging entrance every thirty minutes or so. Although they were letting five rigs in at the time, our timing was always off. It was after 3:00 p.m. before they let us in.

Once inside the staging area, at least we felt part of the gang. The party had started with festivalgoers pulling on cans of beer (and yes, we smelled reefer as well) and congregating in small groups to talk. The temperature was about ninety-four degrees that day, and the RVs provided only a sliver of shade along their eastern sides.

"Look at how happy all these people are," I said. "Despite long delays and the heat, no one is complaining. Incredible!"

"It's festival time," Michael said. "This is all a part of the experience."

Volunteers were leading five rigs out of the gate at the time, at perhaps twenty-minute intervals, and allowing another five rigs to enter. We learned from folks who had been coming to this shindig for decades that these delays were unusual. There had reportedly been one festival fifteen years ago that was comparable. "Mud," everyone said. They described the camping area this year as soft and mushy. Instead of three entrances to the campground, volunteers told us only one was passable, especially by some of the huge 45-foot Class A motorhomes.

Our turn came around 5:30 p.m., and we were far from being among the last to get in. Tired, hot, and hungry, my nerves had frayed. Michael dealt with these sorts of problems better than I. But even he began to lose patience when an old beat-up Class A broke down a couple of rigs ahead of us on the muddy, potholed dirt road. We sat in the heat for another hour until somebody got the thing running again. Ten minutes after we finally started moving again, an ancient Volkswagen bus—at least thirty years old if it was a day—broke down two vehicles in front of us. Volunteers called in a big farm tractor, which towed the old relic to its assigned campsite. Those Volkswagen folks would have to figure out repairs later. The rest of us in line were relieved and happy to have them out of our way.

Finally, at almost 7:00 P.M., a volunteer directed us into our spot. Even though we were on higher ground and at the back end of a row four rigs deep, the ground was soft from all the rain. When we got out of the rig and looked, our tires had sunk about four inches into the mud.

"Think we'll ever get out of here?" I asked Michael.

"We'll worry about it Monday morning. Right now, it's time to relax." Out came the beer for Michael and the beloved red wine for me. It had been a long day.

We were too exhausted to do much socializing with our neighbors that first night. There was more space between the rigs than what we had expected. We were happy to learn we were close to the golf cart pick up point where we would catch rides to the main gate. A huge truck offering showers for seven dollars each sat a short distance away. (We did not use the pay showers, opting instead for sponge baths and one full shower each in our RV for the time we were there.)

We began hearing about Fest kids early that first afternoon in the staging area. These were the children whose parents had brought them to the Philadelphia Folk Festival every year, beginning when they were babies. The festival had been an annual event in their lives—every summer, they would see and hang out with the same kids at the Old Pool Farm. Now they were adults, with children of their own. It helped explain why there were so many people camping in groups. Some of these groups had been meeting up every summer for decades.

We learned some people would come to the campground for the four-day festival but never set foot in the mainstage area where the stages and vendors were. For these folks, the party in the campground was the festival. They might miss the big-name headliners, but they did not miss music. Impromptu and planned jamming went on all night long.

HOME IS WHERE THE RV IS

At the Philly Folk Festival in 2017, there had been a medical emergency when a woman experienced carbon monoxide poisoning from the exhaust pipes on RV generators. Generator exhaust vents are generally down close to the ground, underneath the house at about the same level as a car muffler. Because of the medical incident the previous year, festival organizers this year required that every RV have a Gen-Turi Exhaust System to divert fumes up into the air rather than blowing them out at ground-level.

Michael spent almost $200 on our Gen-Turi. He was not pleased to note that less than half the RVers had complied with the new rule. We were even less pleased to find that a few folks also failed to adhere to the 'no generators after 10:00 p.m.' rule, choosing instead to run their air-conditioners all night. Granted, we felt tempted to do the same—nighttime lows dropped only to the upper seventies, and the humidity was high.

We adhered to the rules and did not run our generator, primarily because of our next-door neighbor, a woman in her sixties in an old pop-up camper. She had lost her husband a few months earlier, and this was her first Philly Folk Festival without him. The only place her pop-up camper had ever been, for over forty years, was to this festival every summer. Her own Fest kids, now in their thirties and forties, helped her set up the camper and dropped by several times a day to check on her. Michael and I agreed that this widow-woman did not need to listen to our noisy generator outside her window every night. We chose to sweat it out.

The Philadelphia Folk Festival was the indisputable highlight of our 2018 road trip. For both of us. Hands down. However, there were a few surprises.

Our first shock was realizing our expensive festival package did not include any meals. Our blues festival in Chippewa Falls, Wisconsin, had included two gourmet dinners, and Michael was incorrectly positive that

Philly promised the same. Exhausted from the heat and the eight hours it took to get into the festival campground, we managed to find a package of spaghetti sauce in the freezer and a box of spaghetti in the pantry for our first festival dinner. Food vendors in the main stage area offered fast food and limited choices. We ended up going out to local restaurants several times during the four-day festival. Next time we will be better prepared.

Our big festival trauma, stamped into my mind for eternity, occurred our first day. We had turned off our generator on arrival day at about nine o'clock at night, per festival rules. When we woke and turned the generator on the next morning, nothing happened. The RV house battery would run a few lights, but it did not have enough current even to run the electric coffee maker, let alone the air conditioning. Our RV sat in full sun and had minimal overhead insulation. By nine o'clock, the outside temperatures had reached the mid-eighties. The inside of our RV was not far behind.

Among thousands of festivalgoers and dozens of festival-volunteers, somewhere there had to be a person who would be able to diagnose our problem and fix it. Luckily for us, we found two such people. Not that either of these guys would have wanted to spend hours of precious festival time working on someone else's RV, which they did not, but between the two of them, a couple of hours apart, our generator arose from the dead. We will never know for certain what the problem had been. The first helpful stranger said our GFCI breaker in the bathroom had gotten wet and needed disassembly and drying. We did that. Two hours later, our second Good Samaritan said an emergency switch on the generator was in the 'off' position. He flipped it on, and with the now-dried GFCI breaker reinstalled, the generator sprang to life.

It was noon by the time we finally got our power back. According to our indoor-outdoor thermometer, the outside temperature was ninety-eight degrees, and the inside was ninety-six. We cranked the A/C down low and headed for the main gate, hoping when we returned in a few hours, the temperature inside our little home would be habitable. It was.

Another disappointing surprise concerned our reserved seating at the main stage. To accommodate an audience of over 30,000 people, the stage sat at the bottom of a large rolling hill. Most attendees would spread blankets or unfold their short beach chairs on the hillside. The reserved seating was wonderfully close to the stage and offered perfect acoustics. However, due to a long summer of rain, the ground squished, and there were spots when, if not careful, you would sink to your ankles in mud. Although volunteers threw down a steady, ongoing supply of straw to try to make the slippery, muddy downslope passable, it still challenged anyone wanting to take advantage of those front-row seats. I refused to risk ruining my sneakers to get close, so we sat near the back of the reserved area. Although they were not muddy, those back-row seats also had their problems. The hill was so steep that all the chairs pitched forward to an uncomfortable degree. I felt like I was going to fall forward on my face.

Vendors offered the expected hippie-festival fare—long skirts and off-the-shoulder tops, tied-dyed t-shirts, jewelry, candles, herbal teas, and every other sort of memento one could imagine. Michael and I both bought Philadelphia Folk Festival shirts. His was a typical short-sleeved t-shirt with a large festival logo stamped on the front. I opted for a long-sleeved, tie-dyed hoodie with the festival logo raised on the front. Because of all the pastel blues, pinks, and yellows, Michael dubbed my purchase 'the cream-sickle shirt.'

"This is all pretty amazing," I said to Michael on day three of the festival. "I feel like I'm nineteen years old."

"How can you say that? Look around—I'd say two-thirds of the folks here are our ages."

"I know, but I didn't get to do this when I was nineteen. I missed out, being stuck down South."

We ambled through the children's section of the festival, which was an area more interesting than almost any other. Swarming with children who ranged from little ones who toddled to teenagers who swaggered, parents and volunteers provided multiple activities for them all—tight ropes and balance beams, mimes and clowns, face-painting and finger-painting, and dozens of hammocks suspended between trees for the use of anyone who wanted a rest.

"Can you believe all the children wearing tie-dye?" I asked Michael.

He shrugged, not considering my question worth his time, I guess.

"Looks exactly like all the pictures I've seen of Woodstock. Look at that little girl over there," I said, pointing to a baby in a tie-dyed romper. Covered with mud, the tot stomped in a puddle as her pony-tailed dad, barefooted and wearing only shorts, laughed at her antics.

The lineup of folk singers did not disappoint us—David Bromberg, Christine Lavin, Tom Paxton, and Trout Fishing in America, to name a few.

We had wondered, based on weather forecasts before festival time, if our experience might mirror Woodstock with thunderstorms and deluges of rain. The heat that Friday afternoon broke records as the mercury reached ninety-nine degrees. Around 6:00 p.m., a thunderstorm provided relief and delayed the evening concert by a couple of hours. Organizers chopped a few minutes off the allotted time for every performer that evening. Weather for the rest of the weekend stayed cloudy with only a couple of brief showers. We were relieved that temperatures stayed under ninety degrees for the remainder of the festival.

As we pulled out of the Philadelphia Folk Festival campground that Monday morning around ten o'clock, we realized that we had not heard a single irritable or unkind word during the entire four-day festival. We would wear our souvenir shirts with pride. We would cherish the two parking stickers on the front windshields of the RV and the car even more. The stickers measured maybe two inches by six inches, brightly colored and with the Philadelphia Folk Festival logo easily visible from yards away. We vowed never to remove them. They would be our visual prompt to go back to one of the happiest places we had ever been.

Tired, in need of showers, and with heavy hearts, we pulled away from the Old Pool Farm and the now-dissolving 57th Philadelphia Folk Festival, promising each other we would be back for number fifty-eight.

CHAPTER 17

Easy Rider, Old Coot Style

In the early days of our RV travels, we were high with excitement over our newly discovered freedom. Everything about RVing exhilarated us. I felt like 'queen of the road' in my passenger seat perch, despite ongoing protests that I did not want to be an RVer. I imagined every passing motorist looked at us with envy. Everything we were doing seemed very cool. I could not quite put my finger on why I continued to feel reluctant.

Being out on the open road, traveling across the country, planning the trip as we went along—it was inevitable that I would eventually compare RVing with motorcycling. The long-ago scenes of Captain America and Billy riding choppers cross-country in *Easy Rider* had remained strong in my memories for decades. It had been my first motorcycle fantasy, although I had never wanted to stash cocaine in a gas tank.

Easy Rider hit the movie theaters in 1969 and triggered in me a lifelong fascination with motorcycles. Motorcycling became a dual symbol for being bad and for being free. Back in my college days, I had had similar nonconforming sentiments as I marched down streets and protested at rallies.

Politics aside, there were times when the image of tooling down the road on a motorcycle, side-by-side with an amigo, and passing a doobie back and forth between the bikes for the sheer fun of it tickled my imagination. I could so totally see me doing that.

But I never did.

For years, I had hounded Michael. "We need to buy matching Harleys and take off across the country."

"Dream on," he always said.

About ten years ago, while we were on vacation, I watched a huge, fully dressed Honda Goldwing, 1500cc three-wheeler pull into a parking lot at Mount St. Helen's, Washington. An older couple climbed off.

"Let's go talk to them." With eyes wide and jaw dropped, I was drawn to this couple and their bike like a cat to catnip. I had to hear their story.

My reluctant husband followed me across the parking lot. We learned the couple had retired a couple of months earlier and were celebrating with a three-month trip across the country.

"That's what we need to do," I said later. "Wouldn't you love that?"

"Maybe going across the country, but not on a motorcycle."

Through the years, at least twice a year, I brought up the possibility of buying matching bikes, maybe three-wheelers. Michael never wavered on wanting no part of it. Motorcycles scared the bejesus out of him, and he made it adamantly clear that he would never, ever, under any circumstance, climb on one to even go to the end of our street and back, let alone take off on a cross-country road trip. He wanted to go to every state in the United States, though, which is why he wanted the RV after retiring. (Had I planted this itch in my husband with my motorcycle obsession? Shame on me, if I had.)

When we bought the RV, Michael tried to convince me that traveling in an RV would produce the same thrill of open-road adventure as riding on a motorcycle, and maybe it would. For him. I did not even try to explain how untrue that would be for me. But by the age of seventy, and with my orthopedic issues, I had reached a tentative acceptance that I would never get on a motorcycle again. I had made my peace with this unrequited dream. To some extent.

Two aspects of the *Easy Rider* movie trip had appealed to me. The first was its nonconformity and badassed-ness. Even now, more than six decades after the release of the movie, I still looked at motorcyclists on the road and made many assumptions about the personalities and politics of the riders. I felt a kinship and imagined they flaunted conventions and leaned to the left politically. I knew it was not so. For example, I knew a right-wing Republican, NRA gun-loving, straight-as-an-arrow, retired police detective who rode a big Harley. The ultra-liberal, left-wing folks I hung out with would view this conservative biker as a freak. My own biases assumed that tattooed, leathered, and bandanaed, helmetless scruffy bikers shared my politics. I admitted to dramatically flawed thinking with these notions.

When I compared bikers and RVers, initially, there appeared to be little, if any, overlap in their profiles. Motorhomes were as common as SUVs, and there was nothing eyebrow-raising or pushing-the-envelope about either. I did not like the motorhome stereotypes though, the ones of old retired geezers out and about, slowing down traffic, clogging up the intersections, making all kinds of stupid mistakes as they crept across the country, spending inordinate amounts of money to keep gas or diesel fuel in the damned things, and forgetting half the places they went or things they did because of senility. I did not want to be in that RVing demographic.

The picture became even more unclear when I remembered some of the observations Michael and I made of our fellow RVers on our Alaska Caravan trip. For the most part, those were retired, right-wing Republican, NRA gun-loving, straight-as-an-arrow folks, much like the Harley-riding retired cop I knew. But . . . wait. My retired cop friend, in addition to his super-cool Harley low-rider, also tooled around the country in a 40-foot Class A motorhome.

My bottom-line understanding and a great conclusion for me to reach was that stereotyping did not work in this country and never had.

Try to put a person into any kind of category, and you would likely be surprised. And wrong.

Although I did not yet see that RVing could be a countercultural political statement, I began to entertain the possibility that an RV could indeed lead to feelings of freedom unavailable when living in a fixed location. Granted, an RV could never trigger those feelings of wind in my face or of being a part of the scene as opposed to looking out a window at it. But I admitted it felt liberating to toss aside appointment books, calendars, alarm clocks, and the daily routines we had settled into back home.

Out on the road, we lived a flexibility that we would never have been able to adopt in our sticks and bricks home. Even something as simple as not taking the most direct route from Point A to Point B felt liberating. We tended to wake up whenever we wanted, eat when we felt hungry, and go to bed at night when we ran out of energy. On the road, almost everything was new. Whether we moved from one campsite to another or not, things changed because the rigs and the people around us constantly changed. Sometimes it felt like the country was a huge anthill, with vehicles disguised as frenetic ants going about their business, passing but never touching each other.

There was something incredibly exhilarating about being anonymous amid such intense activity. Unnoticed, untouched, and unscathed. I began to see myself as a spectator, an observer of life rather than a participant. How easy it was to imagine ourselves in hiding. Could a nomadic lifestyle be the 'drop out' I had longed for back in the late sixties? Could all these campgrounds be contemporary communes, except now with an ever-changing population? Instead of working the land for physical sustenance, perhaps this new breed of silver-haired nomad worked the land for mental and emotional sustenance. Maybe these twenty-first-century RVers were satisfying a need for ongoing stimulation, with sound and visual bytes now matching the flashing images on television and in video games. Maybe electronics really had changed our brains.

I experienced another change in thinking. Rather than looking at this new breed of senior citizens with disdain and condescension, maybe

I needed to start embracing them as the New Age trailblazers they might well be.

Shame surrounded me as I confessed to my obnoxious thinking. How could I be such a snob? Regardless of political affiliations or attitudes about guns and war, or gay marriages, or anything else, most RVers reflected courage, resourcefulness, flexibility, intelligence, and financial solvency. Perhaps I should try to cultivate the perspective that dropping out of one's life and taking off in an RV was very similar to the sixties when young people dropped out of society and went off to live in communes. Except retirees were doing it in a much smarter way. We went with our Medicare and Visa cards and all sorts of other safeguards for any trouble we might get ourselves into.

We RVers had each other. Despite the superficiality of interactions among fellow campers in these fluid RV parks, below the surface was profound respect and acceptance of each other. There was a nonjudgmental recognition that divergent religious, political, and lifestyle differences existed among us but that they did not matter. If a truck engine did not start in the morning, or an entire electrical system in a rig blew out, or if a medical emergency occurred in the campground laundry room, every camper within hollering distance would be there to help.

Michael and I saw it often—the raised hood on a vehicle, and five minutes later, five guys were all poking at the engine. Three old men sitting in the sunshine talking about where they were last week and where they planned to go next. Old women sitting in the rec room, passing around cell phones showing off pictures of grandchildren. Simple recipes shared in the laundry room. RV parks were indeed like small towns in America, something Garrison Keillor would have treasured and admonished us to cherish and protect.

With a new understanding and interpretation of *Easy Rider*, I looked at my husband and his beloved 26-foot Class C Thor Four Winds with a changed attitude. Maybe I got it. At last.

Freedom was more than passing a doobie back and forth while tooling across the country on motorcycles. It was more than wearing long skirts and going without bras or living on communes and trying to grow food organically. It was more than what music you listened to or whether you chose to relax with alcohol, drugs, or a walk in the woods. It had nothing to do with anything visible to anyone else. Freedom was a state of mind. Or maybe once again, my music icon, Janis Joplin, had it right with the line from "Me and Bobby McGee" about freedom meaning simply that one had nothing left to lose.

Was I the last adult on the planet to figure this out? It was not profound and would probably be of only passing interest to most of my contemporaries. I doubted many folks in my age bracket had held on so many years to such a silly pipedream as riding off into the sunset on a big Harley Davidson. I chalked it up as a testament to the power of unrequited longings. (Or a reflection of my OCD personality that had trouble letting ideas go.)

I had always managed to get almost everything I wanted despite not always knowing what that 'want' actually was. There were times I thought I had to violate middle-class norms to assert my independence. I now saw the *Easy Rider* symbol of the motorcycle as too literal and restrictive. An RV served the purpose, and it had made the actual break-away a hundred times easier. I could now literally act out my desire to take off and see the world.

I wondered what had made me cling so many years to the notion that I wanted to ride a motorcycle. I did not like sitting for long periods in one position, and it was almost impossible to shift around and stretch on a bike, both of which I could do in a truck cab from the passenger seat. I did not like getting hot and sweaty, especially when my hair got wet and plastered to my scalp, which happened under motorcycle helmets. I did not like harsh wind and brutal sun on my skin, and unless I wore long sleeves and pants, riding a motorcycle was nothing but exposure to the elements. I did not like being unprotected during thunderstorms, in roasting and freezing temperatures, and in all the other weather extremes one encountered on bikes. I did not like close calls with other vehicles driven by distracted and texting drivers who failed to see motorcycles. While motorcycle riding was indeed thrilling, I may have grown too old to appreciate those kinds of thrills anymore. Safety was now more important to me than excitement.

Our RV had given me every opportunity those *Easy Rider* choppers had given Fonda and Hopper but with greater physical comfort and increased safety. My real freedom was within myself and not even peripherally related to any external trappings. I had come full circle. I was where I need to be.

With my new understanding of personal freedom, I now viewed our RV differently. The more months we spent on the road, the more at home we felt. Our RV still needed a name, something to anchor it in the world, like a street address anchored our cinderblock house in Tampa.

Easy Rider just might be the perfect name.

CHAPTER 18

It's Too Hot!

Our RV trip up the East Coast, despite the excitement of getting back on the road, began with less of a thrill than previous trips. This lackluster beginning surprised me since it would be the trip that would add many stickers on our United States sticker map. Michael was super-psyched about all those stickers and was beginning to wonder if perhaps we could somehow get to Hawaii in a motorhome. I did not understand his enthusiasm this time around, especially considering we had already been in almost all the States where this trip would take us.

"This is not exciting. I'm bored," I said. We were on day four of a trip meant to last over five months. About ten miles outside of Savannah, Georgia, our current nondescript RV park looked like most of the others we had stayed in during the past two years. Although it was a beautiful sunny day, hardly a soul stirred. Our trip along the coastal lowland area had included an uncanny number of bugs. While mosquitoes generally limited their feeding to sunrise and dusk, the damned no-see-ums loved hot, bright days like this one. Temperatures were already approaching ninety degrees even though it was only 10:30 a.m. I suspected both heat and no-see-ums had kept folks inside their air-conditioned motorhomes.

"We're old hat at this stuff now," Michael said. "You're not really bored."

"Not sure I agree, and it's not only the heat and all these bug-bites that make me say that."

"Weather will be nicer when we get to the Outer Banks. Then you'll be putting on a hoodie at night." We sat inside our RV, and Michael was reading *The Tampa Bay Times* on his iPad. "This heatwave is breaking all kinds of records. It's the global warming thing. I just read that the temperature in Fairbanks, Alaska, got up to eighty-six yesterday. Can you believe that?"

I grunted a noncommittal response. We had left home five days ago and spent three nights at an RV park in St. Marys, Georgia, a little coastal town I had always thought would be a cool place to visit. The saltwater marshes and water grasses provided homes for millions of birds and water-loving animals. The air teemed with mosquitoes and the ubiquitous sand gnats that almost ate me alive but never bit my charmed husband.

"You didn't find that trip to the Cumberland Island National Seashore a bit tedious?" I asked. "We were trapped. For an entire friggin' day." Cumberland Island, originally owned and settled by the Carnegie family, was the largest of the Georgia barrier islands. The family gave most of the island to the government for a national park, stipulating that everything on the island had to age and weather naturally. We had gotten up at dawn, driven ten miles into the little town of St. Marys, and took a forty-five-minute boat ride to get to the island. After arriving at Cumberland Island, we boarded a shuttle bus that took us on a six-hour tour of the place, driving us on the worst, bumpiest, pot-holed roads imaginable.

"At least we got to see the wild horses," Michael said.

"Yeah, and learn about the horrible ethical dilemma of letting them die of starvation and disease because of their hands-off policy of letting nature take its course." The image of those scrawny, sick animals had upset me. "I wish I hadn't heard that story."

"But you did hear it, and now you need to forget about it."

"How can I forget it when it's bothering me? The average lifespan for a horse is twenty-five to thirty years, and those horses die at twelve or thirteen." I stood up from our dining table and stretched. "Maybe I'm just tired. That six-hour tour almost did me in." I had fallen right before leaving home and bruised my tailbone. Every single bump on the dirt road during the tour had made my lower back scream in pain. The no-see-ums were even thicker on the island than on the mainland, and my insect repellant lost its effectiveness about halfway through the day.

"I'm focusing on the dinner we had that night," Michael said. We had gone to a local seafood restaurant, a dive bar really, where Michael tasted his first Low Country Boil—a concoction of crab legs, shrimp, corn on the cob, potatoes, and lots of spices.

"I don't like this trip, Michael." I sat back down, not believing I had said the words out loud. "Even that trip to the Okefenokee Swamp was boring. I'm simply not a tourist. I don't like spending all this money and going to see things that disappoint me."

"How could the Okefenokee not disappoint you? You'd built that place up from your childhood memories to be the greatest place on the planet. It had to be a letdown to go back as an adult."

"I suppose you're right," I said. "I'll shut up."

"What's the plan for today, Mr. Trip Planner?" We had moseyed a little farther up the east coast and were now in Savannah, Georgia. Sticky sultry weather and blood-sucking no-see-ums continued to dominate my thoughts.

"Let's get the laundry done, and the house cleaned. We'll go into town later in the afternoon, maybe go to Paula Deen's restaurant for dinner. There's a carriage ghost tour at night that might be fun."

We did it all—laundry, house-cleaning, The Lady and her Sons Restaurant, and the Ghost City Tours. Laundry and house-cleaning took a predictable couple of hours and went smoothly. Although the waitstaff seated us quickly at Paula Deen's, we were disappointed with our dinners. We both found the food too salty and too rich. The richness probably came from the old Southern adage about cooking that "everything's better with butter." We thought the ghost tour was overpriced, lame, and disappointing. Temperatures had remained in the upper eighties well into the evening. A couple of drinks in an air-conditioned bar on the Riverfront salvaged that evening in downtown Savannah from being a total bust.

"We're going too slow," I whined as we struggled to make ourselves get out of the RV and go at least somewhere each of the four days we stayed in Wilson, North Carolina. It had been our layover spot while we waited for our spot in Kitty Hawk, North Carolina, to become available. I had begun to realize that what we initially viewed as exciting, we might later view as humdrum.

"It's what you asked for. You wanted to slow down, spend more time in each place."

"Not places like this though, and not in ninety-five-degree heat. I feel like I'm permanently wilted," I said. The humidity matched the thermometer, and every day the skies threatened rain. Rain only occasionally came though and lasted thirty minutes at most.

"At least there's a nice big Food Lion in town," Michael said. "Want to do Sloppy Joe's for our gourmet dinner tonight?"

"Pretty sad when a dinner of Sloppy Joe's becomes the highlight of the day."

"Tomorrow we'll drive over to Raleigh, see the Capitol, check out the city market area. That should be a good day." We were taking turns planning outings for each day, and tomorrow was Michael's day to organize.

His planned outing did not prove any more exciting than things I had been able to come up with. The three-mile hike along the Neuse River Trail was in full sun much of the way. We found the City Market District boarded up and practically abandoned, and the State Farmers' Market was closing by the time we arrived.

"When do we get to go home, Michael?"

"In another five months," my husband said. "It'll get better. Be patient."

Things did get better, despite the omnipresent brutal heat everywhere we went. Still, few destinations lived up to my expectations. For example, Cape Hatteras National Seashore looked precisely as it did on postcards as did the other things we saw on the Outer Banks. At least the wild horses on Corolla Island seemed in better health and enjoyed longer lifespans than the ones on Cumberland Island. My favorite touristy thing in Kitty Hawk was the Wright Brothers National Monument. It was the site of the first airplane flight in 1903, an achievement that changed the world.

Heat followed us everywhere we went that summer. "It's global warming," Michael said, "but I've got to say, you've become one really hot woman on this trip."

"Cut it out. It's not funny, and you're not funny either." Sweat dripped from the ends of my hair, my face flushed red with heat, and my energy level registered about zero. We were in Montreal, Canada, and the friggin' thermometer read ninety-six degrees. "How come you're not sweating?"

"It's not that bad. At least the humidity is low. Think what it'd feel like if we were back in humid Tampa?" Michael never got as hot as I did. At least he had stopped with the menopause jokes a few years back.

"Can't tell you how much I'd love to feel Tampa's weather right now." It was true. I would have chosen the unbearably sultry, humid weather in Tampa over what we had been experiencing all summer. Everywhere we went, temperatures soared above normal and broke records. If I had been back home in Tampa, I would have stayed in our air-conditioned house and would not be trying to go places and see things.

"Maybe summer is not the best time to travel," I said. "This is insane. It's Canada. It's supposed to be cooler than Florida. Do you realize the temperature in Tampa today is only supposed to get up to ninety-three?"

"But the humidity here is much lower than in Tampa. You'll be okay, Little Gerri," my husband said.

Jerk, I thought. Sometimes his nickname for me felt warm and affectionate. Other times it felt condescending. Like now.

"Okay, Big Mike." I snarled my retort.

I nevertheless registered a profound insight. The air conditioning in our house back in Tampa worked quite well. This little-house-on-wheels my husband so loved had little insulation. When the outside temperatures climbed into the upper eighties and nineties, even with the A/C running full blast, the inside temp never dropped below seventy-eight or so. Too hot for me. I would have been much happier in this kind of heat back home, going from one well-air-conditioned place to the next. There would be no need to go outside and see anything because we would already have seen it. I could stay inside and stay cool.

Of more importance to me, I would be able to go outside early in the mornings and garden. It was the rainy season in Florida, the time when all my tropical plants doubled in size every month. Although I had paid someone to keep the shrubbery under control while we traveled, I still worried about how my plants were doing. I liked to do my own gardening, make my own decisions about when, where, and how much to prune.

As a Master Gardener, I had learned about heat-related dangers that threatened those of us who did not have enough sense to come inside out of the heat. Gardeners often started projects and lost track of time. They refused to stop working until they finished the job, often ignoring their bodies' warnings of dehydration and over-heating. Heat stress could quickly escalate to heat exhaustion, which could result in a potentially fatal heatstroke.

All summer, I had been listless, sluggish, and only quasi-interested in my surroundings. I interpreted my feelings as boredom. Now I realized I might be experiencing physiological reactions to the extreme heat. How could anyone ever relax and enjoy something when they were sweating like a stuffed pig?

"I think RVers are at risk for the same kinds of heat-related problems as gardeners," I said to Michael. I had had this epiphany as we strolled through the Montreal Botanical Garden that afternoon in full sun and ninety-six-degree heat. "I don't think boredom has been my problem this summer. I think I'm a victim of heat exhaustion."

"Could be," my husband said. "But I don't see any way to get around it."

"I do. We could stay home."

Michael rolled his eyes and gave me a playful, but real, jab in the ribs.

CHAPTER 19

Nest-Building

The longer we traveled, the more I realized we could do a better job of making our rig reflect who and what we were. I started noticing ways other campers individualized and decorated the outsides of their rigs. I knew we would never stay in one place long enough to plant flowers or create a fairy garden—both of which would have mortified Michael anyway—but we could make a few small changes that could have a big visual impact, at least in my mind. I had come to believe that most RVers gave little thought, if any, to their fellow travelers. Still, I thought we needed to decorate, and I did not mean adding a wood-burned plaque saying, 'Michael and Gerri from Tampa' and not by plugging in an artificial palm tree covered in twinkly white lights.

Our first home-decorating purchase had been Michael's vinyl United States sticker map. It fit perfectly on the freezer door of our refrigerator. We second-guessed the positioning every time we saw other RVs with sticker maps affixed on the outside, often on the wall of a slide. Later, we added a sticker map of Canada, placing the Canadian map on the refrigerator door. Now, every time I looked at the two maps, I felt irritated. We had done it wrong. Canada should have been north of the United States, not south. We had made the rule that we had to spend at least two nights in the state or province before adding a sticker.

We also had a small herald flag, a gift from Michael's sister. It read: Weekend Forecast: Camping with a Chance of Drinking (Drinking May Be Heavy at Times). When we remembered it, and when we planned to stay in one site for a few days, we would plant the little flag out in front of our house. Many RVers had similar flags, and most had the common denominator of first names and hometowns. I hated that our little flag was so common. At least our message was funny, to us anyway. We would occasionally see our same flag at someone else's rig but with different names stamped on it. I would then feel anything but unique.

"We need more than sticker maps and a flag to stick in the ground," I said to my husband. The Philadelphia Folk Festival had inspired and motivated me. Most of the old hippies camping in our area at Old Pool Farm had spent years collecting paraphernalia to express their politics and interests. Tie-dye had been everywhere—from shirts to pants to tablecloths to shade sheets. I purchased the obligatory tie-dyed lightweight hoodie at the festival, and Michael dubbed it my cream sickle attire. In fact, he made a Facebook post of me hiking a trail at Franconia Notch in New Hampshire that read: *Hey, let's dress up like a cream sickle and go hike in the woods.* Michael found the post terribly funny, and I guessed many other folks did, too, based on the Facebook responses.

Multiple ideas for decorating our rig crystalized in Woodstock, New York. Although the ideas were not original or even particularly creative, they excited me. The place was hippie-ville on steroids. Forty-nine years after the music festival, Woodstock still attracted a pilgrimage of folks from the sixties subculture of long ago. With block after block of quaint little shops, Woodstock offered a plethora of consumer goods that could make tripping-out our rig an almost instant accomplishment.

I was a skinflint and often said with a smile that I worked too hard for my money to spend it on silly, superfluous things. However, I plunked down almost thirty bucks for a tie-dyed sheet ingeniously marketed as a tapestry. It had loops on all four corners for easy hanging. I had seen sheets like these suspended from awnings in the campground at the

Nest-Building

Philadelphia Folk Festival. Yes! I snatched it up and handed my Visa card to the clerk. A few minutes later, I spent almost the same amount on a batik tapestry to use as an outside tablecloth.

The tapestry proved easy to attach to our awning. It provided shade from the sun, depending upon our orientation, and offered a small suggestion of self-containment and privacy. It created a feeling of boundaries, like we had an additional room outside of our little house. I loved the way the burnt orange and black batik tablecloth complemented the funky, multi-colored hanging shade sheet. I patted myself on the back for my purchases, not regretting the sixty-five bucks one bit.

I viewed both the tie-dyed sheet and the batik tablecloth as political statements. I sometimes heard folks my age utter disparaging remarks about *hippies*. I felt both the sheet and the tablecloth said something about us, and I felt proud of the message. I may have lost a few right-wing Republican friends when I posted a picture on Facebook of our rig, all decked out with our 1960s memorabilia. I did not care. At least not then.

Who could go to Woodstock and not buy Woodstock precision-tuned windchimes? The Woodstock Percussion Factory was eight miles away in Shokan, New York. Unfortunately, the warehouse outlet for bargain sales was not open when we were there. I ended up paying a retail price (almost seventy dollars) for medium-sized chimes from a store on Main Street. I planned to hang the chimes from the awning of the RV, along with my tapestry. I chose chimes tuned to *Amazing Grace*, which I have always thought to be the most soulful song ever written. I felt like I had baptized and sanctified our Four Winds with these Woodstock purchases.

We sometimes saw rigs with bumpers and windows covered with stickers, anything from places visited to political messages to funny jokes. While that would be a unique way to personalize our RV, Michael did not want to mar the exterior shell of our little home with paint-damaging stickers and decals. He took pride in vehicle maintenance and was thrilled when someone had commented that our almost-three-year-old rig looked new. He kept it clean and covered with a nice layer of wax.

HOME IS WHERE THE RV IS

There were infinite ways to transform a rig into something uniquely personal as opposed to something that looked like every other RV. I recently purchased an LED laser strobe light to place outside. When lit, it created sparkly fairy-dust-like particles of red and green light that bounced off whatever surface it touched. When pointed up into a tree, the ambiance was magical and delightful. The lights charmed even when they simply bounced off the side of the RV. However, I admitted to seeing the strobe light's remarkable kinship with an artificial palm tree covered in twinkly lights. I sighed in resignation to my compromises and failures.

The final frontier was to name our home-away-from-home. It was almost obligatory. I remembered John Steinbeck in his 1962 *Travels with Charley: In Search of America*. He named his truck camper *Rocinante* after Don Quixote's noble steed. Or Ken Kesey and the Merry Pranksters traveling across the country in an old converted school bus they had named *Further*. Unfortunately, RV manufacturers had nearly exhausted the English language with colorful and appropriate names for recreational vehicles. For example, some of the names I might have considered are Revolution, Mirada, Pursuit, Zephyr, Journey, Serenity, Renegade, Synergy, Spirit, and Liberty. But they were all already taken by manufacturers.

Michael liked Gopher as a name for our rig—maybe we would spell it Go-fer. He said it would be short for Go for It. I liked it, but it did not feel perfect. I came up with Mariah, which sounded pretty good to both of us when our only association was with the wind. When I looked up the meaning and origin of the word, I found it too religious for our taste and style.

My latest inspiration is to name the Four Winds *Easy Rider*. Not long ago, I witnessed a motorcycle mishap on an interstate highway. The accident aroused dormant memories of my long and convoluted longing for a motorcycle. For me, that movie was about the search for freedom and self-understanding. *Easy Rider* would be a perfect name for our RV since that was exactly what I was trying to find as we traveled.

Nest-Building

We would keep searching for a name, though, since *Easy Rider* did not strike the same chord with Michael. I expected a perfect name would pop into one of our heads when we least expected it. Maybe by then, Michael would be willing to consider having a name airbrushed or stenciled on the cowl and the rear of the motorhome.

There was an adage that said travel changed a person. The last time I hauled out all my Woodstock purchases and displayed them around our motorhome, I felt a whisper of embarrassment. I hoped this whisper would not mushroom into a shout, but I felt sure it would. It was hard for a nest-builder to build a nest while changing who and what she was. It became oxymoronic that traveling people, or even sedentary people who continued to grow and change, could decorate their homes to reflect who and what they are. Dynamic situations meant ever-changing background props.

I reached the inarguable conclusion that while my tie-dye, batik, and windchimes were fun, the bottom line was that they were plain silly. I needed to stick with my minimalistic inclinations and stop trying to be Harriet Homemaker.

CHAPTER 20

If Only It Could Last

Michael called me a negative, critical person. I argued that I was discriminating.

"You're always complaining about something," he said. We had arrived back at the RV after dragging ourselves for four hours through the Montreal Botanical Garden in ninety-six-degree heat. Many parts of the garden were in full sun, and the sky held not a hint of a cloud.

"I don't think saying 'I'm miserable' qualifies as complaining under these circumstances," I said. I had chugged a full bottle of Dasani trying to re-hydrate myself. My eyes stung from salty sweat running down from my forehead. My sticky clothes clung to my body, and I smelled like a locker room of teenaged boys.

Michael's remark set me to thinking, though. In the comfortable and familiar surroundings of home, I rarely complained. At home, I could make choices. I could select places, activities, and times that felt right for whatever the weather happened to be. However, in the RV, we ended up planning activities around our geographic location. For the botanical gardens, we could not have waited four days until the temperatures dropped twelve degrees back down to normal. We either went when we were in Montreal, or we did not go at all.

Maybe I had become rigid and inflexible. Could my complaining be yet another low-volume protest about having had my roots yanked up and being drug around out here on the road for months on end? Surely there had been some peak moments during the many months we had traveled in this damned thing, times when I had thought I could die right then, and it would be okay because I had truly and thoroughly been 100 percent happy. After all, we had had the RV for over three years and had put almost 45,000 miles on the odometer while spending at least two nights in forty-five states and six Canadian provinces.

I let my mind drift, hoping to access travel memories in which I had felt euphoric. Our month-long trip to Alaska in 2017 came to mind—that trip had been transformational in several ways. The Alaska Highway, especially in The Yukon Territory of Canada, had cut through a vast, thick, and untouched wilderness, one that made me feel tiny and insignificant. I registered a few epiphanies about my place in the world on that 1500-mile highway. While the raw, remoteness had triggered a surprising apprehension, I had nevertheless felt a calm connection with the Universe that had felt spiritual. But there had not been any chuckles. Profound, but not fun.

I remembered Skagway, Alaska, a port town where we had stayed four days. It had rained almost nonstop, and temperatures had hovered in the fifties and sixties. We were traveling with the Adventure Caravan company with eighteen other rigs, and by this point in the sixty-three-day trip, we had run out of patience with the caravan schedule and with some of our travel mates. On the day I now remembered, we had opted out of a cold, rainy, rough, twelve-hour-plus boat trip to Juneau and back. Instead, we chose to find our own adventure.

Skagway had a year-round population of less than a thousand people. The little town would hardly be on the map were it not for the dozens of enormous cruise ships that stopped in the port daily during the summer months. Up to 30,000 tourists a day descended upon the little village where they purchased day-trip land excursions, ate and drank in local bars and restaurants, and shopped in stores the town had built just for them.

"Why so many jewelry stores?" Michael had asked a local shop owner.

"They did some research asking what tourists wanted to buy while they were on vacation. Jewelry was the main thing, so now we have two or three jewelry stores on every block. It's all good," he had said.

While our caravan co-travelers were out at sea, Michael and I headed to a local bicycle shop on a side street from the downtown. We had seen a sign advertising a Summit to the Sea bicycle excursion—a fifteen-mile, four thousand feet descent down the White Pass and into Skagway. Vans took cyclists and mountain bikes to the top. The bicycle trip back down the mountain pass and into town retraced the historic Klondike Gold Rush route. As we almost flew down the steep road on our bicycles, probably going twenty to twenty-five miles per hour, I realized that hands to grip the brakes were exponentially more important than feet to turn the pedals. We did not need to pedal. The adrenaline rush produced by the descent was incredible. Even better, the four-hour bicycling adventure served as a perfect segue into a memorable night.

On the bike ride, we became friendly with our tour guide, who later introduced us to his buddies back at the bicycle shop. It happened to be the day of the Floyd Mayweather/Conor McGregor professional boxing match, described as "The Biggest Fight in Combat Sports History." Pay-per-view planned to broadcast the match, and the local Happy Endings Bar, which sat across the street from the bike shop, planned to air the fight that night. The young tour guides and shop employees invited us to join them at the bar to watch it.

We were both in our late sixties at the time, and the excitement of having folks in their twenties and thirties invite us to join them thrilled us. Even if we had not liked drinking in bars (which, fortunately, we both positively adored), or if we had had no interest in boxing or mixed martial arts fighting (we had a teeny interest in the MMA), we would have nevertheless jumped at the chance to join locals at a neighborhood watering hole for an event this noteworthy.

The Happy Endings was located next door to a strip-mall motel with maybe ten or so rooms. We arrived about thirty minutes before the fight began. We expected standing room only and were amazed when locals scooted over and insisted we sit at the bar, directly in front of a huge screen.

"They're old guys. Make way for the old folks," the younger locals said, laughing and slapping us and each other on the backs. They were already a few drinks ahead of us.

A little later, one of our Adventure Caravan friends joined us. He had finally gotten back from the God-awful twelve-hour boat trip to Juneau in the wind, rain, and cold. "Several folks on the boat got seasick from the turbulence," our friend said. "You made a good decision not to go."

Meanwhile, our new buddies at the bar were yelling, "Another old guy. Make room for another old one." Somehow, they found another bar stool for our friend and seated him behind Michael and me. Guys on both sides kept buying us drinks. Michael drank beer, of course. I wanted to try a Moscow Mule, which one of the young bicycle shop women had described as excellent at this bar. After the first sip, Moscow Mules became my drink for the evening.

By the time the fight ended, Michael and I were both so polluted and giddy we hardly even knew or cared who had won. I had paid no attention to the fight and would not have understood the referee's calls even if I had been watching. Instead of watching the main event, we had spent four hours talking and laughing our asses off with folks at the bar. I was sure there were a few locals in the bar, but the folks we talked with were seasonal employees who would leave for other jobs or to go back to school in September when the tourist season ended in Alaska. We liked these young folks. They were living dreams, unfettered and free to come and go, switch directions, try out various things before settling down. They made me feel happy about what Michael and I were doing in an RV, except we were doing it at the other end of the continuum of life.

That evening at the Happy Endings Bar had a happy ending for Michael and me. (My husband later educated me that "happy endings" at a bar or hotel did not refer to lots of laughs throughout the evening but rather to another potential outcome of drinking and partying.) That night stood out as one of the best times we had ever had while RV-ing. Was it the Moscow Mules talking? Could it have been the supreme compliment of inclusion in the gang that these younger people had paid to us old coots? Or could it have been the pure joy of an entire evening with no responsibilities, nothing to do but laugh and have fun in such a cool place a million miles from home?

There had been several other equally fun experiences in which I knew I was exactly where I needed to be at precisely the right point in time—squandering over a hundred dollars in nickel slot machines at the Tropicana Casino in Atlantic City, New Jersey; listening to and watching a Queen video at the Rock and Roll Hall of Fame in Cleveland, Ohio; wandering the aisles of Garrison Keillor's Common Good Books store in St. Paul, Minnesota; selecting aged cheddar cheese at an Amish market in Bird-in-Hand, Pennsylvania; watching athletes train for Olympic ski-jumping competitions at Lake Placid, New York; strolling down quaint streets lined with vintage shops in Woodstock, New York, against a backdrop of hippies who appeared to still live in the sixties in their own stoned minds; or settling into the no-cell-phone-or-internet-service Ammonoosuc Campground in Twin Mountain, New Hampshire, and realizing I could stay there for the rest of my life.

Months after Michael's accusation that I was a chronic complainer, I struck back.

"I want you to know that I'm not a negative, critical person," I said. "That comment back in Montreal hurt my feelings."

"What are you talking about?"

I spent a couple of minutes trying to refresh his memory of our little talk following the Montreal Botanical Garden outing.

"Most of these things we see and do while RVing don't touch me; I don't connect with them. They're things that just happen." I wanted my husband to understand if only a little bit.

Michael rolled his eyes.

"No, really . . . I've said it many times before. I'm not a tourist. When we go to all these places, I want to feel like I'm there as a part of the scene, not like someone who dropped in to observe from a distance."

"You become a part of the scene the minute you enter it," Michael said, a tone of exasperation in his voice. "You're trying to over-think this again."

"No, I'm not." I brought up the Skagway Happy Endings Bar night, hoping that would help explain my feelings.

"I agree that night was a blast, one of the best times we've ever had."

"I think it's because we weren't tourists that night. We became a part of the gang, almost like magic."

"Okay, Miss Smarty-Pants, Over-Analyzer-of Everything, how do you propose we go about re-creating that more often?"

"Great question," I said. "I'm going to think more about it and get back to you when I have the answer."

I guessed Michael forgot my promise. He had never asked me for an answer. However, I had not forgotten the question. I was still trying to figure it out.

CHAPTER 21

Simple Pleasures

My contented feelings outweighed the negative ones many times over. I saw myself as a satisfied person who found a quiet joy in almost everything, especially my little routines of daily living. I liked the order and predictability that allowed me to go inside my head to amuse and entertain myself. I did not need all the outside stimulation and constant changes that Michael thrived on and needed to recharge his batteries. Our friends often commented on how different the two of us were. They were so right.

Given those two personalities, it was not surprising Michael found RVing a perfect fit, and I struggled with the constant changes. I wanted to believe that we had both expanded our minds and extended our horizons in terms of how we saw the world and our places in it. After all, we had compromised our way through three years of RV travel. It had been good for both of us.

I had produced a long list of things I loved about RVing, although I had yet to share my list with Michael. Perhaps it was stubbornness on my part, or at least a need not to let him think he had wholly swayed me to his way of viewing our traveling lifestyle. My husband could sometimes be a formidable force with which I had to deal. I was always aware of the danger that he would trample my quieter, softer ways.

Simple Pleasures

At the top of the list of things I loved about RVing was the sheer joy that came from having less stuff around us when we were out on the road. We packed and traveled with necessities and a minimum of extra items like books, DVDs, and electronics. We packed clothes with a discriminating view of anticipated activities and weather, careful not to bring every item of clothing we owned. Unfortunately, overpacking was my tendency, not Michael's. On our last trip, I somehow ended up with eight pairs of shoes, a totally insane number, and I swore never to let that happen again. I ended up wearing five of the pairs, though. Luckily, we were able to store extra things like shoes in the back of the C-Max. Extreme temperatures made clothing trickier. We had one trip when the mercury rose from a low of forty-two degrees to a high of ninety-eight degrees. The only thing I forgot were my Uggs.

I loved the feeling of self-containment that RVing triggered. Everything we needed was right there at our fingertips. I sat on our little sofa with my laptop, and I could stay there comfortably for hours. I placed our small stepstool beside my right foot, and that was where the coffee cup or water bottle sat. Meanwhile, Michael sat at the table with his iPad opened to the *Washington Post* newspaper or a bestselling thriller. Or maybe he had his headphones on and was listening to YouTube videos or music from Pandora. If I needed a drink refill, I put my laptop on the sofa, stood up, and took four steps to the kitchen. If I needed to go to the bathroom, it was three steps beyond the kitchen. One step got me from one side of the RV to the other, and a simple reaching up or bending down allowed me access to everything in the rig.

We reached an incredible conclusion after several trips in our little peanut of an RV. We had more storage space than we needed or used. Granted, we crammed some of our stuff in the back of the car, but still . . .

When we returned from our Alaska trip, we were ready to sell the house, upgrade to a larger rig, and go on the road full time. Michael shattered those plans when he fell on a sidewalk and shattered his shoulder. All sorts of complications and extended rehabilitation followed, and we had to put the possibility of fulltime nomadism on hold. While we still thought about trading our house for a 30-foot Class A motorhome, I now had trouble visualizing myself giving up my house. I had been so ready to go fulltime when we got home from Alaska. I hated that I lost that momentum. I felt like I reneged on a promise. Had I?

"What would be wrong with alternating between our permanent home and our portable home?" I asked my hubby. Michael shrugged, rolled his eyes, and did not answer. He was disgusted with me for equivocating, for second-guessing whether I would want to go fulltime. If anything, I now thought the perfect solution might be two-month stints in each house. It might be the resolution to our apparently unreconcilable differences when it came to our 'should we go or should we stay' dilemma. For that fifty percent at each place compromise, I might opt to go to an even smaller RV, maybe a Class B Road Tec or a 20-foot Class C Navion.

The actual RV aside, the incredible simplicity and ease of living in such small quarters brought me joy. I stood in the kitchen and could reach every tool, utensil, pot, or pan without taking a single step. If I pivoted and took one step backward, I could open the refrigerator and reach everything inside. One step to the left and I could access the pantry with all our dishes, dry goods, and emergency cans of soup. Two more steps to the left were the drawers with our first aid supplies and medications, tools and insect repellants, and a tall bottom drawer with cleaning supplies, laundry detergent, and an assortment of flashlights and lanterns. An extra set of sheets, blankets, quilts, and towels were in cabinets above the bed. The medicine cabinet in the bathroom held all the things we used daily, and the cabinet under the sink held toilet paper. Although the layout was not perfect, I was not sure I would have been able to come up with a more efficient or easier plan than what our Four Winds offered. RV manufacturers knew what they were doing when they came up with these designs.

A second thing I loved about RVing were the surprises, of which there were many: taking an open-air, under-the-stars shower in a campground at Land-Between-the-Lakes National Recreation Area in Golden Pond,

Simple Pleasures

Kentucky; seeing a bobcat at Cumberland Island National Seashore in St. Marys, Georgia; watching toddlers in tie-dyed rompers stomping in mud puddles at the Philadelphia Folk Festival in Schwenksville, Pennsylvania; discovering that our campground in St. Charles, Missouri was right beside the 238-miles-long Katy Rails to Trails bicycle path; sitting in folding chairs on our cliffside RV site in Malibu Beach, California, and looking down at dolphins playing in the Pacific Ocean; or finding myself politically enraged when learning of the Mexicans transported daily on school buses to work in the fields at below-minimum-wage pay in the lettuce fields of Yuma, Arizona. My list of surprises could extend for many chapters. The list gave me things to think about, and maybe write about, long after we had left the site of the surprise.

Although problems were rarely pleasant when they popped up, we felt satisfied and competent when we resolved them. Many things could and did go wrong in our RV, which explained why folks laughingly said RV stood for 'repair vehicle' or 'ruined vacation.' So far, we had managed to solve every problem. Our turn signals had stopped working. Tires had gone flat. Someone backed up and destroyed an open basement door (I was the guilty party). Someone else pulled forward and tore off the awning (Michael's mistake). The computer board for the water heater stopped working. Water seeped into a bathroom GFCI breaker and took out the entire electrical system. One side of the Blue Ox Tow System failed to engage and left our tow car straddling the middle line of a narrow two-lane road in the mountains. All these things and more had happened to us on the road.

We found it true: money solved problems. It had worked for us every time so far. We had never found ourselves stranded beside the road for more than an hour, and some of our delays had been delightful, like the nine days we sat in a campground in Rapid City, South Dakota, waiting for a manufacturer to ship a new awning from God-knows-where. While waiting for that awning, we had visited the Badlands, Custer State Park, Mount Rushmore, and Crazy Horse in some of the most beautiful country we had ever seen. We had spent time in downtown Rapid City hanging out with the locals, attending street concerts, and eating and drinking in local bars.

Even nonmechanical challenges offered us opportunities to feel good about how we were doing. We successfully got rid of a stinkbug infestation that had started in Jonesborough, Tennessee. I had felt pretty good about my eye-hand coordination when I managed to swat and kill more than a dozen huge blackflies that had invaded our house in the Upper Peninsula of Michigan. We had also managed to stave off the permanent residency of sugar ants, and we had yet to suspect or see evidence of rats or mice, both known to make homes in RVs. Houseflies had become old hat for us.

Problems on the road and the challenges of navigating our way to their resolutions made us feel confident. From our initial shakedown cruise of almost side-swiping the tow car at a gas station, we had come a long way in knowing how to handle our rig. At first, everything about our little Thor was scary and intimidating. Now we felt we knew her well inside and out. We loved the feeling of knowing what we were doing and believing we could resolve any obstacle thrown our way on the road.

Weather in Tampa, Florida, could be redundant. It was hot, and it was humid. There was not much of variety, unless a tropical storm or a hurricane was coming, or unless one of those unusual cold snaps reached us in January or February. Floridians sometimes challenged my perceptions of the weather and argued that average temperatures from December through March were about seventy degrees. I countered that global warming had changed those averages. Furthermore, I confessed to being a post-menopausal woman who rarely felt cold. Florida weather always felt too hot and humid to me regardless of what the thermometer said.

In contrast to the consistent weather in Florida, many extremes were possible out on the road in an RV. We had RVed in horrific thunderstorms and areas with widespread flooding. We had seen hail the size of golf balls. Desert winds with gusts up to forty miles per hour had almost pushed us off the road, and dust storms had reduced our visibility to three feet and scared the bejesus out of us. We had seen the thermometer drop to seventeen degrees. While we had not yet camped in snow, I was sure it would happen in time. I would choose ice and snow over the one-hundred-thirty-degree summer desert temperatures of the Southwest. We planned our trips with the weather in mind.

An unanticipated joy of RV travel was connecting with old friends and rarely seen family. After the first RV trip, we began to rack our brains to remember former connections and where they lived. We started selecting routes that allowed reunions. We visited my cousin Nancy in Fayetteville, Arkansas, a couple of times. She and I had grown up two miles apart but had not seen each other in over fifty years. Michael and I both visited first cousins in the San Antonio, Texas, area that neither of us had seen for decades. We hooked up with Michael's sister Anne for three extended weekend visits in RV parks in Maine, New York, and Virginia. We had dinner with Michael's cousin Bradley, and his wife Joan, in Burlington, Vermont. We visited my cousin Wayne, and his wife Paula, at their lakeside home in Snelling, Georgia, outside Atlanta.

I reconnected with long-lost friends in Mechanicsville, Maryland. I had introduced them to each other back in the early 1970s, and they had gotten married. As best friends with both, I served as their 'best person' at the exchanging of vows in a beautiful regional park. We visited one of Michael's old bosses in a small town in rural Pennsylvania. We had dinner in Philadelphia with an online writer friend and his wife, previously known only through email communications. The four of us hit it off and had a great time. We also reconnected with friends we had traveled with a year earlier on our Alaska caravan excursion, first at their home in upstate New York and the second time at the Baseball Hall of Fame in Cooperstown, New York.

Without a doubt, the greatest thrill of traveling around in an RV was how cool it made me feel. While I felt hip even when we were not talking about our travels to each other or others, those feelings of excitement grew bigger and stronger when we bounced our stories off other people, especially when we saw how others reacted to our tales. I sometimes got a little embarrassed when Michael raved on interminably about how exciting and fun it was to go all those places and do all those things. I felt like he bragged, and that maybe it was not in good taste to talk so much about our adventures. But I realized that his audiences were generally captivated. My husband was a good storyteller, and even I conceded that we had seen and done some incredible things.

Some folks told us we were living the dream. That they wished they could do what we were doing. That they planned to take off in an RV the minute they retired. That they were sorry, they had not done it while they were still physically able to travel. That they were jealous. That we inspired them.

Occasionally, someone told us they would not like our RV trips. That they would be too uncomfortable in a little RV. That they would feel claustrophobic. That they would never be able to stay away from family, especially grandchildren, for that long. That they would be too afraid of getting sick or having something terrible go wrong with the RV while on the road.

Michael and I were both risk-takers, of sorts. We had both lived on the edge, had taken chances we probably never should have taken. We drove after drinking too much alcohol. I rode a motorcycle for a couple of years during one of my midlife crises, a dangerous activity in the eyes of many. We both smoked cigarettes for decades, ignoring the compelling evidence that smoking would damage our health. We had been luckier than we deserved in that nothing awful had happened to either of us. Yet.

For us, taking off in an RV was not a scary decision. My initial resistance to RV travel had nothing to do with things that could go wrong but rather with the things I had to leave behind: my garden and orchids, my Toastmasters clubs, my writing buddies, my life. None of the worries expressed by our unimpressed audiences ever crossed our minds. Michael and I were both drawn to the novel and the unknown.

However, while selling the house and living fulltime in an RV felt scary to me, it did not feel that way to Michael. He would do it in a heartbeat.

Sometimes when we were out on the road, and something happened that flooded my soul with unbridled fullness and joy, I wondered why I held myself back from committing to a fulltime life of nomadism.

Simple Pleasures

It took only a second for the answer to manifest itself. There were indeed aspects of RVing that I adored. There were, however, aspects of living on my little street in Tampa, Florida, that triggered the same amount of excitement and joy.

Bottom line: I wanted it all.

Gerri behind the wheel

Vollis Simpson's Whirligigs in Wilson, North Carolina

Mailbox in memory of Wesley Belisle in Kitty Hawk, North Carolina

A creative RV home in Medina, Ohio

Michael encounters Big Foot in the Upper Peninsula of Michigan

Boat trip on Lake Superior to see the Pictured Rocks in Munising, Michigan

Along the Kancamagus Highway in Conway, New Hampshire

Pretending to be Jimi Hendrix and Janis Joplin in Woodstock, New York

Tripping out the RV in Lake George, New York

2018 Philadelphia Folk Festival

Winter Olympics Training Center in Lake Placid, New York

2018 Willie Nelson Outlaw Festival in Saratoga Springs, New York

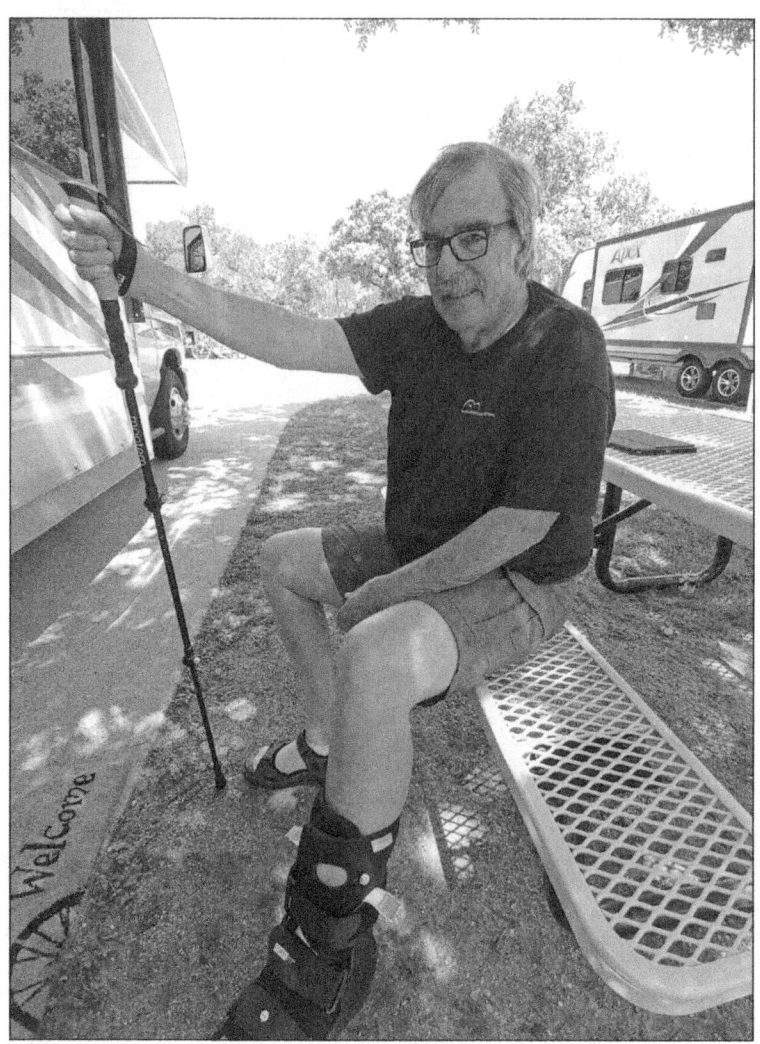

My broken-legged husband

National Baseball Hall of Fame in Cooperstown, New York

Somewhere along the Blue Ridge Parkway in the Smoky Mountains in Virginia

CHAPTER 22

Better to Say No

"You should've known better," my mother used to say when I did something stupid. However, she was a kind, gentle mother and would say it in a teasing way. She was nicer to me than Michael is, or than I am to myself.

"Where the hell are you taking us?" Michael asked.

"We're driving through the Mark Twain National Forest," I said. "It's fall, and the leaves are changing. I thought it'd be a pretty drive."

I had directed us off the main highway somewhere in northern Arkansas and onto a two-lane road that cut through wooded, rolling hills. Michael drove, and I navigated. He had agreed this time to let me choose the route. We were on our way to Fayetteville, Arkansas, to visit my cousin and her husband. A mile off the highway, we lost cell phone service. We saw another vehicle maybe every ten or fifteen minutes.

We had been less than three hours from Fayetteville when I selected this scenic route. Now, two hours later, we were still nowhere close to our destination.

"Did you think this would be a short-cut?" Anger was now audible in Michael's voice.

"No, not really. On the map, it looked about the same distance. With the lower speed limits, I figured it might take an additional forty-five minutes at most."

"I'm thinking you really miscalculated on this one."

Michael was right. By the time we got to Fayetteville, my 'let's look-at-the-fall-foliage detour' had taken over five hours.

"But now we can say we've been to the Mark Twain National Forest," I said. "Don't you like Mark Twain?"

"Whether or not I like him is beside the point. This was pointless."

I realized he could have said stupid, but he did not. That scenic tour was our first and last time-consuming detour from GPS directions.

"We're in Nashville, and I think we ought to check out live music, and I mean something more than a bar band down on Broadway." Michael was so excited he bounced in the truck seat. "As soon as we get set up at the campground, I'm going to start looking for something. That okay with you?"

"Sure." I shrugged. We had been driving for five hours, and I was tired. Michael had become such an aficionado of music that I did not have the heart to break his heart by saying no. If I had said to him, "I'm too tired. Let's wait until tomorrow night," he would have been disappointed. Then I would have felt bad.

Two hours later, Michael yelled his success. "I found two tickets at Cannery Row. It's an old converted warehouse district that's supposed to be super-cool. There are a couple of bars and a huge ballroom where the concert will be."

"Are you going to tell me who we'll see?"

"Bob Mould. You've probably never heard of him. He's a punk-rocker, songwriter, musician who plays alternative rock stuff. It'll be interesting to hear something different."

Hear it, we did. The Bob Mould concert was so loud my ears rang for three days afterward. The music, which I thought was a stretch even to be called music, was pure head-banging funk. We both hated it. However, we ended up standing with an interesting couple, probably in their mid-forties, and who appeared almost as much out of place in this venue as we did. They had driven over sixty miles into Nashville from their farm to attend this concert. Bob Mould was the wife's favorite musician. Conversation was impossible except for brief pauses between songs and during a ten-minute break. I found the contrast that this beef cattle ranching couple who lived surrounded by Amish farmers could now be drinking and partying at a head-banger's concert absolutely mind-boggling.

We left the concert before ten o'clock. We stopped at a nearby bar for a couple of drinks before heading back to the campground.

"Thank God this bar doesn't have live music tonight," I said. "My ears couldn't take it."

"It was pretty bad," Michael said. "Sorry about that. If it's any consolation, though, I was ready to leave even before you were. I hated that music."

Our take-away from the experience was that not all live music was preferable to listening to recorded music on CDs or Napster.

As we tried to make our way along Route 66, also known as The Mother Road, we felt as though we had time-traveled back to the fifties.

"That's what Route 66 is supposed to be about," Michael said. "It's a trip back in time. Back to when folks took these tedious road trips across the country. They needed interesting things to stop and show the kids."

"Jeez, but it stinks in here," I said. We had stopped for lunch at a funky-looking roadside diner in a little town somewhere in Missouri. "Smells like stale cigarette smoke."

It was cigarette smoke, but it was not stale. Folks were still smoking inside the place. We learned from our waitress that Missouri still allowed smoking in many of its restaurants and bars. "Us mid-westerners aren't going to be told what we can and can't do," our server said.

As recent ex-smokers, Missouri proved difficult for both of us. We found a cigarette smell in many of the restaurants. While it made Michael sick to his stomach, it made me want to start smoking again. I would not have even noticed the dreadful odor if I was the one producing it.

"Happy to be leaving this stinking state," Michael said. We had crossed the state line separating Missouri from Oklahoma.

"The State is lovely, Michael. It's those hold-on-to-the-past businesses that are the problem."

"Probably owned by Republicans," my husband said.

"Be nice."

Oklahoma had its fair share of Route 66 funk. We went about seven miles out of our way to see Ed Galloway's Totem Pole Park in Chelsea, Oklahoma. We regretted the waste of time, somehow failing to appreciate Ed's love of totems and his dedication to creating his lasting monuments reflecting his passion.

The Big Blue Whale in Catoosa, Oklahoma, snared us out of the way again by its claim of being one of the best of the remaining Route 66 relics.

"It's a relic, all right," I said. We had gotten out of the car and walked down to the thing.

"It's a swimming/fishing dock," Michael said, "made into the shape of a whale. Bet it's challenging trying to keep this monstrosity painted."

The whale was huge. If the covered entrance had been wider and the roof higher, two or three cars could have fit on the dock. However, I would not have wanted to see cars try this; the wood under our feet felt rather rotten. Overall, the Big Blue Whale did not impress either of us.

What would a trip down Route 66 be without seeing the Wigwam Village Motel in Holbrook, Arizona? Or any of the other dozens of quaint, somewhat-preserved roadside inns? Some of the older lodgings looked like the small cabins now found in occasional RV parks. Our Route 66 guidebook said that in the twenties and thirties, when Route 66 was new, many travelers camped along the way. Some of the restored roadside motels had evolved from what initially might have been parcels of land for communal camping. They had bathhouses, drinking water, and a cooking facility shared by overnight travelers. The sites reminded me of roadside places where the Tom Joad family might have stayed during their migration from Oklahoma to California in John Steinbeck's classic, *The Grapes of Wrath* (1939).

The first travel-trailers in the United States appeared in the mid-1920s. However, it was not until the end of World War II and the need for affordable housing for returning veterans that mobile homes became popular. John Steinbeck, driving across the country in the 1960s researching *Travels with Charley,* expressed fascination with these mobile homes and wondered what they meant for the country. I tried to wrap my head around history and trends.

"RVing along Route 66 might be retro," I said. We bounced along cracked pavements, at times losing our way while trying to follow the old road. When construction crews had repaired dilapidated sections of the original highway through the years, engineers had sometimes shifted the improved road several miles away from the original road.

"I don't know about retro," Michael said, "but it's certainly a challenge trying to follow it."

"The road was completed in 1926." I continued to read from my Route 66 guidebook and shared tidbits with my husband. "Early travelers going across the country often camped along the way. The way I understand the history, campgrounds evolved into these little roadside inns and motels. But now it seems like half the world has gone back to camping, and the country has returned to having all these RV parks and resorts."

"I think the number of people traveling by car across the country and staying in motels far exceeds the number traveling in RVs and staying in campgrounds," Michael said.

"How do you know that? Seems to me half of all the retirees in America are out here in their motorhomes."

"I don't know it. It's what I think. I have no idea how we'd find an official answer to the question."

"Along these old sections of Route 66, the motels far outnumber the RV parks," I said. "This is not easy traveling for an RV. So far, I'd have said 'no' to almost every single roadside attraction we've seen."

Our RV bounced along a narrow backroad in the Texas Panhandle near Amarillo. We were still trying to follow the famous Route 66, and I was close to dubbing it infamous because of the difficulty.

After traveling for three years in the RV, I could think of many things we had seen, heard, or done to which 'no' would have been a good answer. Things like thinking we could stay out and party all night in Kansas City when I was two months post-op from a total knee replacement. Or believing we could ride mountain bikes on unbelievably rough, overgrown bike paths in the Land Between the Lakes. Or the silliness of thinking we might look like we fit in at Muscle Beach in Venice, California. My list could go on. We were not always realistic about who and what we were, especially when it came to our ages and physical fitness.

At some deep level, I think we both considered ourselves invincible and immortal. It was the way I believed it should be and the way we needed to continue living our lives. While the Big Blue Whale and the Wigwam Village Motel might have been best left unseen, we were more than compensated for all those wrong turns and wasted hours when we reached Cadillac Ranch. I was so glad we said 'yes' rather than 'no' to everything we saw. Otherwise, we would never have recognized the gems when we found them.

CHAPTER 23

Smoke Gets in your Eyes

A blazing bonfire, drinks in hand, music in the background, twinkling stars overhead, the soft murmurs of other campers sitting by their roaring campfires—what could be better? Bonfires at night were indeed one of RVing's greatest pleasures. Michael would have loved building one every single night we were on the road.

Unfortunately, those fires were also one of the most expensive aspects of camping, and a bonfire for one night could end up costing as much or more than the camping site. That was why Michael and I have had frequent "discussions" about whether to have a fire.

"Please, pretty please," Michael would say in midafternoon, maybe before we had even arrived at our campground.

I laughed. I did not even have to ask what he was talking about. I knew.

"We had one three nights ago."

"So? That was three nights ago. The weather is going to be beautiful tonight, down in the sixties. Perfect for sitting outside."

"Let's see how much this KOA charges for a bundle of wood." We had seen prices range from four to over eight dollars for one small bundle. Depending on the cost and how long we planned to sit outside, a bonfire for one night could cost anywhere from eight to thirty-six dollars. Even if we assumed an average somewhere in the middle, a nightly bonfire could easily become costly. To have one every night, as my hubby wanted to do, would be extravagant. Or at least it would from my Poor Richard, child-of-the-Depression-parents' perspectives.

One time early in our RVing days, we thought we would get smart and save money by scavenging from our woodpile at home. Michael carefully stacked the wood in the back of the C-Max on an old blanket, thinking he was doing a great job of protecting the upholstery in the rear storage compartment. Unfortunately, our firewood was old, and Michael did not see signs of an ant infestation as he loaded up. That proved to be a rather unpleasant experience.

We considered trying to stock up in places where we found firewood cheap. For example, we found large bundles of firewood selling for five bucks apiece sitting beside roads in the Adirondack Mountains. We soon realized bringing our wood into campgrounds was not an option for anyone with half a concern about the environment. We learned beetles and insects were doing terrible damage to vast tracts of timberland all over the country. Many campgrounds posted warnings not to bring in wood from other locations lest we introduced and released invasive, destructive insects in the area. So, even if we had had the space for storage or the inclination to go to all that bother, we would have felt unconscionably guilty setting up camp and burning our stash of firewood.

The longer we RVed, the more willing I became to splurge on a bonfire. We settled into a routine of maybe once a week. Often we would get lucky, and a neighbor in an adjoining site would have a bonfire. We could then sit outside and enjoy someone else's bonfire, albeit at a distance. However, I felt like I was stealing or cheating when we did this.

"You're such a cheapskate," Michael said. "We could do this every night, you know."

"I'm rationing out our resources so you can enjoy bonfires forever," I said.

Bonfires sometimes proved to be a mixed joy of camping, though. While charming to behold and warming when a chill filled the air, a sudden gust of wind could send smoke right in one's face.

"God, it's burning my eyes," I said.

"Move over here, dodo," Michael said. "You're sitting right in it."

"The wind will change again as soon as I move. Watch."

After a night of bonfire sitting, even if the wind never blew smoke in our eyes, we would realize the next morning the clothes we had worn the night before reeked of smoke. Sometimes we would not care, depending on what we had on tap for the day. Other times, we would toss clothes we had worn for only a few hours into the laundry bag.

We sat imprisoned in the RV in rainy mid-fifty-degree weather in what should have been a positively delightful place in December—Panama City Beach, Florida. We had taken the bicycles and had hoped to log between twenty and twenty-five miles a day along the flat streets that lined the Gulf of Mexico. Instead, we huddled inside our tin-can house and racked our brains for ways to entertain ourselves. It was our second month of RV ownership. It was our longest outing to date, and we had anticipated nine glorious days. However, nonstop cold and wet weather was not the only unpleasant aspect of the trip. Red tide had invaded this section of the Gulf of Mexico, and I could hardly breathe from the pollution in the air.

"I'm going to cook a couple of eggs for breakfast. Want some?" I asked Michael.

"Nah. I'm good."

I fork-split my Thomas English Muffin, per the directions, and dropped the two halves in the toaster. Next, I pulled out our little 8-inch nonstick frypan, heated it on our gas stovetop, and cracked in a couple of eggs. I looked forward to Sunny-side-ups as a special treat to brighten the dismal day.

"Yikes!" I jumped as the shrill beep of the smoke detector sent jarring blasts right in my ears. "Michael, what do I do? I don't see any fire."

My husband jumped to the rescue by opening the house door and waving papers up near the smoke detector toward the open door. There must have been smoke, after all. Cold air and blowing rain invaded our warm nest, and the smoke detector calmed down at once.

"I smell it now," I said. "Guess I'll take the eggs up, although the whites are still pretty runny."

"That's one sensitive smoke detector we have," Michael said. "I didn't smell smoke either, until after it went off."

The smoke detector became my nemesis, almost to the point that I had come to dread cooking on the stove or in the oven. It seemed to happen at least once a week, sometimes from a burner, sometimes from the oven. The alarm was so loud I felt sure campers ten rigs away could hear it. Not only did it make me angry, but it also embarrassed me.

"I don't get it," I had said to Michael. "The heat is not too high, and there's nothing spilled in the bottom of the oven that would burn. There's absolutely no goddamn, friggin' thing that should be making that blankety-blank smoke detector go off."

"Calm down. It probably happens to everyone," Michael said.

"Then how come this park isn't constantly filled with the sounds of smoke alarms going off? I'm sure others heard our alarm. Why don't we hear theirs, if they're going off? Why hasn't someone called the fire department for us, for God's sake?"

"Stop being so hysterical."

I did not feel like I was overreacting. I hated the damned thing because it hurt my ears. I thought Michael was half-deaf anyway, so it probably did not sound as loud to him as it did to me.

I have tolerated that smoke detector for three years now. I have quietly set up little tests while using my nonstop frypan, trying to find the magic setting on the dial where food cooks efficiently but does not trigger the alarm. I have tried various experiments with oven temperatures as well, trying to avoid those dreadful shrills.

Nothing so far had worked. Despite my best efforts, the damned smoke detector sounded its warning at least a time or two each week, no matter what I cooked or how I cooked it. I might have felt differently about the damned thing if I ever actually saw enough smoke inside the house for concern. There had been only a couple of times that smoke registered on my sniffing radar.

I considered taking the batteries out of the thing and not telling Michael. He might then think I had become a better cook.

For years, Michael and I had heard about the wildfires out west. They had sounded terrifying, and we had looked at the evening national news with alarm as we watched live footage of destroyed homes and distraught homeowners. The California fires on the hillsides and mandatory evacuations always caught our attention. "Thank goodness we don't live out there," we would say to each other. Then we would get on with our lives and not think much more about wildfires. After all, Florida had its share of them in the dry, spring months when vegetation was brown and bone-dry from freezing winter temperatures and no rain. Our fires, however, did not usually threaten communities. Our densely populated areas were along the coasts, not in the middle of the State. Except for Orlando, of course, and only idiots lived that close to Disney World anyway. Just kidding.

We got our first whiffs of those western wildfires on our return trip from our Alaska Caravan in September 2017. We had made our way out west in June and had seen nothing but clear skies, though the temperatures were above average. We left Alaska at the end of August to make our way back down to the United States. In the Yukon Territory, we started hearing rumors that British Columbia was on fire.

"What'll we do?" I asked Michael. He hung out with some of the men in the caravan and received regular news and weather updates. I believed all old men stayed riveted to news coverage of weather forecasts and driving conditions. Michael thought that was an absurd notion.

As reports of wildfires continued, caravan folks began telephoning friends and family in the U.S. in efforts to get updated information. A couple of folks from upstate New York discussed the possibility of taking a northern route through Canada across to the east coast as a way of dodging wildfires and avoiding delays. As caravanners considered ways to get back to their homes, some of those from the east coast considered heading for the Pacific Coast and following it down to Southern California before cutting to the east. It all sounded rather over-reactive to me.

Michael lobbied hard for the Washington, Oregon, California route home. By this point in the trip, we had already been gone over three months, and I wanted to get home yesterday.

"Okay, we'll do it your way, but I'm warning you, this may not be a good idea," Michael said. He had finally agreed to take my route of choice, the most direct one possible that would take us in somewhat of a diagonal direction from Washington to Florida, a route passing right through the heart of the wildfires.

"We'll be fine," I said. "I want to go home."

We began to smell smoke 500 miles north of the United States border. Another couple of hundred miles down, our eyes began to itch and burn. We found an app on our iPads that would alert us to road closures, locations of new fires, and updates on existing fires. Most of the time, however, we were in areas so remote and rural, we had no Internet service, so the app was of no use. For the most part, fire-fighting efforts consisted of trying to slow down the speed of the fires and changing their directions. There were too many fires in too many places to ever think firefighters could put them all out. Officials adopted containment and the minimization of damage to lives and residences as their major goals.

Opting for the quickest way back to Tampa, we came down the eastern coast of Washington. Occasionally, we encountered road detours due to new fires and had to take alternate routes.

"Michael, look at the map." We had stopped for gas and had enough Internet service to pull up the weather service map showing locations of fires. "We are completely surrounded. This is scary!"

Michael studied the images and glared at me. "You're the one who insisted we go this route. Look what you've gotten us in to." He shoved the iPad back to me and stomped off to go back inside.

I felt like screaming after him, "And you're the one who dragged me off on this stupid trip. I never wanted this damned RV to begin with." I bit my lip and maintained my composure.

Spokane was our first urban destination on our return-home trip. We arrived to find smoke so thick we could hardly breathe. Emergency broadcasts interrupted regular programming on both radio and television, telling people to stay indoors and to keep their air-conditioners running. In addition to smoke from fires on three sides of the city, a heatwave had descended, and temperatures had climbed to the upper nineties for the past several days.

On our first morning in Spokane, I walked out of our RV about 10:00 A.M. in that miserable RV park. The air was so thick with smoke that I could hardly see the street 300 feet away. When I looked up at the sky, the sun looked like a little orange ball, the air so smoke-filled I could look directly into the sun without even squinting.

The orange sun had freaked me out so much I went back inside and insisted Michael come back out and look at the sky. "That's got to be one of the strangest things I've ever seen in my life," I said.

"I heard on the news that the temperatures today should have reached ninety-five," Michael said. "However, the smoke is so thick the sun can't penetrate to get down to the ground. They're saying the high will probably be about eighty-six."

"How long do you think it'll take us to get out of this?" I asked.

"We'll leave here the day after tomorrow. We have to get new tires for the front of the truck before we go any farther, to be safe." The Alaskan Highway had done a job on our treads.

We stood together, arm in arm, staring up at the orange sun for a long time. I wanted to memorize this experience, in case I ever had options again of either driving into wildfires or trying to avoid them.

While Michael cursed me for insisting on a route that had landed us in eerie, smoky Spokane, we would learn within a couple of days that Michael's suggested route of following the Pacific Ocean down through Oregon and California would have resulted in as many, maybe more, delays and closed roads than the route we had chosen. The only smoke-free route would have been to drive several thousand miles across deserted roads in northern Canada with no cell phone or Internet service and little towns of 200 residents situated fifty to seventy-five miles apart. None of our options had been good.

As soon as Firestone mounted our new tires on the RV, we hooked up the C-Max and boogie-shoed across the northern perimeter. We left Washington and sped through Idaho, Montana, North Dakota, and South Dakota. We did not breathe clean air again until we hit Iowa ten days later. We zipped through beautiful country, and what I am sure would have been gorgeous places to stop, such as the Badlands in North Dakota. Thick smoke and broiling hot temperatures destroyed any desire on our parts to play tourist.

We would go back again one of these days to those smoke-filled places we could not enjoy that time around. Maybe we would even hang out a bit in Fargo, North Dakota, the town made famous by the infamous Cohen brothers of movie fame.

We would make sure we went in either the spring or early summer, or we would wait until late fall. The smoke from bonfires in campgrounds and gas-stove cooking was child's play compared to smoke from a wildfire covering several thousand acres of timberland.

I would never complain about our smoke detector again.

CHAPTER 24

Sweet Places to Live

Like an echo from our initial pre-motorhome discussions, Michael still wanted to go, and I sometimes still wanted to stay, despite continuing to move forward toward acceptance of this alternative lifestyle. Michael needed an ever-changing view, and not only out of the front windshield of the RV. He wanted new scenery in every direction, and I wanted constancy in my external world. I tended to turn inward for stimulation.

The same differences held true once we were on the road. Michael believed the RV had wheels under it for a reason: to move. I looked around campgrounds, and yes, there were lots of folks traveling, people who stayed only a night or two at each stop. But nestled in different parts of almost every park, I had learned, one usually found a rather large consortium of seasonal or full-timers. We had seen and talked to a number of these folks, and they fell into several categories.

The seasonal people had often settled in the area for a reason. Usually, it was the weather, either finding warmth during winter months or cooler temps during the summers. Sometimes they had family nearby, or maybe they liked the recreational opportunities in the vicinity. For some, it was a campground where they connected with long-term friends regularly.

The full-timers were more likely to be employed. They sometimes worked remotely from home offices inside their RVs. They may have had short or long-term work contracts for anything from electrical to construction to nursing to any number of other fields that might hire temporary employees.

Sometimes it looked as if life had been hard for a few of these permanent residents. Perhaps a no-longer travel-worthy motorhome was the only thing the family could afford. We had seen a fair number of deplorably run-down rigs with fulltime residents, often families with children.

"We need to stay put," I had said to Michael. "It's crazy to keep zipping all over the country. We need to stay in each place long enough to get a feel for the area."

"I know what it feels like in North Platte, Nebraska. I don't need to stay here another week."

"You could go to three more rodeos if we did," I had said with a laugh. Michael had fallen in love with rodeos on this trip. I did not think using horses, bulls, and steers for sport was a morally acceptable practice. I did not understand why People for the Ethical Treatment of Animals (PETA) people did not protest and wave signs and placards at every rodeo gate.

"There'll be bigger and better rodeos down the road." Michael grinned at me and walked away.

The previous evening, we had gone to the Buffalo Bill Rodeo in North Platte. Sitting next to and talking nonstop with old ranchers in the grandstands, Michael's passion for rodeos had surged.

North Platte sat in the middle of a gazillion acres of cornfields. And while it would not have been an area I would have chosen to stay in for very long, it had its appeal. We had visited the Union Pacific Railroad Yard, which was the largest train yard in the country. We had seen film clips from World War II showing the famous canteen set up by community volunteers for deployed soldiers. The infamous Orphan Train had made stops in North Platte, and an entire section of the station had old photographs plastered on its walls of orphans and the farm families who waited to take them in. The orphan trains had run from the mid-1800s to the early 1900s. I had read books about those orphans and loved having their history brought to life in that train yard. The day before, we had watched a downtown Nebraskaland Days Parade.

Our layover in North Platte helped me understand what it would be like to spend more time at the various places we visited. A list started to form in my mind.

What were the places where we might negotiate a good campground rate for a month rather than paying a nightly rate? Where were the places that had captured our interest for some reason or another?

"I think we ought to consider a different use for our RV," I had said to Michael. We were back home from our four-month-long trip to Alaska, the one that had included over two months of traveling in a caravan with thirty-eight other people. We now sat on the lanai, our dinner trays in front of us, enjoying the space, the seventy-degree temperatures, and, for me anyway, my plants and what remained of my orchid collection.

"What do you mean?"

"Instead of traveling all over, let's pick out a place we've been to that we loved, like Austin, Texas, and go stay there for a whole month? We could get to know those places inside-out, upside-down."

"That'd be an interesting way to do it," Michael said. "First, though, we have to get stickers on our map for all the states we haven't been to yet."

His answer did not surprise me.

With four states left, I returned to my mental list of neat places we had been to, and I tried to rank them in terms of preference. Michael and I talked about each one.

"Woodstock would probably be my number one pick," I said, "but we were there last summer. Guess we'd need to wait a while before going back."

"How about New Orleans?" Michael asked. "That'd be a great place to start."

We had stayed a few days in New Orleans on our way home from our Route 66 trip back in December 2016. Except for our conveniently located, reasonably priced RV park that had felt and smelled like a kitty litterbox, we had had a great time. We had taken the perfunctory stroll down Bourbon Street, but we felt really hip to shrug it off as a tourist attraction. We were among the in-the-know insiders who were aware that the real music scene was now on Frenchman Street, especially for the blues. We met up with some friends from Tampa and hit several of the clubs. It was a purely coincidental occurrence that we were both in The Big Easy at the same time. It felt especially vogueish to snag reservations at The Spotted Cat Music Club.

I googled the top restaurants in New Orleans. Sometimes we pretended to be foodies and checked out trendy restaurants when we visited cool places.

"We could go out for 5-star dinners about seventy-nine consecutive nights in New Orleans before getting close to the bottom of the list," I said.

"Then we should put New Orleans at the top of the list if we decide to stay in one place for a while in the RV," Michael said.

"But we were there a couple of years ago. Maybe it's still too new."

"Probably so." Michael paused. "But now we know so many other places. Remember Ann Arbor, Michigan? What a surprise that was. I'd never even thought about the place, but then suddenly we're sitting on a roof-top restaurant, listening to live music, looking down at a little street fair, and I'm thinking what a great little place this is."

"We'd fit in politically, for sure. It's described as one of the most liberal towns in America," I said.

"We certainly don't have much to keep us here in Florida anymore."

"I'm not ready to pick up and move, Michael. I'm envisioning a month or so in each place." Inwardly, I groaned, long and hard. Why does he keep saying that? He may not have any roots in Tampa, Florida, but I certainly do. I have the Master Gardeners, Toastmasters, a couple of writers' groups. I have connections that motivate me and support what I do. I was too old to start over trying to build up a new social network. I did not think I had it in me anymore.

We stood up from the table to move our dinner trays to the kitchen. Although our RV talk had ended for that evening, the subject continued to arise, and we gradually added other places to the list of places where we would like to stay for a while.

"How about Sault Ste. Marie, Minnesota?" I asked. We had spent a few days there, the nose of the RV pointing directly at the Saint Mary's River. We could see Canada on the other shore.

"I think Sault Ste. Marie, across the river in Canada, might be better."

"We'd never be able to find another campground right on the river like that. Remember how we didn't even have to put up the shade in the front windshield, how we woke up in the mornings, and looked out at that beautiful view?" I thought it was about the best campground we had ever stayed in.

Three days later, Michael remembered another one. "San Diego, California. Oh my God, I'd love to spend a month in that place. Remember driving up to La Jolla that day and signing up for the kayaking trip over to see the sea lions?"

"Oh, yeah. The water was so rough we kept capsizing. I was lucky I didn't lose my glasses when we tipped over that second time."

"But we got a full refund for the excursion, even though we'd already decided we were too old and infirm to handle that kayak." The kayak rental place had to cancel the excursion and give full refunds to everyone in the group because of a hammerhead shark sighting.

"Oh, what good times. I'd completely forgotten all that," I said. "Why go to San Diego? Why not just go to La Jolla?"

"San Diego has more bars, you dodo."

Two weeks later, I remembered another place we had liked. "Traverse City, Michigan, right on Lake Michigan," I said. "We took that sunset cruise and drank too much."

"Weather was certainly beautiful there."

"Bad traffic, though. I still think about that Grand Traverse Campus, though. Remember how it was a former mental hospital and had been re-purposed into an upscale community of shops, restaurants, and condominiums. What a cool place that'd be to live," I said.

"But not in the winter. You would not like the below-freezing-level winds and snowstorms blowing off that lake."

"Chippewa Falls, Wisconsin, was a nice little community," I said.

"Yes, it was, especially with the Leinenkugel's Brewery right there in town. But you'd never get me back to a place where over ninety percent of the ticks tested positive for Lyme's Disease."

"You're right." I had forgotten about that terrifying little blues festival experience.

Over time, many other places came up as possibilities for one-month stays: Duluth, Minnesota; Lake Placid, New York; Memphis, Tennessee; San Antonio, Texas; Tucson, Arizona; Seattle, Washington; Santa Fe, New Mexico; and the list could go on for pages.

"Let's hurry up and get the rest of the states over with so we can shift gears with this RV travel," I said. "I'm ready to do something different. I'd like us to stop spending so many hours bouncing down highways and start spending more time relaxing."

"One more long road trip, and we'll get that one done in the spring and summer of 2019. Then we can switch breadth for depth. You'd like that better, huh?"

"Yep, and I think a month is a short enough time period that you wouldn't get too bored." My husband's ADHD restlessness did not always mesh well with my need for time—time to mull things over mentally, to let reactions incubate, to sleep on my feelings, to process the reactions, to look at every possibility from thirty-seven perspectives. Maybe we were too different ever to reach a consensus on where to live, how to live, and how to spend the rest of our lives.

What did it mean if we could not? We both might end up needing places to stay for longer than a month.

CHAPTER 25

The Meaning of RVing

I wanted our RV travel to mean something. Being a tourist did not cut it. I wanted the travel to be for a reason, and I wanted to document the significance of what we saw, what we did, and what we felt. I wanted 'to live deep and suck all the marrow from life' like Henry David Thoreau had said he planned to do. My internalized Protestant work ethic lived and thrived, demanding I be productive and useful. It mattered not that I had retired seven years earlier and no longer had to work or prove anything to anyone. And like Thoreau, my 'work' could be observing, thinking, and extrapolating the meaning of what we saw and did.

That a journey in an RV could serve as a metaphor for a journey through life was too simple. There had to be more to it than that.

My questions became: What did RV travel mean to me, to us, and for our relationship? Could I look back at our experiences and extrapolate something deeper or more important than simply seeing what we saw or doing what we did? Could I develop a framework for organizing my thoughts? What content areas could I explore?

Health popped into my head as a place to start. Could RV travel improve health and physical fitness? Could it increase longevity or at least produce a better quality of life? Maybe I would find meaning in a damned RV if I thought I would live longer or feel better.

We were so cool; I remembered thinking as we prepared for our first RV trip. We had finished packing our little house on wheels and were pulling out of our driveway in Tampa, the C-Max hooked up behind the Thor Four Winds and the Trek bicycles loaded on the bike rack on the back of the RV. Our first road trip!

"I'm thinking this RV means we'll be able to have a healthier lifestyle. Maybe we should pledge to get exercise and take good care of our bodies on every trip we take. What do you think?"

"Great idea," Michael said. "RVing and being outside go together. On the road, we have nothing to do other than focus on taking care of ourselves."

While we did not do an actual high-five across the truck cab, I remembered the conversation ending in mutual agreement that from that point on, we would pay more attention to diet, exercise, and sleep. Theoretically, it should have been easier to do that on the road, away from the phone calls, doctors' appointments, home maintenance, gardening, Toastmasters meetings, errands and shopping, dinners with friends, and all the other things we did at home.

Yes, I had thought; I would do my Yoga stretches every single morning. I would ride my bicycle at least fifteen miles a day. Maybe I would even add some dumbbell exercises. I needed to get rid of the flab on the undersides of my arms. My intentions were good, and my motivation was high.

That first outing in Flagler Beach did indeed prove rather healthy, beer and red wine notwithstanding. We ate fresh, healthy food. We rode our bikes for three consecutive days, averaging about twenty miles a day. We slept like babies at night from our outside exertions and held our heads high with an air of self-righteousness. We might be old coots, but we could be active and stay healthy.

While we had good intentions, we underestimated the power of several factors. We hadn't realized how exhausting a day of travel in this rig could be and how we would not have the energy to even think about exercise by the time we settled in at the next campground.

We did not anticipate how hard it would be to cook a decent meal or to plan healthy meals ahead of time while traveling. We often defaulted to eating out in restaurants, adding calories, sodium, chemicals, and all sorts of other undesirables into our diets.

We had not understood how significant weather would be on our motivation to get outside and exercise—anything from extreme temperatures of both heat and cold to rain to strong winds to polluted air from raging wildfires.

I had not realized how uncomfortable I would find sitting in one position in the truck cab for hours at the time. With my arthritis-riddled body, I felt more comfortable up and about, in constant motion. When we pulled into a campground after three of four hours of travel, I experienced excruciating pain when I tried to straighten out my body and walk. While exercise would have been absolutely the best proactive remedy for that arthritic agony, I did not often force myself to take that appropriate action.

Drinking became an almost daily treat for us both. Cocktails at five o'clock became a habit. We saw this pattern at campgrounds all over the country and in Canada. Retired RV folks like us celebrated the end of each day with alcohol. We understood this logic, and we joined right in. For Michael, a Heineken call proved effective in easing whatever woes or discomforts he might be experiencing at the end of the day. For me, the lure of a red wine cure for my aches and pains proved stronger than any healthier alternative I could imagine.

We are older, I thought. We deserved our daily alcohol infusions. It did not matter if it cut a couple of years off our lives. Being out here on the road in an RV at our ages deserved daily congratulatory toasts. Yeah, right.

When looked at from a perspective of entitlement because of age, one could view RVing as a magnificent, final celebration of life, done by the participants themselves rather than waiting for survivors to perform the final rites. We were the survivors!

I liked this interpretation. The meaning, however, might have been more complicated. I continued to dig.

People make all kinds of claims about the benefits of travel: the required problem-solving made one smarter and more confident; personal growth occurred through the new experiences and challenges; one understood their own country better after visiting another one; people who traveled were happier, healthier, and lived longer; one's mind expanded as it took in new ideas, making one a different person. I was not sure I believed any of these claims. They were all made by travel enthusiasts and posted ad nauseam on the Internet.

"I'm thinking I need to make my own post," I had said to Michael. We sat on the lanai, and I had finished scanning yet another list of what travel could do for me.

"What are you talking about?"

"The Benefits of Staying Home," I said, a smile on my face. "There are all these outrageous claims of how travel changes one into a better, wiser person. I think it's a boondoggle."

"You're becoming quite the cynic, aren't you?"

"Nope. I'm trying to find truth, and I'm horrified by all these clichés and pithy little sayings. Don't people think for themselves anymore?"

I knew I sounded obnoxious, but I could not help myself. We had had one travel experience that had touched me to my core—The Alaska Highway. The epiphany struck before we even reached Alaska.

We were traveling in The Yukon Territory in Western Canada, a vast and remote area beyond anything I had ever experienced. We would travel for miles, sometimes over fifty, before reaching a tiny settlement with a couple of gas pumps, a small store and restaurant combination, a strip of four or six motel rooms, and maybe a cleared field where RVs could park. The settlement's electricity came from a huge generator. The owners at these small settlements had to haul fresh water in and haul the waste out. The tundra, which lay below the ground's surface, remained frozen year-round, which meant they could not drill for freshwater.

The Alaskan Highway remained impassable for much of the long, dark winters. As we looked on either side of the Highway heading west towards Alaska, we saw tight, virgin hardwood forests, sometimes so thick I had wondered how any but the smallest of wild animals could squeeze between the trees. Sometimes we would see steep drop-offs into ravines and canyons, no guardrails of any sort to prevent inattentive drivers from going over. A friend told me a story about her parents losing their tow car while traveling the Alaskan Highway one late fall many years earlier. The RV's tow bar had failed, and the car went over one of these unprotected drop-offs. It was not until the snows melted the following year that rescue teams finally spotted the lost vehicle.

My great moment of learning as we drove along that famous road was a regenerated epiphany from a trip three decades earlier to India. There was nothing original, unique, or even particularly deep about the thought. My insight was simply a reminder of my insignificance in the universe. In India, the sheer number of people, the mass of humanity that stretched forever in metropolitan areas like Mumbai and New Delhi, had triggered the feeling. Now, driving along the Alaskan Highway, the vast emptiness of anything but wild, untamed nature sparked an identical feeling.

But that was not a meaning that rang entirely true for me. It did not explain how traveling around the country in an RV could change me or was in the process of changing me. I must be missing something, I thought. Or maybe my expectations were too high.

I had been a bit rebellious my entire life. As a kid in school, I completed my assignments quickly and then acted out. It was not unusual for teachers to send me to the principal's office for a lecture or punishment of some sort, such as staying after school to wash walls. I gave my parents fits and grey hair by misbehaving and talking back. I embarrassed them by asking heretical questions at the local Baptist church and writing provocative stories for English classes at school. In college, my acting out expanded to sex, drugs, and rock n' roll, although I somehow managed to graduate on time and with honors. My adult rebellions included riding a motorcycle for a couple of years and divorcing a couple of husbands before finally settling down.

When I looked back on my life-long pattern of challenging authority and social norms, I often thought I simply wanted freedom, the kind of freedom expressed in the movie *Easy Rider*. I now realized I had found my freedom; I simply needed not to let the reactions of others bother me when I did what I wanted rather than what others expected. My problem was still feeling guilty. I both loved and hated being 'bad' and had never outgrown a silent thrill when I shocked or horrified others.

RV travel suddenly made sense for someone like me. If the opinion of others bothered me that much, living on the road surrounded by strangers should be the perfect answer. I could act out, be outrageous, or . . . be as calm and tranquil as a tired kitten, which was closer to my truth these days. No one would care. Probably no one would even notice. RVers were mind-your-own-business people, a live-and-let-live, I-will-stay-out-of-your-face if you will stay out of mine breed.

Contrary to the above suggestion that this insight came upon me like a lightning bolt, it took three long years of RV travel to understand that seventy-five percent of my resistance to cultural mores stemmed from unresolved issues originating from my dysfunctional family. I was not critical of my family—I believed all families were a little off, and no one came through unscathed. I did feel a little embarrassed, however, that it took me seventy years of living and several years of RV travel to figure it all out. Maybe I am a moron.

I now believed that traveling around the country in an RV was an ultimate expression of one's freedom. I had been guilty of stereotyping RVers, and I suspected the entire younger world tended to do the same. Maybe my next area for political activism should be showing the world that not all RVers were the same. That they came in as many political, religious, social, and intellectual variances as there were points along each continuum. Not all RVers were golf resort people. Or folks who dressed their miniature Schnauzers in frilly little dresses. Or are even among the obnoxious who filled in sticker maps and deluged Facebook with photographs of all the cool places they went.

I realized it sounded trite almost to the point of being inane, but not all RVers were created equal. Nor could anyone sort, categorize, and insert them into little stereotyped compartments. Every rig tooling down a highway housed someone with his or her unique reason for being in that place at that specific time. It was not that different from the residents living in the homes that lined my street in Tampa, Florida. Duh!

I finally understood what our RV trips meant from a metaphorical perspective. They were simply additional miles along our literal and figurative journeys home. In many ways, RVing might have been another word for freedom. Maybe that was the quintessential meaning of this nomadic way of living.

CHAPTER 26

Marital Trials and Tribulations

Sometimes the constantly changing campgrounds, towns, and scenery of RV travel boggled my mind. It was too much newness, too many unfamiliar intersections, and too much time spent bungling down yet another grocery store aisle trying to find 3x5 ruled index cards. Struggling with so many things stressed me out. It was easy to remember life back home as problem-free and efficient because we knew where most everything was, and we accomplished things on autopilot. We knew where to find the health food store, on what aisle Publix shelved the catsup, and which Italian restaurant had the best lasagna. I had always believed that having the decisions of daily living on automatic freed one up mentally to be creative and productive.

Michael viewed this kind of theorizing as pure hogwash. He loved visiting unique places and encountering new challenges. He believed successful navigation through the unknown kept us younger, more flexible in our thinking, and more adaptable. Travel offered opportunities to solve problems and feel competent. On the road, one learned to shrug off the compromises and inevitable changes in plans. For example, back home, I ate pre-made fresh salmon cakes from the seafood department at our Publix supermarket for breakfast a couple of times each week. I spent the first few weeks of our last road trip asking at every grocery store we entered if they had this specialty item. Not one store said yes. I quit trying. By the time we got back home, those spicy salmon cakes were no longer even on my radar screen. I had completely forgotten about them.

Change and constancy are two sides of the same sword, though, and I would be hard-pressed anymore to select which of the two was the most challenging and which was the most satisfying. Living as gypsies and moving from campground to campground was simultaneously the most stressful and the most carefree lifestyle I could imagine.

However, living for days on end in about seventy-five-square-feet in an RV could turn up the volume on getting along with one's spouse. Tiny space living created challenges that would never have popped up at home.

I loved my home routines, and I have been able to recreate a few of them on the road. For example, consider sleeping and waking habits. In both places, I went to bed about two hours earlier than Michael every night and got up about two hours earlier than him in the mornings. I used the early morning time to write. At home, when Michael got up, he mumbled a 'good morning' as he stumbled past my office to the kitchen for coffee. Then he would sit either at the dining room table or out on the lanai for the next two hours reading the news, either on his iPad or in the newspaper. As I sat at my desk working, I would be aware of his movements. I would return a grunted acknowledgment of the 'good morning' and never miss a beat in what I was doing.

I would have thought the same routine would be possible in the RV, and Lord knows I have tried. I did not have an office in the RV. I sat on the sofa that was along one wall of the house and directly behind the passenger seat of the truck cab. I worked with my laptop on my lap, and any notes or references spread out on the seat to my left. My coffee mug sat on a small step stool on my right. (I had initially tried to work at our table but found it too high and the ergonomics wrong for my laptop. Plus, the table was too small for my computer and papers and all of Michael's stuff, like his iPad, Post-It notes, headphones, and ballpoint pens.)

When we lived in the RV, this early morning routine became another animal altogether. When Michael first got up, in the nine steps it took for him to travel from the bed to the front of the RV, it was not unusual for him to trip over my feet, bump my laptop, kick the stepstool, and slosh my coffee at least once a week. The mishap happened despite my hysterical warnings when I saw him heading my way.

I had thought that once we got over the initial bungling and Michael had settled down with his newspaper; I would be able to refocus and get back in my groove. However, my excitable husband did not seem able to let me work without interruption. He was a news junkie and needed his daily fix of government chaos. At home, he was at the other end of the house or outside when he read the titillating details that television anchors had covered superficially in the televised coverage the night before. But in the RV, he had an audience only four feet away. He could not seem to resist blurting out stories and updates. I did not understand his apparent inability to curb his impulsivity or stifle his amazement over the next installment of whatever the current top story was in the news.

I kept telling myself that I could write while we were on the road. I probably needed to add the caveat that I was about half as productive on the road as I was at home in terms of a daily word count. But since I often wrote about RVing, in fairness, I needed to add that I collected experiences to write about all day long while we traveled. Maybe I needed to suck it up and accept that living in the damned RV was equally as productive as writing about it. The experience gave me things to say.

Were all men obsessed with food the way my husband seemed to be? I have talked with other women, and I sensed that 'yes, they were.' Dinner was perhaps the most important part of my husband's day. Sometimes he asked what we were having for dinner before he even opened his eyes and got out of bed in the mornings. By the time he had finished the newspaper, he would most definitely have asked the question. Making the perfunctory trip to a grocery store for food and supplies became a priority for the day.

Michael adored supermarkets. I considered having a custom t-shirt made for him that read: "A Day without a Grocery Store Trip is Like a

Day without Sunshine." Once inside the store, Michael paid attention to name badges and made a point of addressing each employee by name. He talked with the folks behind the deli counter, the produce unpackers, the canned goods stackers, the meat cutters, and especially the cashiers and bagging people. By the time we left a supermarket, which usually took twice as long as it would have taken had I been alone, Michael had a bounce in his step and a smile on his face because he had made new friends. If we were in that town for an additional day or so, those grocery store folks remembered him, for he most likely had made them smile.

I kicked myself sometimes for my irritability and impatience. On those supermarket trips, I found myself rolling my eyes and gritting my teeth, wishing my husband would hurry the hell up so we could get on with our day. I thought of how boring someone like me must seem to the rest of the world. I moved through the world quickly and efficiently, a serious expression on my face. I tried to minimize extraneous distractions and streamline the process of getting from Point A to Point B. At least I was not boring to myself—I enjoyed a rich-and-racing nonstop internal dialogue. In fact, I never got bored. I could find things to think about while sitting and watching grass grow.

I watched Michael with awe and amazement—how could he be that way? I saw the smiles he triggered, the impressions he made, and all the folks who remembered him the next day or the next time around. It was as if he spread sunshine wherever he went. (Of course, all those new friends from the supermarket and everywhere else probably never considered what it would be like to live with my husband's intense effervescence on an hourly basis. They would probably never think to ask if there was a flip side that arose when he was not out in public.)

Still, I had stopped groaning and inwardly saying "not again" when my husband got on a roll. He was funny. He could be hysterical. He was quick and smart. He added extroverted humor to my life that I would probably never have found anywhere else. Not with my shy introverted seriousness.

RVing could be a lonely activity, and despite having a partner with whom it was easy to share space, sometimes one needed to talk to others. I needed outside interaction, fodder for my fire, for my writing. I made myself seek out conversations with strangers because the stimulation was essential and necessary.

As the quintessentially outgoing one in our relationship, Michael found himself engaged in conversations with others far more often than I did. I did not believe he went out looking for interactions: they came to him. As a retired salesman, he had never met a stranger and could talk to anyone about anything. As my mother used to say, "He certainly has the gift of gab."

It was unavoidable that sometimes I found myself in situations in which my garrulous husband was off and running with a new friend. He would leave me standing there with nothing to say, unable to find a break in the conversation to interject a few words. I felt left out and ignored. Aware that I was about to hear Michael tell his latest story for the seventeenth time this week, I felt angry and trapped.

"You take over the conversation. You forget I'm there and act as if it's just the two of you talking," I told him.

"Sorry," he said. But it was a mumbled apology, and I sensed he had no idea what I was even talking about.

Was it fair to get upset with my husband when he did not have a clue what he was doing? Or when he was so excited, he could not help himself?

Sometimes I thought it was fair. Sometimes I thought not. He was who he was, and after over twenty-six years of living with him, I knew I was not going to change him.

I considered myself an excellent traveling partner, despite my seriousness. While I did not think Michael found me boring, I did not think he found me funny. Which was not to say he did not laugh at me often, because he did. His laughter was a pointed, pointing-of-the-finger at how serious and uptight I could be.

"Relax," Michael told me often. "You'll live longer."

He was probably right. Maybe someday I would figure out how to do it.

CHAPTER 27

Holidays on the Road

Our family had shrunken to a nominal size, so small as to be almost nonexistent. That landed us in challenging positions during holiday seasons. Sometimes we cooked big meals for those special occasions, sometimes we ate in restaurants, and sometimes friends took pity on us and insisted we share a traditional meal at their homes with their families.

My daughter had a large family on her dad's side, and that made any holiday gathering at his house more exciting and appealing than a small get-together at my house. Occasionally, we invited assorted friends and neighbors over for a holiday meal. At times we had as many as twenty guests filling our dining room table, three tables on the lanai, and a card table thrown in for good measure in the living room. My daughter liked those kinds of holiday meals, and while Michael and I did, too, they were too much work and too expensive to want to repeat them often. After the last huge celebration of that sort, I announced when the last guest had left, and we had crammed the last dish into the dishwasher, "I'm too old for this."

When we bought an RV, a world of other options opened for us. No longer did we have to apologize for not having more relatives or feel like charity cases when we crashed our friends' holiday celebrations.

Long before the RV purchase, we had spent a few Christmas and New Years' holidays in several, super-cool places—Venice, Italy; San Francisco, California; New York, New York; Key West, Florida; and Austin, Texas. Now that we owned an RV, it seemed a perfect time to reinstitute the practice of getting away for the holidays. We now owned a house on wheels that would let us go anywhere in the country.

With the RV in our possession less than six weeks and having taken it out on the road only one time, we lacked the courage to go far during that first year of ownership in 2015. We even lacked the courage to miss Christmas that year, opting instead to leave the day after Christmas for eight days in Panama City Beach, Florida. The small beach town had a tradition of dropping 50,000 beach balls on New Year's Eve at midnight down on the ground. We thought it might be a fun thing to see.

Being new at everything even remotely related to living in our tiny mobile house, we managed to stay happy on that trip despite polluted air from red tide in the Gulf of Mexico and non-stop rain in mid-fifty-degree temperatures. When New Year's Eve came around, we hardly even thought about those promised beach balls at midnight. The weather was too miserable to want to stay up that late to see them. We never asked, but we suspected the town canceled the beach ball drop anyway because of the rain.

In 2016, we again found ourselves on the road for New Year's, this time on a return trip from the West Coast.

"What's with rain every year on New Year's?" I asked Michael. We had left our Christmas in New Orleans and stopped in Biloxi, Mississippi. The Internet listed over a dozen casinos in town, so we assumed it would be easy to have an evening of great food and drink, followed by feeding penny slot machines until we had each lost fifty dollars. We had planned to enjoy a New Years' eating, drinking, and pretending we were gamblers, which we were not.

The evening did not work out as we had anticipated, and Biloxi would not be on our top ten list of places to hang out for the ushering in of another new year. Dinner was okay, though neither of us could remember the name of the restaurant or what we ate. We traipsed through the pouring rain, trying to find a decent casino. The two places we found were both tiny and reeked of cigarette smoke. We were back in the RV long before midnight, having gambled less than twenty dollars each in the penny and nickel slots.

We both had birthdays in February. Were two Aquarians supposed to be compatible? How could we be so different and still be born under the same astrological sign eleven days apart? Maybe the two-year gap between our births accounted for our differences. I was the oldest and loved being able to say, "I married a younger man." While many people might not consider birthdays to be holidays, we did, which made it surprising that we had yet to celebrate either of our birthdays in the RV.

We RVed twice over Fourth of July holidays. The first time, we celebrated the occasion with thirty-six Americans and two Canadians in a campground in Hill Springs, Alberta, Canada. Our Adventure Caravan Alaska trip group had left Great Falls, Montana, on July 3, 2017, and crossed into Canada. It was our first stop on the trip. Our campground sat on the top of a hill, surrounded by blazing yellow fields of canola and with a view of the Canadian Rockies to the west. The cookout with hot dogs, hamburgers, and more sides and desserts than I could remember was the first of many potluck dinners on that trip. Everything still seemed new and exciting at that point, including those people we would be traveling with over the next two months. At the time, we thought it was very cool to celebrate our Independence Day in a foreign country.

We spent our second Fourth of July RVing holiday (2018) in a beautiful campground on the St. Mary's River in Duluth, Minnesota. The owner told us his campground sat beside the largest fresh-water estuary in the United States. We have had several friends challenge that bit of trivia. Regardless of the accuracy of the claim, we enjoyed miles of hiking trails that followed the shoreline through a woodsy swamp.

Michael was disappointed when Duluth canceled its big Fourth of July fireworks display that year due to a forecast of heavy rain. We drove down to the port area along Lake Superior that evening anyway and enjoyed an expensive dinner at the Bellisio Restaurant. We chatted with a Canadian couple from Thunder Bay, Ontario, who sat at the table next to us. Thunder Bay was our next destination, and we enjoyed getting insider tips on what to see and do. Although this Independence Day did not feel patriotic, we found it memorable, fun, and probably better than anything we would have done back in Tampa.

Our best holiday on the road ever was Thanksgiving Day in Amarillo, Texas. We landed in Amarillo on a cold, windy Thanksgiving Eve and set up in a campground next to The Big Texan Steak Ranch and Brewery. The first thing we did was to make sure the restaurant would be open on Thanksgiving Day, and we made reservations. We knew from all the Internet hype, the billboards that began appearing twenty-five miles outside of town, and the crowd of patrons in the place at 5:30 p.m. that we had made a great choice of a restaurant for a holiday meal.

We woke up Thanksgiving morning to temperatures in the forties and wind gusts that felt thirty miles per hour strong. The weather did not damper our spirits or alter our agenda for the day. Bundled in our warmest clothes, we drove about an hour to the Palo Duro Canyon State Park. The Internet reported this canyon as the second-largest one in the country, with only the Grand Canyon being bigger. With that kind of description, we expected something far more substantial and grander than what we found. Nevertheless, we enjoyed hiking up and down steep hills for a couple of hours. For me, it represented a celebration of mobility. At that time, I was only a few months out from two total knee replacements.

After Palo Duro Canyon State Park on that brisk Thanksgiving Day, we searched for the most famed of all the Route 66 roadside attractions. "Just wait until we get to Cadillac Ranch," Michael had said. "You'll think you're hallucinating." Our RV bounced along a narrow backroad in the Texas Panhandle.

My husband was right. Cadillac Ranch was surreal, and it blew my mind.

Cadillac Ranch intrigued as none of the other funky, bizarre, and whimsical roadside attractions along Route 66 had done. Stanley Marsh 3, a Texas artist, businessman, billionaire philanthropist, and prankster, conceived the idea. He wanted something that would baffle the locals. In 1974, he commissioned three artists from California, all part of a hippie-alternative architectural practice called The Ant Farm, to create the monument. Intended as a tribute to Cadillac tail fins, the artists collected ten junked-out Cadillacs, all built between 1949 and 1963, and buried them in chronological order, nose down, in a cow pasture.

The site became a mecca. Visitors came from all over the world to pay homage. In time, those gawking tourists stole every removable part, including the revered tail fins, to carry home as souvenirs. Stripped-down and battered frames remained, and they changed daily as visitors swarmed the site with cans of Day-Glo paint.

Route 66 was built as a direct route from the Midwest to the West Coast and preceded interstate highways by several decades. It began in Chicago, Illinois, and ended at the Santa Monica Pier in California. When interstate construction began in the mid-1950s, the Mother Road began to fall into disrepair. By 1985, Texas had completed a long stretch of Interstate 40, two miles north and parallel to Route 66. To preserve Cadillac Ranch as a shrine, Marsh moved the cars in 1997 to a field abutting an I-40 frontage road.

We found Cadillac Ranch and joined the long line of folks waiting to pass through the open gate. The atmosphere felt party-like. As we entered the pasture for our hike to the middle of the field, we noted the subtle humor of a No Trespassing sign and a padlock on the fence, not the gate. Later I read that Marsh and the artists had deliberately created what they hoped would become an interactive piece of art. Although Cadillac Ranch probably exceeded their expectations, I suspected the loss of those hallowed tail fins saddened the creators, at least a little bit.

Through the years, Marsh had periodically had the cars re-painted. Once, they became solid white for a television commercial—another time, pink, in honor of his wife's birthday. When one of the Ant Hill artists died, the cars ended up flat black, in mourning. In 2012, painters covered the cars in rainbow colors to celebrate Gay Pride. With every change, the new colors lasted only a few hours before visitors again arrived with paint to leave their marks.

Cadillac Ranch was not Marsh's only public art. Folks have called him a prankster, and in fact, he created a few other bizarre things. For example, he had hundreds of mock traffic signs made up, with sayings such as "the road does not end here" and "I have traveled a great deal in Amarillo." He had the signs put up all over in Amarillo and Lubbock, Texas. Another time, he painted a broad white band around the top of a huge natural mesa and called it a "Floating Mesa."

Marsh had critics, and many of them viewed his art as nothing but eyesores with little or no artistic value. Marsh's response? "Art is a form of legalized insanity, and I do it very well."

Marsh reportedly loved those buried Cadillacs, feeling that all the graffiti and vandalism gave them a real patina, like the Chinese vases that increased in value with every new crack.

Despite a howling wind and fifty-degree temperatures, we lingered in that desolate site for more than an hour. Everyone did. We walked around and between cars, studied details, tried to decipher scrawled names and messages. Paying our respects to this vintage America symbol felt sacred. Almost religious.

Sadly, we had not known we could leave graffiti, so we felt a little like idiots. Next time we would know. And we would take pictures the minute we finished painting, for nothing at Cadillac Ranch remained static very long.

There *would* be a next time. I knew it in my heart.

We went to Palo Duron Canyon State Park a second time two years later. It was twenty miles from Cadillac Ranch, and we planned to revisit the ranch as we headed west. But alas, it had been a rainy summer, and we were told we would sink to our ankles in mud if we tried to go. So we put it on the list for a later time. A wonderful thing about being old and retired was that you could be flexible that way. Of course, another side of that old and retired coin was that you never knew how much time you had left. But I believed we would make it back to Cadillac Ranch one day.

I think we all see and do things that have the potential of expanding our minds a bit—of opening us up to possibilities that we had never considered before. Cadillac Ranch and Stanley Marsh 3's story did those things for me.

It was a shame Stanley Marsh 3 died in infamy. He began having strokes when he was seventy-three and became debilitated relatively quickly. At about the same time, lawsuits began popping up with allegations of his sexual misconduct with underaged boys. All the lawsuits were settled out of court by his estate. Marsh died at age seventy-six.

It was interesting to note that those Cadillacs had now been buried in the ground longer than they were ever on the road. I wanted to believe they would be there, inspiring visitors forever. But if they did not last, I was comforted to believe they would live forever in the minds of us lucky ones who had seen them.

Our already perfect Thanksgiving Day got even better with dinner at The Big Texan Steak Ranch and Brewery. It began with the free limousine service that picked us up at our campsite and drove us across the street to the restaurant. We gave the driver a generous tip.

Part of the marketing hype of The Big Texan was the humongous size of their steaks. (However, everywhere we went in the state we heard the claim that everything in Texas was 'bigger and better.') The restaurant ran an ongoing 72-ounce Sirloin Steak Challenge, saying the steak and all the sides were free of charge for anyone who could eat the entire meal in under one hour. The meal consisted of a shrimp cocktail, a 72-ounce steak, a baked potato, salad, and bread and butter. If any food remained on the plate at the end of the hour, the diner had to pay seventy-two dollars for the meal but could take any uneaten food home in a doggy bag. In case you did not do the math in your head, 72 ounces is four-and-a-half pounds.

A special section of The Big Texan featured a table reserved for any diner accepting the free-meal challenge. Part of the dining entertainment sometimes consisted of watching someone try, and usually fail, to consume all that food. Wait staff filled us in on stories of the few folks who had managed to stuff it all down, including one very skinny woman who came in about once a year, just to prove she could do it. We were disappointed that no-one tried to finish that humongous meal when we were there. Staff told us it was hit or miss with patrons accepting the challenge, with an average of two or three challenges per week.

Michael and I found ourselves hardly able to finish the 16-ounce ribeye we split between us. We had thought about ordering a traditional turkey dinner but changed our minds. It was a steak house, for God's sake. Nothing wrong with a juicy ribeye on Thanksgiving Day.

"I hate turkey dinners," Michael always said when we spent holidays at home. "I vote for ham. It's easier and quicker, and everybody likes it." For us, a ribeye steak on that Thanksgiving Day was a special treat we would always remember.

"We're in Key West! Let's eat out," Michael said. The year was 2018, and once again, we found ourselves discussing a holiday meal. "Look at that sign right there." We sat in a dirt-floored bar by the water, drinking beer and waiting for our sunset Sip and Sail boat ride, complete with appetizers and an open bar. The sign indicated the bar was serving a Thanksgiving Dinner the next day for $17.95 a person. "You couldn't cook it at home for that price."

"Yes, I could, and I'd have left-overs to eat the next day," I said. "Sorry, but that little Boar's Head turkey breast is in the refrigerator, and we're cooking it." I had dug in my heels. This year I wanted turkey for Thanksgiving, and I wanted it in our RV. Somehow, it would make the holiday seem more like Thanksgiving if we ate a traditional meal we prepared ourselves.

Publix Supermarket sold Boar's Head turkey breasts pre-cooked. We selected one that weighed about two pounds, a perfect size for two adults. I wanted Michael to cook it on our Weber grill. He had been boasting for months that he could bake things in this grill but had never done it. Now was his chance. I had bought Publix's oven-ready, uncooked cornbread dressing and a large container of turkey gravy. I would snap and cook fresh green beans. We did not need the mashed potatoes, sweet potato casseroles, cranberry sauce, rolls, or any other supplemental dishes for our tiny RV table.

While our dinner did not prove elegant or gourmet, even Michael agreed that the turkey was moist and tasty. Our Key West jaunt had already included several nights of eating out, and I was thrilled to have a non-greasy, low-sodium, and no-additive meal with a bonus of leftovers for later. I did not even care that we might end up throwing much of that turkey breast in the garbage because it had been too large for the two of us.

We added our Key West Thanksgiving to a list of memorable holidays. It might have competed with Amarillo, Texas, had the night ended a bit differently. Key West was the kind of town that never stopped, not even on time-hallowed occasions or traditional holidays. We had been downtown earlier in the day and found three out of every four shops and restaurants open for business as usual. We had planned to go to a 9:00 drag show on Thanksgiving night. Unfortunately, I hit a curb with the car while parking and blew a tire. Our entertainment for the evening was having the car towed to a repair shop and getting ourselves back to the RV park.

If you ever wanted to grab a bite to eat on Christmas Eve, you should go to Bulldogs Corner in Paulina, Louisiana. My husband and I made the forty-mile jaunt north from New Orleans along the Mississippi River and landed squarely in Cajun country. It was our first Christmas on the road in the RV, and we wanted to see the centuries-old tradition of lighting bonfires along the levee on Christmas Eve. Their purpose? To light the way for Papa Noel, the Cajun version of Santa Claus. We had heard an alternative explanation—to light the way to the nearest Catholic church for Midnight Mass—but I liked Papa Noel as the reason.

Folks in New Orleans had warned us of horrendous traffic along River Road, a route that paralleled the Mississippi for hundreds of miles. We headed out from the city early and snagged a parking spot one block from the levee and not too far from the only business in sight—Bulldogs Corner. We heard music from the Bulldogs' jukebox a block away. Harleys, choppers, and an occasional Japanese bike lined the front of the bar in a precise, backed-in formation. Dozens of people loitered and milled around the building's perimeters, most with a beer in one hand and a cigarette in the other. A handwritten sign out front advertised an all-you-can-eat buffet of jambalaya, gumbo, and other local food specialties for five bucks per person.

"It'll cost ten bucks to get in," Michael said.

"That's pretty steep for a dive."

"Maybe, but where else are we going to find restrooms for the evening? Plus, we have to eat somewhere."

As we neared the bar, we saw and heard lots of activity out back. Lights from emergency vehicles flashed with urgency, and gawking bar patrons hooted and cheered. We walked to the rear and saw paramedics hauling a stretcher to a waiting ambulance. Another medic leaned over the stretcher pressing blood-saturated gauze pads to the patient's cheek. Cops surrounded a second guy, whom they had in handcuffs, and were hauling him towards a cruiser.

We circled the bar and joined the long line out front to get inside. We could hear yelling and laughing, even above the blaring music. The atmosphere sounded pumped and charged with electricity. The energy felt almost palpable.

"Fight broke out," someone in line explained.

"They were arguing over a girl," another said. "I know 'em. She broke up with one of them 'bout a week ago. Came in tonight with a new boyfriend—that's when the fight broke out."

Someone else added, "And that new dude bit him on the cheek. Can you believe that shit?"

Finally, we reached the door where we would pay our cover and get our wristbands.

Michael, ever the comedian, said to the employee collecting the cover, "I hear this is a good place to get a bite." He somehow managed to keep a straight face. The bar employee did not crack a smile—I am guessing he did not understand the joke. Later in the evening, Michael tried the same line with the bartender, who said, "Yeah, the food's pretty good in here."

We ordered beer and clinked our bottles at our good fortune of getting in before the place reached its capacity. We decided to check out the unlit tree-looking, tepee-shaped structures along the levee in the daylight and return for the Cajun buffet after the bonfires were lit.

The structures were immense—some as tall as two-story buildings—and almost every one reflected the same layering of logs and boards for proper airflow and a long-lasting burn. We heard folks say that some of the fires would still be burning at daybreak, though most would be a pile of glowing embers. Some of the displays reflected themes, maybe of religion, or hunting, or patriotism. We saw one structure with an old baby grand piano positioned on the edge.

"You're not going to really burn up that piano, are you?" I asked.

"Couldn't give that damned thing away. It's missing half its strings. Figured this'd be a good way to say goodbye to 'er."

Excitement mushroomed in the crowd as the sun set and the sky darkened. The dousing of the structures began around 6:30, with two or three men working together on each one, flinging can after can of liquid on the lower logs.

"Is that gasoline?" Michael asked.

"Nope. Kerosene. Gasoline jumps back at-cha too quick."

The air along the levee went from smelling fresh and cold to smelling like an oil refinery before twenty-first-century pollution restrictions.

I could have set my watch by the lighting of the fires. At seven o'clock sharp, the levee went from being almost entirely black to a fairyland of blazing light, all in a matter of seconds. The fires whooshed upward in a driven fury the moment matches touched those kerosene-saturated logs.

I had expected a cheer, or least some applause, from the hordes of people who now lined both sides of River Road. It had been a dramatic, magical, mystical moment when those hundreds of bonfires, extending over fifty miles, erupted and transformed darkness to light, stillness to roaring energy, coldness to fiery heat. There was no piped-in music, no live news coverage broadcast on Jumbotrons, and no flashing neon lights. The ritual felt primal in its raw simplicity. Later I would interpret the crowd's silence as reverential respect for this ancient tradition.

We watched the bonfires in silence for more than an hour. There was nothing to say. Eventually, we headed back to Bulldogs Corner for restrooms, more beer, and food. The Cajun buffet for five bucks each was worth every penny.

The next evening, we ate Christmas dinner at Irene's, an upscale Italian restaurant in the French Quarter of New Orleans. We were lucky to snag a last-minute reservation. Although the food at Irene's was exquisite and our final bill totaled almost $200, I would choose a bite at that biker bar along River Road for a Christmas celebration any day of the week. Those bonfires continued to blaze in my mind.

Holidays on the road had been good, at times, exceptional. If we ever upgraded to a larger RV that accommodated more sleepers, maybe we would take pity on some of our friends and invite them to share a holiday at our house for a change.

CHAPTER 28

Woodstock, At Last

We were going to Woodstock!

The name Woodstock alone had held power for fifty years. That insanely phenomenal music festival in upstate New York in 1969 continued to capture and summarize an entire era of philosophy, politics, and lifestyle in its name. Although I had missed the festival, I had not really missed Woodstock. I had been there figuratively in the sixties and seventies, and now our RV travels were about to take me there literally.

I did not know what to expect. Would we see anything in Woodstock, New York, even faintly reminiscent of the social movement that had characterized the late sixties? The long hair and tie-dye, peasant tops with no bras, anti-war demonstrations and marches against racism and sexism, drugs and free love, anger at the injustices wrought by the Establishment—would we find a single trace of the spirit that captivated us back then? We had believed in that long-ago time we had the power to make a difference in the world.

I had been trying for the past fifty years to sort out the meaning of that turbulent, high-energy period of idealism and rock-bottom-conviction. I had always felt blessed to have been born when I was and to have been in college in the late sixties. The anticipation of visiting Woodstock as a seventy-year-old tourist triggered a floodgate of memories and sensations. I felt as if our pilgrimage might offer me a second chance at youth. Would I feel any vibes in the place, or have any epiphanies that might make me second-guess choices I had made decades earlier? Did I foolishly think that at my age, I might have a chance to make different choices and somehow effect a different outcome for the world? Or even for myself?

Woodstock had not been on our itinerary during this 2018 road trip. The thought of going there as a tourist had never crossed our minds. But when we had looked at rendezvous destinations in New York to meet Michael's sister Anne for the Labor Day weekend, the Catskill Mountains looked like a perfect midway spot. We would be driving north from Atlantic City, New Jersey. Anne would be heading northeast from the Mansfield Center, Connecticut, area. Perfect! Especially when Michael was able to snag us buddy-sites at a KOA campground minutes from the center of town.

I had wanted to go to Woodstock back in 1969. I was a student then at Florida State University in Tallahassee, Florida, partying hard but somehow managing to stay on track for graduation. Only a handful of political issues were on my radar screen at that time. Racism was one, and Tallahassee had an active Ku Klux Klan. I had gone to an anti-Klan rally once and saw a hooded, white-robed mannequin set on fire and burned in effigy. It had left a powerful impression on me, more so than the antiwar demonstrations and marches. But for me, those undergraduate years were mainly about sex, drugs, and rock and roll. Exactly what Woodstock had been about.

Given that I had missed the real thing, I seized upon the opportunity to visit the little town that summer. With a population of 5,823 per the 2016 census, the surrounding area looked like many other upscale communities in upstate New York—communities made up of two or three-story immaculately maintained houses sitting on large manicured lawns.

Within the first minute of driving down the main street of Woodstock, we realized the village was still a hippie mecca. We found the main street lined with vintage clothing shops, head shops, organic food markets, vegetarian restaurants, and, of course, souvenir shops filled with tie-dyed everything. There were even Janis Joplin and Jimi Hendrix clothes that one could don for photos.

One would never have been able to guess from the appearance of that quaint little village that the famous Woodstock festival had not taken place in Woodstock but instead in Bethel, New York, sixty-seven miles away. Back in 1969, festival organizers had selected Woodstock as the festival site, promoted the event by that name, and lobbied hard with stubborn town officials. Those town officers refused to the end to grant the necessary permits. In retrospect, did they rue their recalcitrance? Probably not. Town officials were able to capitalize on the name without having had to deal with the mess left behind by 400,000 festivalgoers, over half of them crashing the party without a ticket.

We paid ten bucks to park the car and started our exploratory stroll down the busy but slow-moving sidewalks. I realized I could sort all the people into three categories. First, there were the tourists, like us, who were almost all gray-haired seniors who looked solidly middle-class, despite our apparent attempts to dress in a manner suggesting we were still cool. I noted lots of Birkenstocks, long skirts and peasant blouses, men with ponytails, and rock-concert t-shirts. I speculated that all us old coots had probably wished we had been in Woodstock back in 1969.

The second and smallest of the groups was made up of business owners and their employees. This was a diverse and motley mix in terms of age and appearance. I suspected that in the backs of the shops, these owners and staff laughed their asses off at how much money we spent on tacky, tasteless souvenirs, many of which distributors had imported from India or Thailand. How politically incorrect was that?

We saw the last and largest group loitering in the little town square, sitting or sleeping under trees, or engaging in listless, flat conversation with each other. These were the folks who looked like hippies. They appeared to be mostly over sixty years old, although some younger folks were mingled in the mix. Almost without exception, they appeared dirty, in poor health, and stoned out of their minds.

I looked at these hippies with a mixture of horror and relief. How could a half-century of time have passed them by? I saw rotten and missing teeth, even in some of the younger people. Had methamphetamine replaced pot for these newcomers, or did they simply have no money for dental care? I saw a guy who looked about seventy years old, puking his guts out under a tree as his two companions sat in silence, not even reacting. I saw another old man with a beat-up bicycle laden with what appeared to be everything he owned, including a filthy sleeping bag secured to the bike with Bungie cords. This guy carried on an animated conversation of pure gibberish to an unseen audience. Schizophrenia? Or maybe dementia from too many fried brain cells? Or perhaps he had simply turned super religious and now spoke in tongues?

Looking back, I was thrilled to have gone to Woodstock in 2018, one year before the planned 50th Anniversary Woodstock Festival. I would bet the town fathers, this time around, would not have balked at allowing the commemorative event within the Woodstock zip code. However, the village of Bethel had beaten them to the punch. The Bethel Center for the Arts was already in full-tilt-boogie planning for the big celebration.

Back in the late sixties, I was a lost soul. I somehow managed to overcome my pointless overindulgences and find my way to a little more discipline and self-control. I still did not understand how or why it happened or what had saved me, but I mustered enough conformity with mainstream values to have stayed out of trouble and to have lived a good life.

I could only imagine where I would be today if I had gone to Woodstock back in 1969. I might have ended up being one of those who never left, neither literally nor figuratively. It was probably just as well I had not gone to Woodstock in 1969. This trip in 2018 felt perfect. The magic and charm of the word Woodstock continued to exert a powerful pull, even now that I had become a crotchety old lady. I believed my fantasies were much more satisfying than the reality of that music festival could ever have been.

CHAPTER 29

A Porta-Potty of our Own

Boondocking required RV skills which Michael and I lacked and had had little opportunity to cultivate. Maybe most important, boondocking required courage. Although painful to admit, glamping might have been more our speed, especially since we did not want to suffer any more hardships or inconveniences than necessary. Getting old was hard enough without deliberately testing our fortitude with challenging inconveniences.

Boondocking was the term for RVing overnight in a spot other than one designed for an RV. It meant no water connections, electrical hookups, and sewer drains. Boondocking might take place in a parking lot of a Cracker Barrell or Walmart, in someone's driveway, on a dirt lane in the middle of the woods, or any other place one might stop and spend the night. I had heard some RVers loved boondocking and could survive in the middle of the desert for several weeks at the time. Those folks had generally equipped their RVs with solar panels for power and additional storage tanks for fresh water. I had not yet met such hardy souls, but I hoped I would soon.

We had boondocked a few times, but only when we had no other choice. We had boondocked at the Columbia Icefields in British Columbia, at the Philadelphia Folk Festival, and the Miami/Homestead National Speedway. At the icefields, we parked in a paved parking lot with a capacity of perhaps thirty-five or forty RVs. The parking lot was about half full. At the folk festival, we camped on rolling hills amongst several hundred RVs, with lots of mud and with everyone squeezed in very tight. At the racetrack, we RVed in a vast open field in an ocean of RVs, several thousand at least, at a championship NASCAR race.

Of our three boondocking experiences, NASCAR should have been the easiest and most comfortable. Instead, it proved the most difficult in terms of sanitation because it involved massive amounts of beer consumed by thousands of men. Maybe women were also drinking lots of beer and getting rowdy, but I did not see them. This racetrack campground took on a life of its own.

Our introduction to NASCAR camping happened many years before our RV purchase. In those days, we camped in a tent with our Coleman lantern, Coleman stove, and a couple of sleeping bags thrown on the ground. While we appreciated campgrounds with bathhouses, we figured we could manage for a couple of days without a bathhouse since the camping area had lots of Porta-Potties. We could cook on our little hibachi grill, make sandwiches, or buy food at the track. We had clearly not understood what racetrack camping was about, or what we would experience in our little pup tent when we signed up for a campsite at a NASCAR race.

This NASCAR camping induction had taken place in Talladega, Alabama. My brain had erased many of the memories, probably because they were so horrific. We found ourselves in a huge field of RVs, almost every one powered by loud, carbon monoxide-producing generators. We felt dwarfed and smothered in our pup tent. The huge motorhomes that surrounded us cast shadows so large and dark it felt like dusk at three o'clock in the afternoon. It was the closest either of us had ever been to one of these large RVs. This took place in the late 1980s.

"Okay," Michael had said, "we're all set up. Now what?"

"Let's take a walk. These RVs are really something to look at."

We strolled up and down several lanes, impressed with the organization of the pasture-turned-campground. Organizers had done an excellent job of utilizing almost every square inch.

"Isn't it nice they've put up these Porta-Potties everywhere?" Michael said. "They've placed one on every third or fourth camping site."

"I think I'll use one, as long as it's this convenient." We had reached the end of a street, and a Porta-Potty sat at the corner, the door facing the side of a big Class A motorhome.

When I emerged from the Porta-Potty a couple of minutes later, an angry man waited outside the door. "You can't use that," he said, almost screaming. "It's ours. Get your own goddamned toilet if you want one, but these out here are private. His voice boomed loud. Folks all around had stopped what they were doing to watch.

Michael had walked on ahead as soon as the owner emerged from his RV. I stood alone, stunned at my mistake, and cowering under the man's wrath.

"I'm so sorry," I said. "I didn't know."

That error was only the beginning of our weekend troubles. The closest water was over a mile away, and we ended up trying to haul in gallon jugs for our limited use. It was mid-July, and Alabama was in the middle of both drought and a heatwave. Temperatures reached the mid-nineties both afternoons of our three-day weekend. At the entrance to the camping field, a line of about a dozen Porta-Potties had been set up for general use. We had arrived on a Friday afternoon and planned to leave on Monday. By Sunday morning, every cubicle in the Porta-Potty row was filthy beyond description, but these were the only options available to use for eliminating our bodies' wastes.

As if the lack of water, the heat, and the nasty porta-potties weren't enough, a group of six large Class A motorhomes had parked in a campfire circle next to our little pup tent. We never figured out how many people shared those six RVs, but it looked like at least forty. Organized by a bar somewhere in Mississippi, they had traveled as a group. The middle of the circle had been designated as communal party space. They had erected three stages, with a pole in the center of each one for dancing. A professional DJ spun the records at an ear-piercing volume. The scene each night had made us wonder if we were in an outdoor, under-the-stars stripper club. We never learned whether the bar sponsoring this trip featured exotic dancers back home or had imported them as part of the weekend's entertainment. The drunken orgy went on all three nights until almost dawn. We found ourselves trying to sleep in our little pup tent while music from next door assaulted our senses, and the dancers in G-strings and pasties assaulted my sensibilities.

By Monday morning, as we packed up to leave, we had both said 'never again.' I meant it—Michael had not, obviously, since the suggestion that we boondock at a NASCAR race came up again, more than thirty years later.

"But it'll be so much easier this time," Michael said. "We'll have our own RV, our own obnoxious generator, our own bathroom." He lobbied long and hard.

"Michael, it just gets too nasty. NACAR fans are sloppy drunks." The memories of those Porta-Potties in Talladega flooded me—urine all over the floor, feces on the toilet seats. I had felt like I needed to bathe in bleach to disinfect myself when we had finally gotten away from that place. We had even considered tossing our clothes in the garbage rather than trusting Tide and hot water to get them clean.

"Hey, it's just boondocking, and we've done it before. It's three nights. We spent four at the Philly Folk Fest. You can do this."

"NASCAR fans are all drunks," I said. "Our other boondocking times didn't include heavy drinking like we'll find at a race. At the icefields, our co-travelers were cocktail hour drinkers, never loosening up enough to even get a buzz on. There were lots of folks enjoying buzzes in Philadelphia, but the highs weren't coming from alcohol. Pot didn't result in sloppy, excessive urination or poor coordination in wiping one's butt." I was on a roll. "I can't believe you're asking me to do this."

"The only place you'll need to use a public restroom is at the racetrack during the races, and those restrooms will probably have fulltime attendants in them the entire time for all three races." Michael eventually wore me down, as he usually did.

Michael purchased a weekend package for the Ford Championship Weekend at the Homestead Miami Speedway. The package included a World Truck Series Championship race on Friday night, an Xfinity Series

Championship race on Saturday afternoon, and a Cup Series race on Sunday afternoon. Michael was beside himself with excitement.

Once again, reminiscent of Talladega, we found ourselves in a vast grassy field filled with thousands of campers. Our reserved camping area consisted of an orderly arrangement of RVs on large grassy sites. The weather could not have been better—cool and dry, with partially clouded skies that helped to prevent sunburn in the open stands. South Florida was at sea level, resulting in flat, level campsites.

This racetrack campground with reserved parking for RVs had a long row of Porta-Potties for public use, reminiscent of the ones in Talladega, Alabama. Also, this campground sported a huge trailer with 'Porta Kleen Showers.' We had seen the same brand-name trailers in Philadelphia but had not taken advantage of them. The showers had cost seven dollars each at the folk festival but only five dollars at the speedway. On Sunday morning, after no shower on Saturday for either of us, Michael took advantage of one of our free shower coupons. He described them as large, clean, and wonderful, with the water being perfect in both temperature and pressure. I opted to shower in the RV since our fresh and grey tanks seemed to be holding up. I did not think one shower would put us at any risk for a backup.

Being a much larger event than our Talladega race, tickets for this 3-day event were pricey—over $800 for the two of us. Maybe this helped to keep out the riffraff. We did not see any pup tents in this section of reserved camping, but we did see a fair number of Class C rentals, the kind in which Cruise America specializes. The rentals made me a little nervous, especially when I realized how many folks seemed to be sleeping in each rig.

We had now passed our third anniversary of RV ownership. In the beginning, Michael had wanted our black tank to remain virgin concerning solid matter. "Only liquids," he had vowed. "Not even toilet paper. Even the marine kind that disintegrates in water can eventually get stuck in the bottom and on the walls of the black tank and cause big problems. I'm requesting your compliance," he had said, looking me long and hard in the eyes.

I did not like it one bit, having to make those treks to bathhouses for my daily constitutions. Sometimes the bathhouses were quite a distance away. In bad weather, we would end up driving to them. But I complied with gritted teeth for almost three years. Then, God bless the day we landed at that Outer Banks RV park in North Carolina and found it did not have a bathhouse. I mistakenly assumed that once christened, there would be no going back on black tank usage.

"I'm so impressed," I had said. The truth was that I felt double-crossed and guilty. I had christened the black tank in our RV. My husband had not.

When we set up our Thor Four Winds at this Homestead Miami Speedway campground, I could not help but note that we were several miles and many traffic jams away from the closest convenience store or coffee shop. Maybe, finally, Michael would christen his sacred black tank.

Next thing I knew, I looked out the RV window and saw a guy wrestling a Porta-Potty from the back of a sanitation truck and walking it across the back of our site to the corner of our RV.

"What's that?" I asked.

"It's our very own Porta-Potty," Michael said, a twinkle in his eye. "Surely you didn't think I was going to defile that tank like you have done and continue to do." He laughed.

"How much is this costing?" I could not believe how my husband squandered money, or that he would be willing to *pay* for a Porta-Potty rental when he had a perfectly well-functioning toilet and sewer system inside his own little house.

"Ninety bucks, for all three days."

I quickly did the math. "Ninety dollars for three days for two people, forty-five dollars each, divided by three equals fifteen dollars for each daily constitutional. That's pretty expensive."

"Look," Michael said. He pointed to the outside latch on the portable toilet. "We could put a padlock on it when we leave, make sure no one else uses it."

"Or lock someone in if they do use it," our camping neighbor said. "I've already explained to your neighbor on the other side that the campground didn't put these things out for the convenience of all us RVers. I told her it was yours."

"Thanks," I said, remembering the mistake I had made at Talladega many years ago. To myself, I marveled at the level to which my husband was willing to go to maintain his non-defilement track record. Stubborn beyond words, I thought. But while I refused to cower in shame over my past toileting weakness, I used our porta-potting for the weekend. Why not? It was right outside our door.

I was so happy that Michael did not get too sloppy with his beer-drinking during the weekend. Our very own Porta-Potty remained clean for the duration.

CHAPTER 30

Why Janis Sang the Blues

We stumbled upon unusual and interesting places in our RV travels. Port Arthur, Texas, was one such place because it had been the birthplace and hometown of Janis Joplin. We spent a couple of days in Port Arthur on our way home from our mildly successful tracing of Route 66 across the country. We had left San Antonio, Texas, where we had caught up with a couple of cousins we had not seen in decades. We planned to spend Christmas in New Orleans, Louisiana. When we looked at the atlas, the long stretch between San Antonio and New Orleans loomed too long without a stop along the way. While Beaumont, Texas, filled the bill from a geographical perspective, Michael noted that Port Arthur sat a few miles south of Beaumont.

"Let's go there," he said, excitement in his voice. "That's where Janis Joplin was born. Maybe we can find something interesting to do or see."

I jumped on the Internet. "Here's a place in Port Arthur called the Pleasure Island RV Park. That sounds pretty interesting."

"Book it."

Off we went, excited to be on a new adventure.

The long drive across southern Texas felt interminable. It was hard to imagine such a massive state until you started driving across it. To help pass the time, I did some online research about Port Arthur and shared my findings with Michael as we bounced along Interstate 10.

"My God," I said. "Port Arthur is the home of the largest oil refinery in the United States. In 2016, it was producing 636,500 barrels of oil a day." I paused to read a little farther down on my iPad. "The refinery is owned by the Saudis and employs approximately 1,200 workers."

"What's the population of Port Arthur?" Michael asked.

It took me a couple of seconds to find the answer. "Fifty-three thousand, eight hundred and eighteen, per the 2010 census."

"Reading about Janis Joplin is a lot more interesting than reading about Port Arthur and oil refineries," I said a little while later. "Janis's dad was an engineer in that refinery. Her mother worked as a registrar at a little college in town."

As we approached Port Arthur, we noticed a haze in the air at least twenty miles before we saw billboards and businesses. And we saw billowing, grayish-white clouds of pollution pouring from the smokestacks of the refineries long before we could see the buildings.

"It stinks," I said.

"Hard to tell whether it's from the refineries or the Gulf. Sort of smells like dead fish."

"Here's hoping we're not running into red tide again. Remember Panama City Beach?"

"It's winter," Michael said. "I think that Gulf of Mexico fungus only blooms when the weather is warm."

"This is December—we went to Panama City in December. I'm not sure the weather has anything to do with red tide."

"Whatever. Let's hope the smell isn't this bad at our Pleasure Island campground."

"Think there'll be a strip of honky-tonks within walking distance of the park? With a name like Pleasure Island, I can only imagine what goes on there. Are you sure this is where we should be going?"

"You're too weird," Michael said. "Look at all the bridges we're going to cross. According to the GPS, we'll be there in about ten minutes."

"According to Wikipedia, the Neches and the Sabine Rivers converge here and pour into Lake Sabine and then into the Gulf of Mexico. One of these bridges takes us across an intercoastal waterway. Our RV park is right on Lake Sabine. Should be beautiful."

The road narrowed. It was after 4:00 p.m., later than we liked to pull into a campground and set up for the night.

"Look at all these buses," Michael said. Suddenly, we saw military-looking olive-green school-bus-looking vehicles filled with workers, all heading north back toward the town of Port Arthur. "Must be the end of a shift at the refinery."

"I thought we'd already passed the refineries."

"From the looks of all these buses, a huge part of this production is obviously south of here, maybe at the actual port on the Gulf."

We would never get to see where all those buses were coming from. We missed our turn to the RV park and had to drive another four or five miles before we could even turn around. The turn-around was at an entrance gate to the port. Two armed men in uniforms guarded the gate and directed us back the way we had come.

"Wow," I said, feeling alarmed. "These Saudis mean business with their oil, huh?"

We pulled into the Pleasure Island RV Park at dusk on a Friday night, setting up as quickly as possible in the howling wind and plummeting temperatures. As we looked out, we were surprised to see many of our RV neighbors packing up their vehicles with suitcases and battening down their rigs, obviously vacating the premises. Later, the RV park manager explained that the buses we had seen carried refinery workers. The refinery employees who stayed at the RV park were almost all managers and bosses. The place emptied on the weekends when these workers went back home to be with their families. By the time our fellow campers completed their exodus, only a handful of people had remained. The closest store was at least five miles away on the other side of the intercoastal waterway. The park felt desolate, abandoned. It surely did not feel like Pleasure Island would be hopping on this chilly December night.

"So much for the hot times on Pleasure Island," I said. "Glad we don't have to go shopping for food tonight. It's too cold and windy to even step outside."

The next morning, we awoke to temperatures in the mid-fifties, sunny skies, and little wind. The air felt thick and heavy on my head and shoulders. Was it fog? Pollution? Salt from the Gulf of Mexico? I could not decide, but Michael later offered the answer.

"Here's an interesting bit of trivia for you," Michael said. "I read this morning that Port Arthur ties with Lake Charles, Louisiana, and Astoria, Oregon, as being the most humid place in the United States. The average daytime humidity here in the mornings is ninety percent. It drops to seventy-two percent in the afternoons."

"That's worse than Tampa," I said.

"I'm beginning to understand why Janis Joplin turned to drugs and sang the blues." Michael laughed. "Port Arthur, so far, has not impressed me as any place I'd ever want to live."

After breakfast, we unloaded the bicycles from the back of the C-Max and took a twelve-mile ride around Pleasure Island. We found several small backroads lining the perimeter of the island, with the intercoastal waterway on the north and Lake Sabine on the south. Occasionally we would pass an old pickup truck or car parked by the road and see a couple of folks down by the water fishing. At the end of Pleasure Island opposite the port, we found another campground, this one more of a trailer park than an RV park. Capitalists had indeed discovered Pleasure Island and its raw beauty, though. They had built a gated enclave of multi-million-dollar homes along the Lake Sabine coastline.

We could not leave Port Arthur without eking every tidbit of Janis Joplin trivia and memorabilia possible from her hometown. We visited the small museum where we learned more about her life, including the fact that her childhood in this little town had been miserable. She reportedly never fit in and spent her high school years taunted and bullied by her classmates. She had been an obese, acne-marred teenager who painted and loved blues music. A docent at the museum remembered that she used to practice "screaming" and had a reputation of almost shattering windows with her powerful voice. I bought a Janis t-shirt at the museum, a purchase which surprised my t-shirt-collecting husband. I don't even wear t-shirts, but for Janis, I would.

A fire destroyed the Joplin family's first home in Port Arthur, but we were able to find the house where the family lived during Janis's teenaged years. A small plaque marked the property, now owned and inhabited by folks other than the Joplin family.

I had revered Janis Joplin back in the 1960s and had mourned when she died in 1970. I had not realized until recently that she died precisely sixteen days before Jimi Hendrix and that they had both been twenty-seven years old. Heroin took out two superstars that year. I liked a later comparison of Janis Joplin to Elvis Presley, the one saying that Janis was the female version of Elvis in terms of being able to captivate an audience.

Later I learned that twenty-seven was a popular age for musicians, artists, and actors to die, so popular in fact that a list referred to as the '27 Club' exists and is available on the Internet. A few other famous musicians who died at this age were Brian Jones, Jim Morrison, Kurt Cobain, and Amy Winehouse.

"Port Arthur contamination may have caught up with her even if the heroin hadn't," Michael said. He had his iPad out, reading as we finished eating breakfast. "Listen to this. Research has shown folks in Port Arthur have higher than normal levels of just about everything—lead in their bloodstreams, heart and respiratory problems, nervous system and skin disorders, headache and muscle aches, and ENT disorders. Listen to this . . . the folks who worked in the refineries are off the charts in terms of all kinds of cancers—brain, stomach, blood; you name it."

"So, you're saying Janis was doomed from the start?" I asked. "Why couldn't her family have lived somewhere decent, like San Antonio or Austin?"

"I'm glad they lived in Port Arthur. If Janis had grown up somewhere decent, she might never have turned to drugs and sang the blues. Think what the world would have missed."

My husband is so smart, I thought.

CHAPTER 31

How Many Can Fit?

Sometimes our little Thor Four Winds felt huge, other times minuscule. The difference, I finally realized, was whether one or both of us was sitting down or whether we were both up and about, moving from one end of the motorhome to the other. Even with the cowl space above the truck cab used exclusively for storage, our RV was supposed to be able to sleep four people comfortably.

When I had raised the possibility of inviting my daughter to join us for short visits during our travels, Michael's response had been swift and definitive. "Absolutely not," he had said. "There's not enough room."

I had not challenged my husband on that assertion until we camped with a couple of thousand race fans at the Miami Homestead Speedway for the championship weekend races. Although there had been a fair number of women and children sleeping in all the RVs, the men seemed to outnumber the women and children about two to one.

"I want you to look at that RV over there," I said, pointing to perhaps a 28-foot Class C directly across the dirt lane from us. "See those four old men sitting out front? They all slept in that RV last night, and they're not even family."

"So?"

"You keep saying there's not enough room for my daughter to join us. Those guys obviously have figured out how to accommodate four people in about the same amount of space we have. We could certainly do three people."

"You don't understand. There's no privacy," Michael said.

"For Christ's sake, Michael. You worked in hospitals in the medical field. What's with all this current concern about your body?"

"The quarters are too tight, that's all."

"You don't think those guys over there don't listen to each other cough, and burp, and fart all night long? That's what bodies do, Michael. They make these noises to reassure us they're still functioning, and to remind us when we've abused them, which is most likely the case with ninety percent of the folks sharing tight spaces at this race weekend." I plowed ahead with my hissy-fit. "You need to loosen up. Get over it. We could be inviting our friends Laura and Ralph to join us for weekends. We could have flown my daughter to Alaska. Come on . . ."

"I don't like the idea of being that close physically to other people."

"Then, maybe I need to start going without you."

I looked around at this NASCAR campground. To our left, we had Vinnie, Darryl, and James—three beer-drinking, race fan buddies. They had rented a 30-foot Class C for the weekend.

On our right was a party of five people—an older man and his wife, his younger adult niece and her boyfriend, and one other old geezer (we never figured out how he fit into this group). The five of them were sharing a 24-foot Class C rental from Cruise America. The trick, I came to realize, was to live outside—all the sitting and drinking and cooking and eating and partying done in folding chairs on the grass. Good weather was a requirement. It looked like this group reserved the inside for sleeping and occasional toileting, like in the middle of the night. Otherwise, those folks looked like they walked a distance away for the line of Porta-Potties set up for public use. Or maybe they used our Porta-Potty when we were not there—we would never know.

I thought back to our many RV trips and observations over the past three years. How many grandparents had we seen traveling with grandchildren? I remembered one huge Class A in our campground in St. Ignace, Michigan, our entrance into the famed Upper Peninsula. This grandma and grandpa had seven grandchildren with them, all appearing between the ages of about three to maybe eleven or twelve. Parental units seemed to drop in at least once a day, but they invariably left their kids with the grandparents each time. The grandparents had planned activities so well the grandkids probably felt like they were at summer camp.

On our Alaska Caravan trip, there were three rigs in our group that had adult children and a teenaged grandson drop in for week-long visits in Alaska. If I had been awarding a trophy for tolerance in sharing tight quarters among the caravan group, the trophy would have gone to two sisters, both in their early sixties, who shared a 35-foot Class A for over three months with their two husbands. Their stories did not help my case when it came to trying to convince Michael that my daughter had a place in our travels.

I was not giving up on my mission to make our RV travel a shared event with family and friends. If we limited our consideration to vetted campgrounds, such as KOAs, we could pretty much be assured of finding nice, clean bathhouses. With decent bathhouses and decent weather, we could do most of the living either under the awning of the RV or around the bonfire.

Since I had not yet convinced my husband that we could share our little rig with others, I committed to joining the Family Motor Coach Association of America (FMCA). It had a chapter in the Tampa Bay area, and the group organized rallies and group camping trips regularly. Our RVing friends from other places told us it was the best way to start meeting other RVers and to start having more fun. I had to scratch my head over our friends' words. Michael and I both thought we had been having fun all along.

I believed I could talk Michael into us checking this group out. While I thought it was a group of mostly old people, I had to remind myself that I now fit into that category, too.

CHAPTER 32

A Very Sweet Spot

I entertained a fantasy, everywhere we went, that this was my home. Sometimes I thought I could be happy living anywhere. Almost every place we visited had a charm of some sort, although, at times, we had to look hard to find it.

For the past three years, the U.S. News & World Report had issued an annual report of America's 125 largest metropolitan areas based on affordability, job prospects, and quality of life. I had scanned those reports and registered little surprise at the 2018 top ten list. Austin, Texas, hit the number one spot on the hit parade. It had long been in my mind as perhaps the sweetest spot on the planet.

A recent trip to Key West, however, changed my mind. Key West was a mecca to which every old hippie felt drawn and connected. It was the place that embodied the concepts of chilling, of being kind and gentle, that anything is okay if it did not hurt someone else.

This was my fourth trip to Key West, and on every trip, I had camped. The first two times were in tents, the last two in our RV, the first time with husband number one, the last three with Michael. The layout and rhythm of the area were now familiar, and during our last visit, we felt no sense of urgency to see, to do, or to go.

Since completing a couple of book-length manuscripts, I now thought of myself as a writer. That meant a trip to Hemingway's house, a place I had not visited in at least ten years. In the twelve years that Hemingway lived in this Key West mansion (from 1928 to 1940, both part-time and full-time), he completed over 70 percent of his successful writings. I had hoped to feel inspired as I looked at the small, over-the-garage writing studio where he wrote masterpieces like *The Old Man and the Sea, A Moveable Feast,* and *A Call to Arms.* While I loved looking at that immaculately preserved writing space, my biggest inspiration came from our tour guide, a young man so passionate about his topic that tears flooded his eyes, and his voice choked out several sobs during his presentation. If the guide was faking this kind of emotion, he should have been in film or the theatre, not conducting thirty-minute guided tours to tourists, many of the groups including reluctant children or uninterested spouses. I walked away with increased awe of Hemingway's genius, despite him being a testosterone-driven, animal-killing misogynist who could not be faithful to even one of his four wives.

Mallory Square in Key West was a gathering spot for watching sunsets. Filled with tourists and probably a few locals, the large paved area had room for vendors to hawk everything from handmade Key Lime soaps to custom-painted seascapes on seashells to water-colored paintings of sunsets to humongous tropical drinks in coconut shells with skewers of cherries and pineapple to temporary tattoos guaranteed to last two to three weeks. Musicians provided entertainment, and they strategically spaced themselves so they would not drown each other out. Singers with guitars were most typical, although we heard a lovely flutist who stood behind a small table filled with his CDs.

The acts that attracted and held the largest crowds were the gymnasts, jugglers, sword-swallowers, and fire-eaters. The crowds of spectators that gathered around these acts grew so large that entertainers interrupted their own shows to ask people to move in closer so as not to block the walkways. As tension mounted toward the ends of these performers' acts, the calls for donations would begin and would rise to a dramatic pitch by the last death-defying stunt. I became so mesmerized by one guy's act of balancing on one hand high in the air on one wobbly post that I forgot to watch the sunset.

Drinking and partying were standard Key West activities, and I had read that Café Pepe's, now called Pepe's Café and Steakhouse, had been Hemingway's favorite drinking dive. We walked over a mile to find this little hole-in-the-wall place, which did not disappoint us. The very cool bartender explained that only lame, naïve tourists ever went to places like Sloppy Joe's or Margaritaville. However, we could not resist the Hog's Breath Bar and Restaurant, another well-known tourist spot. We stayed for only one drink.

We checked out the Garden of Eden clothing-optional rooftop bar along Duval Street, thinking it would be a fun and different kind of place. We reached the bar after a perilous climb up three steep fire-escape-type staircases. Once at the top, we realized we had hit rock-bottom in terms of class, for the place was a dive in every sense of the word—dark, reeking of cigarette smoke, and lacking a single item of beauty that might cheer the place up, like a potted plant or a painting on the wall. A few tables and chairs sat in the open area between the bar and the outside railing. A handful of patrons lined the bar. We had no trouble snagging a couple of bar stools.

The bar ran a never-ending loop of body-painting videos on a big-screen TV that hung behind the bar. Anyone entering the bar, whether they stayed or not, and whether they happened upon any nude customers or not, would see naked bodies if their eyes flickered even momentarily in the direction of the television. The images were huge and in-your-face.

The bartender and I were the only two women there. We both remained fully clothed. The bartender said she had been topless earlier but had gotten cold and put her t-shirt back on. I counted eight or ten men of various ages, with a constant coming and going of curious street people climbing the steep stairs, taking a quick look around, and immediately heading back down. Two svelte, silver-haired men—one with long hair and a pointed goatee, the other shaved from head to toe—made a display of stripping down to their fully-tanned birthday suits. It seemed to me they displayed more arrogance than they did nudity. Michael and I drank beer and talked minimalist lifestyles with a clothed forty-two-year-old marine mechanic who lived nearby on a sailboat.

I was not surprised that our conversation in this clothing-optional bar in Key West, with bodypainting of boobs running continuously in the background, would inevitably turn to Fantasy Fest, an annual street party of debauchery known worldwide. Started by locals in 1979 to attract visitors during the slow season, the October event had mushroomed to over 100,000 attendees and over $35 million in tourist dollars each year.

Our marine mechanic bar-mate reported that he had been a regular at Fantasy Fest for the past five years. He shared details I might have been happy not hearing—things like a guy jerking off on the sidewalk with three women filming the event with their cell phones and a couple doing the wild thing while surrounded by a two-deep audience. Although local ordinances prohibited nudity, authorities reportedly looked the other way during this annual street party.

Our bartender joined in at this point in the conversation, sharing an anecdote of a guy trying to jerk off at the bar the previous afternoon. She learned of his activity when he leaned across the bar and asked if he could touch her. She said she asked him to leave the bar, which he did. "Unfortunately," she said, "everyone else left, too. They were too freaked out by the guy doing that."

Later, at another bar, I talked with a woman who came to Fantasy Fest with her husband and two other couples every year. She said the cheapest rooms available on the island during the event were about $500 a night.

"Did you hear that?" I turned to Michael. "How much are we paying a night at Leo's Campground?"

"Ninety dollars a night, and I've already asked—they do not raise their rates during Fantasy Fest. But they do require a four-night minimum."

"I think four nights might be a bit much for that scene," I said. "What do you think?"

"Wouldn't hurt to make a reservation. We'd probably be able to get a full refund on the deposit if we changed our minds. They have seven spots left right now, and Fantasy Fest 2019 is eleven months away."

"Let's think about it." Somehow, I found it hard to pull the trigger to walk into the middle of that kind of debauchery voluntarily.

While parking in the downtown area of Key West was pricey—fifteen or twenty dollars for three or four hours—we did not mind the trek from farther away but less expensive spots to get to Duval Street, the main drag. Key West was a walking kind of town—old narrow sidewalks through residential areas of large two-storied houses with lush, tropical yards. The growing season was twelve months a year. I loved looking at the beautiful plants as we walked and walked and walked, sometimes up to five miles a day. The distances challenged my disintegrated arthritic feet, but I refused to deny myself the joy of walking in perfect weather in a tropical paradise.

Key West was the largest and most distant of the islands off the mainland of southern Florida. The town displayed a huge marker indicating that it was the Southernmost Point of the United States. Cuba was a mere ninety miles to the south, or 103 miles, depending on how much of a stickler one was for accuracy. Every three or four blocks, barkers stood in booths at street corners, trying to sell boat trips to passing tourists. We could have chosen any number of cruises. We picked a two-hour sunset sail that included appetizers, an open bar, and live music. We later agreed our Sip and Sail trip was worth every penny we paid, which was ninety dollars for the two of us. There was nothing like a Key West sunset in the Straits of Florida from a boat in perfect balmy weather with a great musician putting his spin on old songs from the sixties. I drank enough red wine to get a buzz on and sang along at the top of my lungs to most of the songs. Well, maybe I just sang under my breath.

I have heard that one cannot fully know the meaning of an experience until long after it was over, that it took a while for the details to settle and the significance to surface. In contrast, I had also heard that the more typical way of achieving bottom lines was through epiphanies, especially those reaching earthquake proportions, like a sudden light where before there was only darkness. I only knew that by the second day of our most recent trip to Key West, I felt like I had found the quintessential sweet spot, the place I would gladly have never left, not even to go back home to get the rest of my clothes. I recently learned, however, that one did not necessarily even need clothes in Key West, except for grocery shopping or to pick up prescriptions at the drug store.

I started doing the research. What was the livability index of Key West, Florida? I knew various publications listed this kind of information, complete with surveys, summaries, and retirement guides. Key West had not hit the top 125 spots in the most recent U.S. News & World Report compilation. But with a population of 25,366 people per the 2010 Census, the magazine could hardly consider Key West a metropolitan area, and especially not when job prospects were one of the three factors the magazine considered when making their ratings.

Tourism was the principal industry in Key West, and while I could not find any statistics, it appeared on any given day the population on downtown streets swelled to 40,000 or 50,000, all due to tourists. Sort of like Skagway, Alaska—800 people for eight months of the year, with the daily population rising to over 40,000 when the big cruise ships hit the port and let down their gangplanks for shore leave during the four-month-long tourist season.

But for retirees like us, job prospects were not an issue. We had no intention of going back into the fray with day jobs. Other questions were more important for us, such as: could we afford to live here? I learned that the median income in Key West was $57,643 per year. I sighed to think Michael and I might find ourselves more financially comfortable than 50 percent of the people living on the island. So far, so good.

Given that we might qualify in terms of income, would we be able to afford a house on Key West? I learned that the median price of a home on the island was $439,400, which was 184 percent higher than the cost of houses in other parts of Florida. I was not sure, but it would not have surprised me to learn that a house for that price was nothing more than a tiny two-bedroom, one-bath bungalow. If I lived in Key West, I would want one of the stately, two-storied houses with wrap-around porches on both levels, and with a garden overgrown with tropical plants for privacy and charm. That near-half-a-million-dollar price tag for a house in Key West was a bit more than my Tampa house was worth, and I would have ended up with far less house if I made the trade. I decided buying a house in Key West was not a possibility for me.

Maybe I could rent. About 45 percent of the folks living in Key West rented, I learned, and the median rent was $1,514 per month. Maybe I could afford that. But what would I get for that 1,500 bucks? Maybe an efficiency apartment, if I could even find one? I would have to do more research in this area.

I further learned that the overall cost of living in Key West was 42 percent higher than it was anywhere else in the State of Florida. That made sense. The town of Key West sat at the far end of a string of islands off the coast of South Florida. One had to drive almost 130 miles on U.S. Highway 1 to get from the tip of the Florida mainland to get to the tip of the last of the islands, which was where the town of Key West was located. Everything sold here—food, clothing, gasoline, toiletries, you name it—had to be hauled in by boat or truck. Shipping was expensive.

On our last night, we leaned against a porch railing at our dinner restaurant and looked down on Duval Street. Both the street and the sidewalks teemed with cars, motorcycles, bicycles, and pedestrians.

"Cool place, huh?" I said.

"Yeah, and look how mellow it feels. I bet this is one of the safest places in America," Michael said.

Later, when I looked up crime statistics for Key West, it shocked me to learn that this area had a crime rate 36 percent higher than the rest of Florida. Could it have been drugs brought in on boats? Physician-run pill factories? Prostitution? I could not figure this one out. In most major cities, and certainly in places where the streets were this crowded, one would worry about pickpockets, violent, erratic outbursts from druggies, road rage, any number of crimes. In contrast, these streets felt safe, without any hint of the edge one felt in places like New York City, New Orleans, or Atlanta.

I trusted statistics and the Internet for basic information about places in the United States, although perhaps I should not. Per the reported data, Key West had characteristics that might make it out of my reach financially as well as undesirable as a place to live fulltime. I could not imagine what it would be like with so many tourists invading my hometown daily. Or how sticky and hot it must be down there in the middle of August. Or the sheer terror of following the weather on CNN when a major hurricane was heading straight at the islands. Or the frustration of trying to find a place to park or having to pay twenty bucks to park while running into a CVS pharmacy to pick up a five-dollar prescription.

Still, there were some delightful spots in Key West, spots so sweet perhaps I would not even mind all the irritations and inconveniences. Before making any major decisions, though, a month in the RV in Austin, Texas, was calling. I hoped Austin would be sweeter since it was certainly more affordable.

I had not known that more than a month in Austin would happen soon but that it would not be voluntary. Not this time, anyway.

CHAPTER 33

Sitting on the Dock of the Bay

It could well have been a dock since we were stationary while things around us moved. But it was not a dock. I sat inside our little 26-foot Thor Four Winds motorhome and watched the occasional RV either enter or exit the Oak Forest RV Resort in Austin, Texas. The motorhomes, fifth wheels, and trailers came through at four or five miles per hour, much as boats might ease through a No Wake zone on a river. And while it might have been nicer to sit on a real dock somewhere, or maybe even along a riverbank in our RV, we could not have picked a better town in which to have our travels brought to a screeching halt.

Three years ago, I proposed to my excited RV husband that my RV reluctance might lessen if we stopped traveling as if our motorhome was Seabiscuit heading down the final stretch on the track. "Why don't we pick a place that interests us and go there and live for a month? Why do we have to keep charging back and forth on these cross-country highways, across all these thousands of miles? Let's slow down. Stay in one place long enough to get a feel for what living there would be like."

"We can do that after we get a sticker for every state in the continental United States."

"You and your ridiculous sticker map." I had ordered the damn thing from Amazon after seeing sticker maps affixed to a high percentage of

RVs in our travels. So far, we had made it through forty-five States, with only Colorado, Nevada, Utah, and Oregon to go. We would obviously never get to Hawaii. When I ordered the map, I had had no idea my husband would become so obsessed with filling in all the states with stickers.

We arrived in Austin on day eight of our last RV trip. We had arrived the third week in April 2019 and had planned to stay one week. We wanted to check out the local music scene, eat Tex-Mex food, and do some things in Austin we had not done when we were here ten years ago. We wanted to catch a political satire show at Esther's Follies and see the 1.5 million Mexican bats that made the South Congress Avenue bridge their home from March to October every year. I looked forward to staying in one place for a week. It already felt like we were traveling like a bat out of hell. We had covered over 1,100 miles in the past six days. We had spent two nights in Madison, Florida, one night in Mobile, Alabama, three nights in New Orleans, Louisiana, and one night in Houston, Texas.

We arrived at our RV park late in the afternoon during a downpour, exhausted from a long day of travel in horrendous wind and rain. The rain let up as we pulled into our site. We knew the gap between rain showers would be short, so we scrambled to get everything connected during the lull—water, electricity, cable, and sewer. We also unhooked the C-Max from the RV. When we flipped the circuit on the post to connect to the park's electrical system, nothing happened. We sighed in dismay. No electricity. We drove the car to the office to report the problem.

"Oh, I'm so sorry," the staff person said. "I'd forgotten that pole doesn't work. Let's see where I can put you." She studied her computer screen and then came to the counter with a park map. "Go to Site 10. I'm sure that one will be okay."

As we pulled back into our site to unhook the utilities and prepare to switch sites, the heavens opened up.

"We should wait, don't you think?"

"Nope. Let's get this done." Michael had never been a patient man, and I knew he had been looking forward to popping a beer and watching the evening news once we settled in. "I think I can get the electric and cable hooked up pretty quickly. We can do the water and sewer after it stops raining."

The new site was a short distance away. We worked together in the rain, sweating under our North Face raincoats to connect the two essentials of electricity and cable so we could get back inside as soon as possible. Although only April, it nevertheless felt like summer, much like our hot, humid weather back in Tampa.

As Michael made his last trip down the RV steps to flip the circuit breaker on our outside utility post, he slipped down the wet stairs and wrenched his foot.

"Ah, shit!"

Although he had not broken the skin anywhere, his foot started swelling immediately. "Guess we'll know in a couple of hours whether anything is broken," he said. "I'm thinking it's a sprain."

"A break would almost be better. Bones heal in six weeks. Sprains can take up to three months."

"You don't understand," Michael said. "If it's a broken foot or ankle, it'll mean surgery. And it can take more than six months to heal from foot and ankle surgeries."

I looked at my husband's ballooning foot. "Want an ice pack? I think you should also elevate it."

"No, not now. We'll see what it looks like in the morning." Michael plopped down on the sofa and started channel surfing for his favorite ABC Evening News anchor, David Muir. I started dinner.

Swelling increased during the night. Discoloration never appeared, so the next morning we concluded Michael did not have any broken bones. However, when he tried to put weight on the foot, the pain was so bad it triggered audible moans. "I'm going to find a Doc-in-the-Box," Michael said. "I don't think it's broken, but I could certainly use a boot or a splint of some sort."

It took about an hour and several phone calls to find a walk-in clinic on our side of town that accepted Medicare and United Health Care insurances. The first place Michael called did not accept insurance and said he would have to bring cash. Huh? What medical establishment in the United States did not take insurance in 2019, for God's sake? One of the few advantages to getting older, we had come to understand, happened with our sixty-fifth birthdays and eligibilities for Medicare. We had been enjoying this positively wonderful medical coverage for several years now, having paid virtually nothing for medical care since retiring.

Less than an hour later, X-rays taken and read, Michael shared the news, "Looks like you might get your way. My leg's broken. We'd probably be better off at home."

I winced at the accusation in my husband's voice. "What do you mean by 'I'll get my way'? What are you talking about?"

"You never wanted to come on this trip, to begin with. Now it looks like you'll get to go back home." My husband stared at me, thinly veiled blame and anger in his eyes.

What the hell? How can he say this to me? I did not make him fall. My anger roiled as we walked out of the clinic, the name and address of an orthopedic surgeon in hand. I worried that my husband would never recover from his disappointment if we aborted our five-month-long west coast RV trip. Not with a mere four friggin' states left blank on our damned United States sticker map.

CHAPTER 34

Taking Stock

We spent a long twenty-four hours between the walk-in clinic and the appointment with our charming mid-Eastern podiatrist on the other side of town. Talk about cool doctors; we could not have gotten a better referral. Arush K. Angirasa, D.P.M, F.A.C.F.A.S., Lower Extremity Trauma and Reconstructive Surgery, charmed the socks off us both. Silver-haired, deeply tanned, dancing eyes, and a bashful-boy grin, he was more than a surgeon. He was also a musician who played gigs in a small band as his hobby. Where else but Austin, right?

"You're very, very lucky," Dr. Angirasa said to Michael. He made a crude drawing with a dry marker on his whiteboard of the bones in the lower leg and then pulled out his cell phone to show us the actual X-rays. "You've got a spiral fracture in the fibula. That's this skinny bone right behind the tibia." He grinned. "The dislocation is very small, and it'll probably heal and close up by itself, without surgery. If this injury had involved your foot or your ankle, things would have been much worse."

Dr. Angirasa went on to explain that he would put a plaster cast on the leg. He ordered Michael to put no weight whatsoever on it. This announcement produced some looks of incredulity between my husband and me. How the hell was Michael even supposed to get out of the doctor's office without putting any weight on the leg? The doctor had not handed over crutches or a knee scooter, saying we would have to find those on our own. Meanwhile, my 235-pound husband was already off-balance and impaired from an earlier shoulder injury that had never healed properly. He had experienced trouble navigating his large bulk through space long before he broke his leg. We hobbled out of the doctor's office, mute and stunned, wondering what this catastrophe meant for our trip.

Michael had been sixty-five years old when attacked with a consuming desire to buy an RV and travel the country. I was sixty-seven. As old geezers, we understood there would be risks involved with taking off to parts unknown and so far away from our regular physicians and specialists. Although we felt adventurous and daring, we were not foolhardy. Michael had explored several insurance plans available to RVers who might find themselves far from home and in trouble. He had zeroed in on Good Sam's Travel Assist.

Michael made the phone calls and spoke with a Good Sam Travel Assist case manager. Yes, our insurance would pay a professional driver to deliver our RV and our car to our driveway in Tampa, Florida, if we decided to fly home. Had Michael's injury required hospitalization, Good Sam would have even paid the airfare. But because there had been no hospitalization, we would have to buy the tickets if we flew home. Good Sam requested documentation of the injury and medical clearance from the doctor that it would be safe for Michael to navigate through airports and climb ramps on and off airplanes.

Michael's surgeon was not keen on the idea of someone on crutches or a knee scooter navigating through airports and down aisles in airplanes. We spent a couple of days tossing around options. If the leg could heal without surgery, why cut the trip short and go home? We could not travel for a couple of weeks anyway. We were already halfway across the country to our destination on the west coast. My silent argument was that I never wanted to drive across the country again—it was too far and required too many stuck-in-one-position hours sitting in an uncomfortable Ford-450 truck cab. Out loud, I said, "We've always wondered what it'd be like to live in Austin, Texas? Why don't we hang out here and find out?"

"Sounds like a plan," Michael said. "The timing is good for you to stay in one place for a while, since you need to work on revisions of your book, right?"

The timing was right indeed. But the question was whether my loquacious husband would be able to entertain and care for himself so I would have the uninterrupted time I needed to work on edits for my publisher. Michael needed help dressing, going from one short end of the RV to the other, and almost every other activity of daily living. This was going to be interesting.

Yeah! We would now have a chance to stay in one place for a while. We would stop what I considered frenetic racing back and forth across the country and through Canada, all for the sake of putting stickers on a stupid map affixed to the freezer door in our Thor Four Winds motorhome. It was also for bragging rights. My husband wanted to be able to proclaim to the world that we had RVed in every state in the country except Hawaii.

The end was near anyway. We had RVed our way down to only four remaining states—Colorado, Nevada, Utah, and Oregon. This would be the trip to complete my husband's mission. What would be wrong with staying in Austin, Texas, for a month or so? Hell, yes! The live music capital of the world, a little oasis of liberal politics, a hub of creative output, and a reputation for pure funk. I would love to stay here until Michael's broken leg healed. Maybe I would like to stay here forever.

I had wanted to get my husband calmed down enough for me to feel I was living and working in one place. Maybe it would finally happen here at the Oak Forest RV Resort. I was tired of being a tourist. I wanted to pretend I was an Austinite, if only for the next five weeks.

CHAPTER 35

The Long-Suffering RV Caregiver

"One more thing before you sit down." With his back to me as he hobbled the ten feet from the table to the bed, my invalid husband could not see that I had already sat down. "I need my iPad, headphones, and charger if you don't mind."

With cheer in my voice, I said, "Sure. No problem." But inwardly, I groaned. I even rolled my eyes a little. My life at that moment seemed like nothing more than unending interruptions and requests for service. I moved my laptop off my lap, popped up to grab the requested items from the table, and headed towards the other end of the RV. Michael had just transferred himself from his KneeRover to the edge of the bed. Amazon Prime had delivered this leg scooter to the RV park a couple of days earlier. It had taken us almost an hour to assemble it.

I stood beside the bed waiting, willing myself to show patience. With a broken leg wrapped in a heavy cast, Michael now needed to scoot his body upon the bed so that he could prop himself up against pillows at the headboard. Scooting to get situated in this queen-sized bed had been challenging for both of us even before Michael broke his leg. Arthritic hands and wrists made it difficult for me to support my weight to scoot my body back. Already limited because of his previously broken shoulder, and now further weighted down with a heavy plaster cast on his leg, Michael's scooch took at least twice as long as usual. Once he reached his desired spot, I assisted with the pillow arrangement, inserted a huge package of paper towels and a bed-pillow underneath the injured leg to elevate it per the doctor's orders, and plugged in the charger to his iPad.

"All set?"

"Thanks so much. I won't bother you again for two hours."

"Don't be silly. You're not bothering me."

I sat down again and picked up my laptop, ready to finally get to work.

"Oh, Gerri, I forgot my brown pillow. Would you mind terribly?"

I got up again, grabbed the small throw-pillow from the bench at our table, and took it back to the bed. Michael used the brown pillow on his chest as an iPad support. He could place the iPad on the pillow, and it would be at a perfect distance and angle for reading.

Since I was already up and distracted again, I tackled the KneeRover. Each time Michael moved from the bed to the table or the couch, I had to lift the damned thing and turn it around so it would be facing the correct position for the next time he wanted to move from one end of the RV to the other. It weighed about twenty pounds. Although maneuvering the damned thing inside the RV was awkward, it was not nearly as difficult as getting it up and down the RV steps when we went out. Or worse yet, getting the thing into the back seat of my small C-Max. Ford Motors had not designed my car to transport medical equipment. As a final task, I picked up the almost-full urinal sitting beside the bed and emptied it into the toilet.

"Maybe something to drink before I sit back down. Some iced tea or a bottle of water?"

"Yeah, a bottle of water would be good."

I walked to the end of the house, wrestled a bottle of water from the case on the front floorboard of the truck cab, and placed it on the shelf beside the bed.

"Thank you so much. I feel horrible asking you to do all these things."

"Well, don't. You've got a broken leg. Just don't get too used to all this service." I laughed.

I sat back down with my laptop, wondering if I had anything to write after all. Whatever it was that had been burning in my brain had fizzled out. Kaput. Gone.

Less than two years ago, when Michael had tripped on a chunk of broken sidewalk in our neighborhood and shattered his shoulder, I had spent almost three months as a fulltime caregiver. This included assisting with daily care like bathing and dressing and driving him to medical appointments. It also included daily trips with him to our neighborhood Publix Supermarket for groceries. This was usually his one trip out of the house each day, and he looked forward to it. "Hunting for food for dinner," he would say with a laugh. It was a line we had heard from some stupid musical dance show we had seen at a local community theatre years earlier that had struck us as funny. My hubby loved his daily shopping trips for food, insisting that everything stayed fresher longer and better in Publix than it did in our kitchen.

The year before Michael's shoulder injury, he had nursed me through two knee replacements. Standing beside the bed in our RV, watching Michael struggle to get comfortable, I remembered those 'in sickness and in health' and 'till death do us part' lines we had repeated back in 2006. We had uttered those vows, back when we both enjoyed unlimited mobility and glowed with vibrancy and vim. This getting old business had come without much warning.

Despite our physical deteriorations and limitations, Michael still wanted the RV travel and lifestyle. Maybe even more now than before. Perhaps we both could see the handwriting on the wall. Now, one week into this trip, Michael lay in bed with a broken leg.

In retrospect, we could only laugh that we should have waited until the rain stopped before setting up the RV. One wet slippery RV step had been all it took for Michael to slip and break a leg. Now our trip had changed unalterably.

The Long-Suffering RV Caregiver

While hanging out in Austin had initially seemed like a cool thing to do, the reality of our circumstances removed the glamour factor in short order. Michael's difficulty moving around with a broken leg made any outing a tedious and grueling ordeal. We reconciled ourselves to long days cooped up in our tiny RV, with only each other and our electronics to keep us stimulated and hopefully happy.

It turned out to be a good, productive time for me. My publisher had started the editing/revising process on *The Reluctant RV Wife*, and I needed time to concentrate on the rewrite. As it turned out, I was able to get the job done, despite more interruptions than I would have liked. I found deep satisfaction in knowing the book had been both written and revised from the three-square-foot area on our RV sofa, which I referred to as my 'RV office.'

Michael's broken leg made me think about caregiving, a role I had heard and read about but only recently had experienced first-hand. If this was a test I faced, my competitive self wanted to ace it. Ever the underachiever in so many ways, I had vowed a few years back to leave my mark on the earth by writing a book that would last after I died. Suddenly caring for my husband felt like a much higher calling. Caregiving was more important than writing.

I bucked up a bit more and steeled my resolve not to falter. I remembered my mother and her horrific fall that resulted in a broken neck that ended her life. I realized that most of us did not get to choose how we die. I had always assumed I would live independently, with my faculties intact, until sudden death from a massive heart attack (my father had set this as the bar to reach). I had never factored in caring for a disabled spouse during my final years.

"Can't wait to get this cast off," Michael said. "I'll be as good as new again in a couple more weeks."

"Sounds good." I realized how lucky I was that my husband was maintaining such a positive attitude about his injury. If he could remain so upbeat, it was indeed time for me to make some adjustments.

It was past time to give up my long-suffering attitude and get back to the mission of eking as much marrow from life as possible. With that insight, following a stagnant, bone-dry period of a couple of months in which not a single creative thought felt ready to slip from my fingertips into a Word document, I sat down at my laptop and sighed as the words gushed forth.

CHAPTER 36

My Friends Got Here as Fast as They Could

We arrived at the trendy Parkside Seafood Restaurant on E. 6th Street, downtown Austin, for a quick dinner before the eight o'clock show at Esther's Follies, which was two blocks away. Michael's broken leg, combined with the cracked, uneven streets and sidewalks due to construction, meant moving the car between the two establishments, putting us on a tight timeline to get out of the restaurant and into our seats for the vaudeville/political satire comedy show on time. I had snagged us a couple of stools at the bar—a fortuitous grab—where we would eat. The wait for a table was almost an hour.

I studied the two young bartenders, both attractive women, maybe in their mid-twenties. Both wore olive-green t-shirts, black aprons, and denim bottoms—one a pair of jeans and the other a pair of shorts. The woman in shorts had tattoos covering her arms and legs, designs I did not recognize, and from which I was unable to extract any meaning. She also sported piercings in her nose and on both ears, and perhaps even other places which were not visible to the casual observer. The second bartender, with black-rimmed glasses and a large beauty mark on her left cheek, displayed no ink or piercings. They had both pulled their long hair into ponytails, which was not noteworthy except for the identical olive-green highlights streaking through their locks—a pale olive-green, but unmistakably of the same color family as their t-shirts.

"Think I could turn my hair green?"

"Sure. Just buy some green shit and spray it in," Michael said.

"I'm not sure it's that easy. I knew a woman in my Friday morning writing group with blue hair, and she said she had it done professionally at a salon." I took another sip of red wine. "Think green hair is a requirement for employment here?" Michael shrugged a nonverbal response.

Our sixteen-dollar miniature cheeseburgers, reduced almost to slider-size, dripped juiciness and flavor. The chef had dotted our crispy fries with roasted Italian parsley, minced garlic, and Parmesan cheese. My fifteen-dollar glass of cabernet sauvignon proved the perfect accompaniment, although I felt sure Michael would have argued that his Beck's beer was better.

The multiple-tattooed and pierced bartender asked about Michael's leg. His bulky KneeRover and my awkward maneuvering of it through crowds always attracted attention. This time I had managed to get the damned thing right up to the bar and had parked it behind our stools. While the bartender listened attentively to Michael's long story of how he broke his leg, I sensed this young woman was neither enchanted nor charmed with my husband's recounting of our retirement travels across the United States.

And why should our story interest someone so young? I looked around the bar, realizing once again we were the oldest folks there, probably by a couple of decades. We could have been grandparents to a fair number of customers. My inventory of the patrons revealed well-heeled millennials, straight and gay, uniformly Caucasian, and alternative in dress and presentation. These folks would stand out in the Forest Oaks RV Resort just as Michael and I stood out here in this Parkside Seafood Restaurant. While Michael might think what we were doing in our retirements was cool as shit, these young millennials would not likely be impressed by anything we would have to say. Their lives were just beginning; ours were practically over.

"Are you from Austin?" I asked the bartender with the beauty mark.

"Nope. From Houston originally. Been here about five years, though."

"Always lived in Texas?"

"Of course. Is there any other place to live?" She grinned.

"What brought you to Austin?"

"Are you kidding? This is the coolest place on the planet. Why would anyone ever want to live anywhere else?"

"Are all your friends from Texas?"

"Nope, but they got here as soon as they could."

I had to laugh. "Good answer," I said.

I surveyed the crowded bar again and wondered where all the other old geezers were hiding out tonight. It did not seem to be on 6th Street in Austin. Our RV park out in East Austin stayed filled almost to capacity, and with folks who looked like us—retirees, some fulltime, others on long trips or on their way to their summer homes and away from Texas or Florida or wherever they had wintered this year. It was 7:30 p.m., still daylight outside with temperatures in the upper seventies. Had our contemporary RVers already settled down in their recliners for an evening of television? Even if we were home, that would not have been us. We would have been reading, playing Rummikub, maybe watching a movie. We never watched network television, except for the evening news, which my husband thought he would die if he missed.

Why were Michael and I so different? Why were we out chasing down alternative entertainment in our late sixties and early seventies? Had we failed to grow up somewhere along the line? We sometimes joked that we were on a mission to spend all our money before we died, but this lifestyle of ours went further than that. And it went further than trying to land a sticker on every state on the United States sticker map pasted on the freezer door of our RV. We were not out here in the world just to check things off a list. We were searching for something, even if it only lasted for a night. I suddenly realized I did not know what it was.

There was a time I considered both of us alcohol-dependent—Michael with his beer, and me with my red wine. While I could stop after one glass of my favorite nectar from the goddess, I could also drink with abandon when circumstances permitted. It could not happen these days, though, not with me as the designated driver for my one-legged husband with the broken fibula. I had never gotten a DUI and refused to risk getting one now, especially not in a new city far from home and stranded with an injured husband. I supposed I should have felt lucky that we were stuck in a place dubbed as America's 'healthiest' city. It made it easier for us to find handicapped parking places, a godsend under our current circumstances.

It hit me, sitting in that trendy Austin bar: we were adrenaline junkies. The insight jolted me, but it rang true. We both liked getting the pulse elevated a bit, be it with happiness or excitement or fear or anger or whatever. We craved the unknown, the novel, the not-yet-experienced. We were too addicted to this external stimulation ever to give it up. Despite my previous protests that I was one who would be content watching the grass grow, it was not true. I had lied.

The next day, I thought again about those two bartenders with the matching olive-green t-shirts and hair. And the one who had said all her friends got to Texas as fast as they could.

I figured we had gotten to Texas as well. We had gotten here literally for the first time several years ago, long before we bought the RV. But figuratively, maybe we had been in Texas our entire lives. As we exited the Parkside to retrieve the C-Max for the two-block trip to Esther's Follies, I understood that I needed to be out in the world almost as much as my husband. From now on, I would think of that urge as 'getting to Texas.'

CHAPTER 37

A Juke Joint is Calling Me Tonight

How many hours could a stressed-out caregiver and a one-legged man stay cooped up in a teeny recreational vehicle before going stark raving mad? It was not only the monotony of the same close quarters, the breathing of shared carbon dioxide for hours on end or having only electronic devices and one well-used Rummikub game for our entertainment. When we tried to sit outside, it was the rain, the heat and humidity, and the humongous mosquitos. Those Texas-sized bugs made sitting at our picnic table unbearable without a quarter-inch layer of DEET slathered on our skin. I could not seem to get comfortable no matter where we sat. Our space was too small, the monotony too great.

    The aspect of Michael's broken leg that bothered me most was the sheer tediousness of having to move like a slug. Every trip, even if only from one end of the RV to the other, took three times longer than usual. Michael was off-balance and had poor control of his KneeRover both from his previous shoulder injury and now from the leg. His navigation felt especially ominous as he moved on uneven sidewalks and across four lanes of traffic when we would go downtown. At every crosswalk, we encountered drivers who had been drinking, an erratic stream of battery-powered scooters ridden with abandon by folks of all ages and sizes, and an unpredictable presence of small darting children and unruly leashed dogs. While I groaned to myself when manipulating the KneeRover in and out of the car, I did not dare complain aloud. My 'work' during our outings was nothing compared to what my poor husband had to do.

We tried to get out of the RV every day, even if it was only to an H-E-B grocery store. If there were supermarkets other than H-E-B in Austin, we did not find them. H-E-B was a considerable chain based in San Antonio, with over 350 stores spread across Texas and northeastern Mexico. The H-E-B was short for Howard E. Butts, the name of the oldest son of the company's founder. Locals liked to say H-E-B stood for 'Here Everything's Better.' Maybe it was.

We checked out several H-E-Bs in Austin and settled on a massive megastore in a newer shopping center. With the supermarket being the most exciting outing of the day, we did not mind driving five miles to get there. The store was worth the fifteen minutes of orange-barreled construction and aggressive Texas drivers. The quality of both the produce and meat was incredible. We found a greater variety of fresh, locally grown fruits and vegetables than I had ever seen in a grocery store in Tampa, Florida. Sorry, Publix, but I believe H.E.B. has you beat.

But sometimes a grocery store was simply not enough. Although the logistics of physically getting us there would be tricky, I decided we needed a night of honky-tonk. Or at least I did. The super-hip SoCo area of Austin sounded like an answer. And weren't we cool, talking about SoCo? When we had been here ten years ago, long before RV ownership was even a glimmer in Michael's eye, Austinites had not yet recognized the potential of the seedy, raunchy area of South Congress Street becoming a trendy hotspot. This strip of restaurants and bars south of the Colorado River had been around for decades and featured nightly entertainment from local musicians. It was possibly the best entertainment in the world, where even a house band in a side-alley dive was a highly competitive gig and something special to hear.

We made The Continental Club at 1315 South Congress Avenue, our juke joint destination for our night out on the town. Established in 1955, The Continental was known as the 'Granddaddy' of the local music venues and the premier site in Austin. The dirty, unfinished floors and the torn upholstery on old Continental automobile seats that served as seating along one wall did not suggest anything classy or special about the place. Management had squeezed ATM and cigarette machines into a dusty, cluttered corner behind a small elevated perch where the sound mixer sat with her controls and monitors.

The motley rag-tag old blues musicians who played to a 6:30 happy hour crowd seemed to love their music as much as the silver-haired audience did. Old geezers filled every available seat and created a standing-room-only crowd at the back. Although we were in the back, I managed to snag a seat for Michael. His KneeRover triggered sympathy.

"Hey, what's with all the old people in here?" I asked my husband. "Don't young people like blues?"

"Oh, it's too early for the millennials. You wouldn't be able to get in here with a crowbar by ten o'clock at night."

We talked to several folks, both during the set as well as during the break. It seemed that most of those old retirees were like us, visiting Austin and wanting an immersion in the local music scene, if only for a couple of hours.

The happy hour band and prices lasted from 6:30 p.m. until 8:00 p.m. For the closing, the old black harmonica player said he wanted to end with one of his favorite songs, "A Juke Joint is Calling Me Tonight." The lyrics told the story of someone who wanted to break out, to break free, to do something wild and outrageous, just for one night. In the song, however, his wife caught him, and she did not think he had any business out juking around when he had a wife and kids back home. In the last verse, the singer lamented his choice to go juking while simultaneously realizing he would do it again.

Michael and I left The Continental Club and walked a block down the hill for dinner at JoAnn's Fine Foods, A Diner for Early Birds and Night Owls. The restaurant was attached to The Austin Motel, and both were déjà vu places for us. When we had visited Austin ten years earlier, we had stayed at the Austin Motel and eaten in this funky little diner. While we ate and chatted with folks sitting around us (because everyone in Austin was super-friendly), I thought about that song. It had been decades since I had gone juking. I wondered if a seventy-one-year-old woman could get away with something so outrageous.

Or what if she went to a juke joint, and no one paid a dab of attention to her?

Fortified by live music, Michael ached for more. He combed *The Chronicle*, Austin's weekly entertainment newspaper, to find other clubs and musicians. Several days later, we went to Antone's, one of Austin's original blues bars. Antone's had changed physical locations several times, unlike The Continental Club, which was still at its original location. The performer for this 6:30 happy hour show was The Guy Forsythe Blues Band, and this group knocked the socks off even me. As the set was finishing up around 8:30, I could not stand it anymore.

"I'm going to pass out if I don't eat something," I said. "I've had two glasses of wine on an empty stomach, and I'm getting a headache." I hated to whine and complain, especially since the band had been so phenomenal. However, I was the driver, and I needed food to dilute the alcohol before driving the eight miles back to the RV park. Food was the quickest way to get me sobered up and safe to drive.

"See what the Po' Boys look like here," Michael said. "They told me on the phone they sell several different kinds. We can bring food in here; I've seen several people doing it."

I checked out the Po' Boys, finding them in a small refrigerated case in the gift shop of the club. They looked small and very cold.

"Nope. I don't want a Po' Boy from here," I told Michael when I got back to our table. "I'll walk a couple of blocks; see what kind of take-out I can find. Is that okay with you?"

"Sure. I'd be happy with a hamburger. Anything, really."

Antone's was next door to Eddy V's, a rather expensive restaurant, and right across the street from the Austin Westin Hotel, not a low-rent place either. I walked past Eddy V's, knowing that was not the place for take-out. The Westin had a restaurant and bar on the corner, so I went inside to check out the possibility. I learned I could order hamburgers to go from the bar.

Sweet, I thought, climbing up on a barstool. This was a Thursday evening, and the bar was crowded with businessmen, several of whom had brought their laptops into the bar area, either to continue their day's work or to do whatever.

As I sat alone at the bar waiting for my carryout, I fantasized I was still young and beautiful, that this was the hottest honky-tonk in town, and that I was the sexiest number in the joint. I had on my tightest jeans and a nice hippie-style blouse. So what if I had on my Vionic lace-up walking shoes? There was no way my old arthritic feet were ever going to slip into heels again, no matter how high the stakes or rich the rewards or what kind of juke joint I ended up in. I glanced around, trying to decide if I was disappointed or relieved that not one of those businessmen gave me a second look. I laughed to realize I was probably old enough to be a mother to most of them, the grandmother of a couple.

I pulled out my cell phone and called my daughter.

"I'm at a juke joint, sitting at this bar all alone, and not one man has even looked at me," I said.

"What are you wearing, Mom?"

When I mentioned the hippie blouse, she set me straight. "You have no game! No one picks up hippie chicks." I sighed.

When I got back to Antone's, the second band was up, and Michael had hardly missed me. "Let's eat and leave," he said. "I don't like these guys nearly as much as Guy Forsythe."

"I've been out juking," I said. "Do you care?"

"Oh, yeah? Was it fun?"

I rolled my eyes. "Not sure I remember how to play those games anymore. Nothing happened."

"Oh, sweetie. You're still a hottie in my book. I'll buy you an Antone's t-shirt on our way out, okay?"

"What is this? An offer of a consolation prize?"

"Nope. Your consolation prize would have been any of those juke joint losers you might have ended up with."

While I was not convinced a Westin businessman in an Armani suit would necessarily have been a loser, it nevertheless felt pretty good to stumble back into Antone's to a needy, one-legged husband who loved me.

I now understood that the fantasy of a juke joint calling me at this age was nothing but a flicker of a memory of a life that ended decades ago. Seriously, I would hate to have all those raging hormones still jerking me around. Six-thirty happy hours with grey-haired tourists in this hip town was about all the excitement I could deal with these days.

CHAPTER 38

Not Everything in Texas is Big

"Isn't Texas cute?" read the caption on a t-shirt I spotted in Valdez, Alaska. The graphic on the front showed an outline of the state of Alaska and a tiny inset of a bright red Texas sitting inside Alaska. The t-shirt provided a powerful visual of the vastness of Alaska, a hugeness hard to describe in words. I did not buy that shirt, and I have regretted it ever since.

"According to Yelp, that saying that 'everything's bigger in Texas' is sort of a joke," I said. "This article says it's usually said just to goad tourists since Texas is the largest of the lower forty-eight states." It was pouring down rain, and the TV news warned of tornadoes and flooding. Although it was only 2:30 p.m., we were hunkered down in our RV in a lovely park on the outskirts of Austin, perhaps for the rest of the day and night. I hunched over my laptop screen, trying to learn more about this state that had become our temporary home. Michael sat at the table with his broken leg propped up on the bench.

"Mosquitos are certainly big here." Michael laughed.

"The strawberry buried in that little box from the H-E-B must have been the largest strawberry in the world," I said. We had taken a picture of it and posted it on Facebook. The damned strawberry almost filled the palm of my hand, and for a woman, my hands are large. "And I've never seen so many huge pickup trucks, or so many cowcatchers on the fronts of them," I continued. I shuddered every time I had to drive on these superhighways and beltways around Austin. Almost every road had as many orange cones and barrels as it did automobiles, and every automobile went at least ten miles per hour over the speed limit as it tailgated, swerved, and cut off other vehicles. Austin driving made me want a celebratory drink every time we made it back to the RV in one piece. But I resisted.

We learned shortly after our arrival that not everything in Texas was big. Owners of our Oak Forest RV Park were expanding to include a community called Village Farm, made up of Tiny Homes inside the RV park. Established in 2018, management described it as 'Austin's First Tiny Homes Community.' Six models of Tiny Homes, one of which served as a sales office, sat at the front near the park's entrance.

I did not understand the appeal of those dollhouses. I walked through the furnished models, impressed with how interior designers had decorated them in charming and enchanting ways. The skill of the designers blurred, maybe even hid, an awareness of what was missing in those gingerbread houses. Some of the things would have been a significant lack for us, such as not having room for a table and chairs where four people could sit together for a meal. Most of the models lacked the space to install a washer and dryer large enough to put a queen-sized set of sheets and a few pairs of socks in at the same time. We would have a hard time adjusting to a bedroom so narrow there was no room for bedside tables to hold reading lamps, books, and an alarm clock. A few of the Tiny Homes models had loft bedrooms, but the rooms were too shallow for even a six-year-old to stand up in or for an adult-sized desk and chair. Yes, those Tiny Homes were adorable, but for fulltime living? I knew immediately they were not for me.

While the base price of these Tiny Homes started around fifty-thousand, by the time one added all the a la carte items, such as appliances, air conditioning, and outside decking and a porch, the cost of one of these 399 square foot houses approached $150 thousand. It seemed exorbitant.

"That's more than our RV cost," I said to Michael.

"But a lot less than what most of these Class A motorhomes cost. Remember that two-and-a-half-million-dollar baby we saw at the RV Show in Tampa?"

"I'm trying to wrap my arms around these Tiny Homes," I said. "I think we have more storage space in our 26-foot Class C motorhome than we'd have in a tiny house."

"I don't get it. Why would anyone choose to live in a tiny space like that that you couldn't move around? I'd want my tiny home to have wheels, so we could change locations. Like what we have. What's wrong with our tiny home?"

"Not a thing," I said. "Except it wouldn't be called 'a tiny home.' Ours is an RV. So why are they putting these tiny homes in the middle of an RV park?"

"Wow. I can't believe this." I was on my end of the sofa, laptop on my lap, reading about the tiny home movement. "Says in this article that Jerry Brown, former governor of California, now lives in a tiny redwood cabin in the middle of the desert with his wife and dogs. They have no heat, no running water. Says they cuddle with the dogs at night to stay warm. He was seventy-eight years old when he moved out to the desert to live like this. Think this is all true?"

"Sounds bizarre," Michael said. "I'd certainly try to find some verification before I put that factoid in writing anywhere."

"Think Jerry Brown has lost his friggin' mind?" I could not fathom doing something so physically uncomfortable at age seventy-eight, but maybe Jerry Brown's body was not riddled with osteoarthritis the way mine was.

I conducted additional online research about Jerry Brown's tiny home in Colusa County, California, an hour south of Sacramento. Per *The New York Times*, it was true, except the newspaper reported his age as seventy-seven rather than seventy-eight. Brown's retreat to the desert had not been a spiritual, New Age return to a cave mentality, however. Brown was simply re-staking a claim to the 2,514-acre ranch, Rancho Venada, that had been in the Brown family for the past 150 years. His redwood cabin was just large enough for one air mattress. A compact outhouse sat 200 feet away. Without electricity or cell phone service, there was little for Jerry Brown and his wife to do other than read, take walks with their two Corgis, and sleep. Brown said he was the only one who liked it out there in the desert, a place filled with rattlesnakes and wild boars and where temperatures reached one hundred and ten degrees during the day.

According to the *Times* article, Brown found the solitude and emptiness of the isolated ranch a welcome contrast to the chaos and hecticness of politics. He reportedly looked forward to retirement when his current term as governor ended in 2019. His long-range plan was to rebuild the large ranch house on the ranch that burned to the ground during the 1970s.

Governor Jerry Brown had a plan, and his tiny, unheated, redwood home was a part of that plan.

What was driving contemporary America towards these Lilliputian-sized dwellings? Historically, leaving the family or group to live as a hermit in a cave had deep religious and philosophical roots. Henry David Thoreau's retreat in the late 1800s for two years to his 150 square foot cabin at Walden Pond had been a natural progression from those ancient cave roots. During the 1940s, Buckminster Fuller developed Dymaxion Deployment Units, a sort of miniaturized bombproof shelters that the government manufactured and shipped to military bases around the world to serve as low-cost, secure housing for military families. In the late 1990s, Portland, Oregon, amended its housing regulations to include Accessible Dwelling Units (ADUs), teeny creative habitats for its homeless and low-income populations.

It was easy to understand the attraction of these miniature dwellings as homes for folks who had no other options. While we were hanging out in Austin and learning more about the Tiny Homes movement across the country, we found out that a local nonprofit organization had created an innovative, 27-acre community about a mile from our Austin RV park. We checked it out.

Community First Village, we learned, was a privately funded project that provided "micro-housing" for over 250 previously homeless people. The project placed residents in tiny homes, in salvaged RVs of every shape and size, in tents erected on platforms reminiscent of Girl Scout camp, and in single eight-square-foot cabins with one door and three windows. One resident told us that organizers gave the folks in those one-room cabins a bed, a table, a chair, a small microwave, a crockpot, and a small refrigerator on move-in day. Community kitchens and bathhouses were located throughout the compound.

This Community First Village was intended as a prototype for a cost-efficient way to provide housing and other services for homeless people. The Village required a certain number of volunteer hours of service from its residents, and it also provided jobs for those who were able to work. One job-producing industry was a mobile food delivery service called Loaves and Fishes. The Village had a huge kitchen on the premises where residents prepared food, packaged it, and loaded it in more than a dozen delivery trucks. Residents made daily trips to downtown Austin to deliver meals to the homeless. The concept of previously homeless people now gainfully employed feeding homeless people on the streets was almost too beautiful for words.

Community First Village had several other cottage industries on its campus, van service to transport employed residents to jobs off-campus and back, a free health care clinic, and a cooperative store. The concept and the reality of what that private, non-profit group had accomplished were phenomenal. It was a shame more cities were not paying attention.

I understood very well why those miniature homes might be ideal for single homeless people who lacked the resources to secure shelter for themselves. For charitable institutions providing housing and other services for homeless people, something this small met the criterion of shelter. Folks brought in off the streets and placed in adequate housing did not generally arrive with lots of furniture, household furnishings, and dozens of pairs of shoes.

But what was the attraction of these tiny houses for middle-class people with financial resources? I have talked to folks who would give their right arms to live in one. While at the Oak Park RV Park, I chatted with a couple of people who lived in Tiny Homes, and they remained enthralled, even after several years. I observed visitors walking through the model homes, gushing and oohing over how adorable they found the little houses and how much they wanted one.

I supposed many explanations were possible. The 'hermit living in the cave theory' reflected a longing for simplicity, self-sufficiency, and oneness with the natural world. Marshall McLuhan said, "the medium is the message," and life in a Tiny Home theoretically could both shape and reflect one's thoughts and behaviors.

The manufacturers of Tiny Homes maintained that reduced living space reduced one's carbon imprint. They built the houses to be energy efficient. The sales representatives at Village Farm claimed that a monthly electric bill in one of their Tiny Homes would never exceed fifty bucks, no matter how low one moved the thermostat in the summer or how high one raised it in the winter.

I suppose there would be something undeniably 'cool' about living in one of those little dollhouses. Tiny Home living would most definitely come with built-in bragging rights because it was hip and nonmainstream.

I found yet another explanation on the Internet of what made these tiny houses so appealing. While tiny house living could be both economical and sustainable, a more important but almost unconscious motivation could be an attempt to have nearly total despotic control over one's environment. Conceived as a 'regressive fantasy,' living in something the size of a playhouse could make inhabitants feel like children again. The residents could pretend to be and feel like kings and queens in these miniaturized homes. They could imagine themselves large and powerful, a feeling contrasting sharply to the 'real world,' where most people felt no power over much of anything in their environments.

Minimalistic living was an aspect of RVing that I loved. I liked to travel light, to pare everything down to essentials, and to leave all the fluff behind. As I considered this Village Farm Tiny Homes Community and the Community First Village of 250 previously-homeless people picked up off the streets of Austin and given a chance to revitalize their lives, I tried to sort out why one would choose a tiny home over a recreational vehicle if one wanted to live 'small.' Maybe money, or the lack thereof, drove the decision. Homeless people did not have the resources to plunk down a hundred thousand dollars on a Tiny Home in Oak Forest nor pay the $600 a month fee for the site and amenities.

Lot 10 in the Oak Forest RV Park, where we had landed and felt stranded, felt smaller by the day as our intended one-week in Austin stretched to five weeks. As I thought about those Tiny Homes, I concluded our little 26-foot RV probably had more storage than I had seen in the Tiny Homes models. I knew for sure we were more comfortable than we would have been in a one-room redwood cabin in the middle of the desert, or a micro-house squeezed three feet apart from each other in the Community First Village, or even in one of the Tiny Homes dollhouses nestled among RVs in the Oak Forest RV Park. I found the diversity of how people chose to live amazing.

One could easily view Texas as pure hyperbole. Everything about this State was intense. The hugeness of the State geographically contrasted dramatically with the smallness of the Tiny Homes. I sat at my laptop and, on a whim, googled that 'isn't Texas cute?' t-shirt I had seen in Alaska. It might be time to place the order.

CHAPTER 39

My Worthless Bottle Tree

Coming home was always a weird feeling after being on the road for months at a time. I knew every inch of every surface in our little Thor Four Winds. I knew how that RV looked, smelled, and felt, inside and out. While I was not sick of the RV, nor especially even tired of it, by the end of every trip, I wanted to go home so badly I could taste it. I felt like a horse nearing the stable. The closer we got to Tampa, the more excited I became. If I were a horse, I would have picked up speed at this point in the trip and barreled towards my stall, leaving any hapless rider holding on for dear life. Even if the trip had been wonderful, which they all have been at least most of the time, my 'homing instinct' always kicked in, and one part of me became like a child on Christmas Eve waiting for Santa Claus.

There was another side of homecoming, however, that gradually pushed its way into my consciousness over the years. Mixed in with impatience to see my house and yard, there was absolute dread. I did not want to do it. It went beyond the four or five days of inevitable exhaustion as we reintegrated in a different lifestyle, transferred things from the RV back into the house, washed and cleaned every square inch of the RV as we prepared it for storage, sorted through mountains of accumulated mail, restocked the pantry and refrigerator, scheduled overdue dentist

My Worthless Bottle Tree

and eye exam appointments, and caught up with friends. The list went on almost ad infinitum. I knew I could not begin pulling the weeds out of my flower beds and tending to my plants until we had done everything else. Michael continued to view gardening as my hobby, and I supposed I should, as well.

But there was another reason I felt reluctant to return home. Mysterious things often happened while we were away, and they usually were not good.

Michael and I bought our house in 1997. After living in it for more than twenty years, I knew it well, though possibly not as well as I knew the insides of the RV. Our little traveling abode offered about 75 square feet of living space while our three-bedroom Tampa house offered about 2,300 square feet, not including the garage. In our house, we went into the smaller of our two front bedrooms when we needed to get the luggage out of the closet. Otherwise, it sat unused except for occasional overnight guests. I had set up a computer desk and table along one wall in the larger front bedroom and claimed it as my office. I could sit at the desk and look out the window at my beautiful landscaping, including a bit of Southern funk art.

Shortly after becoming a Master Gardener in 2013, I went on a tear and re-worked my entire yard. One of my projects had been the construction of a bottle tree using a fence post, six-inch nails, and fourteen sparkling empty Heineken beer bottles. (Michael assisted by drinking the beer.)

The bottle tree legend originated in the Congo during the ninth century. Historians believed African slaves brought the tradition to the southern United States during the nineteenth century. According to the legend, upended bottles protected the home by capturing evil spirits that wandered around the property at night. In the morning, when daylight appeared, the spirits found themselves trapped in the bottles, and the sun would kill them.

Traditionally, folks used crepe myrtle trees and Cobalt blue bottles for making bottle trees. The crepe myrtle had Biblical references to the great Diaspora, and the blue color represented a crossroad between heaven and earth, the dead and the living. In folk-art circles, however, a wide variety of ways were now used to integrate bottles into gardens as artistic expressions. I loved this kind of lore, and I had loved making my bottle tree.

I was not a superstitious person. Nevertheless, I had always chuckled in my mind to think that maybe my bottle tree offered our home a small measure of protection when we went off on the road for months at the time.

Unfortunately, with every return home, I found that my bottle tree had failed to do its job in at least a few areas. Sometimes I reeled from all the strange things that happened in our absence.

When we went away on long trips, our next-door neighbor came into the house every couple of weeks to make sure everything was okay. He checked the thermostat to confirm the air conditioning was still at eighty degrees, he looked under every sink for possible water leaks, and he flushed every toilet to help prevent rings from stagnant water. In return, he brought his kids over almost every day during the summer to swim in our pool. We all thought it was a pretty good perk for keeping an eye on our property. (We also paid him for other services, like daily sorting of the mail and notifying us of anything that looked official.) A neighbor with a landscaping business came over every few weeks to trim out-of-control shrubbery and to attack emerging weeds. We paid a pool service to come weekly to make sure the water stayed chemically balanced the way it was supposed to and to vacuum up any debris.

Given that someone was in the house checking on things regularly, we had to wonder how things could have gone so wrong.

We had arrived home a couple of hours earlier, and I was unloading toiletries in the master bathroom. "Hey, Michael," I yelled. "I plugged in my toothbrush, and nothing happened. This outlet is dead."

Michael came from the other end of the house to look. He tried his toothbrush at his sink and had the same result. "That's strange. Look, the phone in here is dead, too."

We always flipped the circuit breaker on the water heater when we went away for even a week and had learned it could take a while for fifty-five gallons of water to heat up. Later that night, when we took showers, we both noticed that the water was barely tepid. We were too hot and tired to complain, though. The next day would be soon enough to carp.

We also discovered that the disposal in the kitchen sink did not work. While Michael successfully revived it with a little wrench we had never used before, our contractor later examined the disposal, declared it to be on its last leg, and said we should replace it.

By the time our contractor arrived to look at the dead bathroom outlets, we knew our water heater was not working right. Given that it was nineteen years old, which was about three times the current life expectancy of new ones, I could only shrug when our contractor told us we needed a new one.

All the inside repairs and replacements cost us more than a thousand dollars. Pretty disheartening for an empty house that no-one had used, right? How did things die when no one had even touched them?

I wished those inside items constituted the entire list. The most significant malfunction, and by far the most expensive, sat in the garage. We had wisely contacted our insurance agent about Michael's Nissan Altima, which we left in the garage while we were gone. The agent told us about a temporary plan that would reduce the insurance rates to about a third of the current cost while the car sat idle. Yeah!

When Michael excitedly got into his car for the first time to back out of the garage, the steering wheel hardly turned, even with great effort. "Oh, my God," Michael said. He had stepped out of the car and looked down to find the entire area under the car covered with greenish-colored, soupy gunk. "I think all the transmission fluid has leaked out." He called our mechanic, who advised him to call a tow service to get the car to his shop.

The car news proved dismaying. We would never know why the fluid leaked out of the transmission. It was a bizarre thing to happen while the car did nothing but sit in the garage. But even stranger, the entire transmission froze up, and we now faced a three to four-thousand-dollar repair bill. Luckily, even though the car was almost seven years old, Michael remembered that he had purchased an extended warranty, and he was able to find the paperwork. The contract would not expire for another three months, which made Michael a very happy and lucky man. It took over two weeks to arrange all the necessary warranty inspections, authorizations, and repairs. In the end, Michael's expenses totaled less than a hundred dollars, and his car now had a new transmission.

So far, we had been covering all the bases and getting our growing list of breakdowns repaired. The demands of the inside malfunctions and the car problem, combined with unpacking, cleaning, and getting repairs made on the RV, kept us focused and busy nonstop during our first two weeks back at home.

Eventually, though, I could no longer ignore the call of my yard. I ached to get back out there and get my hands dirty. I started in the front yard, reacquainting myself with my inground plants and tending to plants in potted containers. My neighbor had done a remarkable job with the landscaping, and the place still looked great from the street. I had to grin when realizing that even though I had been gone for almost six months, my yard was still perhaps the prettiest one on the street. I felt proud of the Master Gardening information I had successfully put into practice by integrating native plants among the exotics and trying to put the *right plants in the right places*. All that research-based information from the University of Florida worked.

The back yard held the biggest surprises, though. First, I found garbage strewn along the fence rows—anything from wads of aluminum foil to plastic containers and lids to crumpled McDonald's wrappers. My neighbors would never have tossed garbage over their fences into my yard. It was beyond comprehension that anyone I knew in my subdivision would litter even their own yards, let alone mine. I removed all the mysterious items but never came up with a satisfying explanation for how they came to rest along my property line. I speculated that the culprits were rats, raccoons, or armadillos, but I did not want to believe those creatures lived in my neighborhood.

The greatest surprise was the clump of papaya trees, two of them over ten feet tall, growing along a back fence. Where had they come from? I had not planted them. I considered that maybe a bird transported seeds and deposited them in a clump. It had rained almost every day we had been gone, and everything had mushroomed in size. But while papaya trees grew fast and strong in Tampa, and ideal growing conditions had prevailed, I could not imagine a seed germinating and reaching ten feet in the five short months we had been gone. It made more sense that someone had planted papayas growing in containers, with strong root systems already. My neighbors and my landscape guy all swore they knew nothing about those papaya trees. I would never know how they got there. Meanwhile, I noticed several small fruits, maybe three inches long, that seemed to grow before my eyes. I might get to eat papaya with my Christmas dinner if the weather held out. I fertilized the trees and vowed to keep them watered.

I thought back to my bottle tree and its job of warding off the evil spirits or at least catching the ones that lurked around at night. I concluded my tree had failed. Electrical outlets had stopped conducting power, elements had corroded in the water heater, the disposal had frozen, transmission fluid had drained out of the Nissan and the transmission had seized, and something strewed litter all over the backyard.

Were the papaya trees a peace offering from evil spirits of some sort? An attempt at redemption following so much mischief? Or maybe the trees came first and were a gift from some positive energy or force, leading the evil spirits to do destructive, damaging things as revenge against the successful planting of something delightful?

At first, it had not seemed unusual that a couple of things had gone wrong around the house while we were gone. It had happened before—we would come home and find something had mysteriously stopped working. This time though, it was a bit too much.

I decided I needed to consider another bottle tree before we took off again. This one needed to go in the backyard. In case it made a difference, I committed to cobalt blue for this second tree, in case blue might work better than green. I knew of a winery not too far away that would save bottles for me if I asked. I called them that afternoon.

CHAPTER 40

Well, Duh!

We had logged almost 50,000 miles on our Ford Triton's 10-cylinder engine of our Thor Four Winds motorhome. We had spent at least two nights in the RV in forty-nine of the fifty United States. I was confident we would never make it in the RV to Hawaii despite my husband's strong desire to do so. We had taken road trips as short as three nights and as long as six months.

We had watched temperatures soar to 108 degrees and sink to seventeen degrees. We had seen rain and hail, fog and smoke, sand and mud, clay and rock, swamp and desert. We had felt humidity so thick it weighted down our shoulders. We had seen tornado funnels in the distance and felt hurricane-force winds in our faces. We had seen flat, endless plains and mountains that rose over 20,000 feet. We had not yet seen snow and sleet, but I knew we would.

We had encountered many species of wildlife, including feared grizzly bears and docile dolphins. We had stood as close as ten feet from a massive bison in the wild. We had managed to avoid the ubiquitous rattlesnakes, despite encountering enough warning signs to put the fear of God in me for the rest of my life.

We had RVed with arthritic knees, both before and after surgeries. We had taken off with a shattered shoulder, having a minimal range of motion and still inflamed and excruciatingly painful. We had experienced a broken leg while RVing that involved casts, a KneeRover, and five weeks of physical therapy. I thought I had had a bad tooth in Portland and prepared for a root canal and crown while on the road. Maybe those evil spirits my Tampa bottle tree had failed to catch had now found us in other parts of the country.

We had camped during every month of the year, and we had spent every major holiday in the RV at least once. We had yet to make a birthday trip, but that was no big deal. Birthdays would be easy enough to do since ours were both in February and eleven days apart.

We had hit the four corners of the country—Florida, California, Washington/Alaska, and Maine. We had driven through fields of every agricultural crop imaginable, except for cannabis. We had seen herds of every species of livestock we could think of, including llamas and ostriches. We had seen tractors and farm equipment that boggled our minds in terms of size, sophistication, and function.

We had camped beside both the Atlantic and the Pacific Oceans. We had crossed major rivers and tiny streams. We had seen all five of the Great Lakes plus many vast and beautiful lakes not considered 'great' but should have been labeled great because they were awesomely fantastic. We had seen ponds so huge they should have been dubbed lakes and lakes so tiny they should have been dubbed puddles.

I completed a draft of a book-length manuscript during a long road trip in 2017 and almost completed another book-length manuscript on the road in 2018. Combined with a handful of essays and nonfiction stories, I had probably written over 200,000 words about traveling across the country in this bouncy tin-can house while doing it. Soon it may be time to write about something other than RVing.

It was time for a final reckoning. My ambivalent reluctance could not continue. Not only was Michael tired of it, but I was also weary of it.

At the beginning of RV travel, I longed to return home after a couple of months on the road. When we would get back, I would walk around my yard and look at all the plants before I stepped inside the house. Sometimes I even picked up the hose and watered a few things or reached down and pulled a few weeds. My heart broke when I saw a plant that had languished or died and rejoiced when I saw one that had thrived in my absence.

Each RV trip became more natural, and each return home less dramatic. When we arrived home the last time after being on the road for six months, I went inside immediately to check things out. It was about five days before I walked outside to look at the plants. Somehow, those plants were not that important to me anymore.

The same held with my writing/critique groups and with my Toastmaster clubs. In the beginning, I missed the meetings terribly and worried that my friends would forget about me while I was away. On the road, I became sad when emails, text messages, and phone calls tapered off.

"You should be glad no one's bothering you," Michael had said with a laugh.

"They've forgotten about me." I almost wailed in despair.

"They haven't forgotten you," Michael said with a snort. "What would they need to talk with you about? You're not working on any projects with them, no business that needs discussion."

After a couple of years and several RV trips of various lengths, I realized Michael was right. My friends had not forgotten about me, and we made enough Facebook posts for them to know exactly where we were and what we were doing. I began to realize that upon our return, my friends and I picked up again right where we had left off. My comings and goings in and out of their lives did not seem to faze them. Maybe it was time to stop letting them faze me.

We had worked on emptying our house for two years. All the stuff that had filled it meant even less to me today than it had two years ago. That recognition reinforced my dawning awareness that maybe I was there, with "there" being that magical point when I could theoretically walk out of my house, leaving everything behind, and never look back.

It was time to tackle the house again, and this time to finish the job. Every nonessential item had to go. It would be powerfully liberating to surround myself only with the items I needed and wanted. RVing had taught me that the list could be very short indeed—toiletries, medications, a few pairs of shoes, a couple of jackets and rain gear, and a few changes of clothes. And of course, because we lived in the twenty-first-century and enjoyed our connections, we had to have our electronic toys. For me, they included a laptop, a notebook, an iPad, and a cellphone. Michael lacked the notebook computer, but he could not live without a television (to stream movies) and a DVD player (for Red Box rentals for those remote areas when we did not have Internet service).

Michael posited his inane notion that we should travel the country in an RV in 2015, a few months after he retired. I had seen him in what I considered mid-life crisis mode. When we bought the RV, I thought his yen to travel was a way to fill the emotional void created by his retirement. Michael denied that a crisis was involved. Instead, he pointed out that he had spent a long career in sales. "I've lived and worked on the road for decades. Why would I want to stay in one place? I'm a traveling man!"

Duh! I had never thought about it in that way, but he was right. He loved driving, loved seeing the open road through the front windshield, and loved the stimulation of an everchanging environment around him. New people, new places, new experiences—my ADHD husband needed and thrived on constant change.

I found it ironic that the solution to Michael's 'retirement crisis,' which in retrospect was not a crisis at all, triggered an emotional tsunami in me. I had been retired five years when we bought this RV, and I loved the life I had built for myself, especially gardening and writing. Looking back, I now realized that all my whining and bitching about being torn away from my 'real life' to go bouncing across the country in a tin-can house was my own crisis. I was getting old. I had been desperately grasping at activities and at people trying to find meaning. I had needed surgery (two knee replacements), and I had never had an operation or a significant health issue before. I looked ahead and panicked at how little time I had left to live. A sense of urgency set in to 'get it right' before

I died. I saw the RV as an impediment to accomplishing the things I wanted to do before it was too late.

Nevertheless, I packed up my stuff and rode shotgun with my husband in our RV, initially with great reluctance. I hoped he would change and become happy to stay home or, better yet, would discover that RVing was not what he had wanted after all.

It took a couple more years for me to realize I was the one who was changing. I began to view this nomadic lifestyle as being closer to my 'truth' than the house in suburbia with its manicured yard, and a couple of hundred orchids on the lanai had ever been. As I looked around my over-stuffed house in Tampa and considered Henry David Thoreau's little cabin at Walden Pond, I understood at last what brought a sense of satisfaction to my soul.

The 'duh' moment finally arrived. I had drunk enough of the Kool-Aid to become a believer. I would never live in a cabin in the woods, but I could sure as hell 'suck the marrow out of life' in an RV on the road. It was as close to perfect as I would ever get in this modern, complex twenty-first-century world. All these 'things' in our Tampa house now felt like cinderblocks pulling me underwater, drowning me in an ocean of possessions that now felt like junk.

I felt embarrassed to have been such a slow learner. I threw hissy fits when I should have been doing happy dances at this opportunity to grow, learn, and change. I had spent over four years feeling angry at my husband for dragging me off on the road for months at the time. I was so busy, hoping he would change that I had not recognized the changes in myself.

CHAPTER 41

Reluctant No More

A stranger approached me at a book festival not long ago. My large cardboard poster of the cover from my book, *The Reluctant RV Wife,* had caught her eye. I was standing in the booth with a few other Sunbury Press authors, with books ranging in content from murder mysteries to Holocaust survivors to mid-Eastern love stories.

"Is that a true story?" she asked me, looking at the title of my book.

I laughed. "Yes, it is. I never wanted an RV—my husband did."

"And he dragged you off in that thing?"

"Well . . . I did agree to it, though I hadn't wanted to."

"Back when my husband asked me to marry him over forty years ago," the woman said, "I looked him straight in the eye and told him there were three things I absolutely would never abide." She paused, then continued. "Cheating, beating, and RVing."

I burst into a deep belly laugh. Other nearby women who overheard the conversation laughed as well. I could not have said it better, no matter how hard I tried. She had nailed it. "I'm going to steal those words," I said. "I love that story."

That woman's words followed me home and would not go away. I had met many women and a handful of men who had said they wanted no part of RVing but had spouses who did. I now wondered how those adverse individuals could be so adamant if they had never traveled in one? Would RV travel have changed them if they had been willing to try it?

RV travel had changed me, and I now found myself backed into a corner. Reluctance had been my schtick when Michael and I purchased our RV in late 2015. I had written an entire book screaming my resistance to RV travel. I continued to cling to my proclaimed status as a reluctant wife, although I now did it with a thinly veiled smile. My reluctance, which had been huge and all-encompassing, had dwindled to a barely discernable level. I no longer hated packing up the RV and hitting the road, and I no longer spent entire trips lamenting all I had left behind. Reluctance no longer fit. It was past time to let it go.

I could not believe how long I had clung to the misguided notion that I needed roots, both literal and figurative ones. It was a mistaken notion that my house in suburban Tampa filled those needs. I now understood I did not need a garden to connect me to the earth or casual acquaintances to give meaning to my life. I had been misguided to think my house and possessions said anything at all about who and what I was.

> *"Simplicity, simplicity, simplicity! I say, let your affairs be as two or three, and not a hundred or a thousand; instead of a million count half a dozen, and keep your accounts on your thumbnail."*
>
> —Henry David Thoreau, Excerpt from *Walden; or Life in the Woods* [Boston: Ticknor and Fields, 1854]

Thoreau said our lives are "frittered away by detail" and that we must simplify. I had resisted RVing as a lifestyle for almost five years, but now it made sense to me on every level—physical, social, political, philosophical, spiritual, and emotional.

I knew that RVs broke down, that campgrounds filled up, and that weather sometimes interfered with plans. But I also knew that life on the road was simpler than life in a large metropolitan area. Everything slowed down when RVing, especially us. We ate when we were hungry, rested when we were tired, and came and went as we chose. There was not much clock-watching. We had few appointments and little need to know what time it was, other than Michael's addiction to the *ABC News* every night.

On the road, we did not have a big house to clean, a pool to maintain, and a yard to weed, prune, fertilize, and water.

We still had bills to pay while we traveled—for cellphones, Internet access, and other electronics, for medical and automobile insurances, and incidentals like clothes and food. But what if we no longer had to pay taxes and insurance on our house, or exorbitant electric and utility bills every month? What if we never had to replace a worn-out water heater, or call a repairman when the ice maker in the refrigerator stopped working, or pay our much-younger next-door neighbor to go up on our roof to clean off the leaves and tree limbs?

Michael and I were now both in our seventies. Our bodies showed signs of wear and tear. But we had learned on our last RV trip that good medical care was available in most places in the country and that almost every medical provider accepted our insurance plans. We needed regular refills on prescription medications, and until we found another community we liked as well as Tampa, we could always go back to our 'hometown' a couple of times a year for medical, dental, and vision checkups. What better place to spend winter than Florida anyway, especially since we had friends, family, and connections there?

In *The Reluctant RV Wife*, I had metaphorically screamed my rage and threw existential meltdowns regularly as I tried to make sense of changes brought about by retirement, aging, and medical issues. I looked down the road of life and understood in my bones that the proverbial light at the end of the tunnel was going to appear someday in the future, probably long before I was ready. I realized the finite nature of time and the need to seize everything I could before I squandered away the opportunities. Thoreau's words returned with a vengeance and brought me full circle, back to being nineteen years old when I had first read *Walden*. Now my insights had matured, and I had over seven decades of experience with which to reevaluate them.

"It's about time you came to your senses," Michael said to me. "Can't believe it took you so long."

"Guess I'm a slow learner."

"You're sure this time?"

"I was sure the last time, but you fell and broke your shoulder. Remember?"

"But you equivocated. You threw another hissy-fit, came up with all kinds of reasons we should keep the house and travel part-time."

"Michael, I am truly at the point I can walk out of this house, leave every bit of this crap behind, and never look back. I'm over it, and I'm ready to go."

"What was the turning point? What finally pushed you to this decision?"

"Let me go look it up on the Internet. I'll read you a quote." I jumped up from the dining room table and headed for my office. As I opened my laptop, I felt chagrined that I could not pick up my almost untouched new copy of *Walden* and find the quote underlined on a dog-eared page. Why had I ever let the original copy that I had read as a freshman in college go to Goodwill during one of my purges? I vowed that on our next road trip, I would give Henry David Thoreau the respect he still deserved, 166 years after the original publication of the book. I found the quote I was looking for and printed it out.

"Here it is, Michael." I returned to the dining room. "Here's the quote that changed my mind." I read it aloud.

> *"Simplify your life. Don't waste the years struggling for things that are unimportant. Don't burden yourself with possessions. Keep your needs and wants simple and enjoy what you have. Don't destroy your peace of mind by looking back, worrying about the past. Live in the present. Simplify!"*
>
> —Henry David Thoreau, Excerpt from *Walden*; or *Life in the Woods* [Boston: Ticknor and Fields, 1854]

We were going to do it this time. We had initiated the black tank, the one my husband wanted nothing but liquids ever to enter, and nothing terrible had happened. What could go wrong at this point?

If it was true that *home is where the heart is,* I had to examine what was in my heart. When I did this, I understood at last that my *home was where our RV was.*

With blue skies out the front windshield and withering roots out the rear, there was nothing left to do now but sit back and enjoy the ride.

ABOUT THE AUTHOR

Gerri Almand started writing after a 40-year career in social work. She found a new voice when her excited husband sweet-talked her into RV travel, which resulted in her award-winning, debut memoir *The Reluctant RV Wife*. Now back for book two, Almand is ready to embrace a life of nomadism and minimalism for the perks of being on the road. Her shorter works have appeared in *The Dead Mule School of Southern Literature*, *The Sun*, *Wanderlust: A Literary Map*, *Kaleidoscope*, *Odet*, *The Florida Writer*, *Orchids*, and other publications. Learn more at **GerriAlmand.com**

Made in United States
Orlando, FL
06 November 2021